Modern Critical Interpretations

Modern Critical Interpretations

Chinua Achebe's
Things Fall Apart

Edited and with an introduction by
Harold Bloom
Sterling Professor of the Humanities
Yale University

CHELSEA HOUSE PUBLISHERS
Philadelphia

© 2002 by Chelsea House Publishers, a subsidiary of
Haights Cross Communications.

Introduction © 2002 by Harold Bloom.

Printed and bound in the United States of America

10 9 8 7 6 5 4 3 2 1

∞ The paper used in this publication meets the minimum
requirements of the American National Standard for
Permanence of Paper for Printed Library Materials,
Z39.48-1984

Library of Congress Cataloging-in-Publication Data
Chinua Achebe's Things fall apart / edited and with an
introduction by Harold Bloom.
        p. cm. — (Modern critical interpretations)
        Includes bibliographical references and index.
        ISBN 0-7910-6336-4 (alk. paper)
        1. Achebe, Chinua. Things fall apart. 2. Igbo (African
people) in literature. 3. Nigeria—In literature.
I. Bloom, Harold. II. Series.

PR9387.9.A3 T52396 2001
823'.914—dc21   2001047602

Chelsea House Publishers
1974 Sproul Road, Suite 400
Broomall, PA 19008-0914

The Chelsea House World Wide Web address is
http://www.chelseahouse.com

Series Editor: Matt Uhler

Contributing Editor: Janyce Marson

Produced by Publisher's Services, Santa Barbara, California

Contents

Editor's Note

My Introduction, unlike almost all of the essays in this volume, attempts a purely aesthetic evaluation of *Things Fall Apart*, as I am not schooled in the resentful stances of post-Colonialism, cross-cultural analysis, and Foucault-inspired historicism.

Richard Begam views the novel as historicized tragedy, while Rhonda Cobham defends Achebe from any imputations of "sexism."

Achebe's rhetoric is studied by Emmanuel Edame Egar, after which the formidable Abdul JanMohamed both praises and deprecates the "sophisti-cated primitivism" of Achebe's employment of the English language. *Intellectual*

The duality of community and individual in Achebe is related to Ibo *biography* thought by Anthonia C. Kalu, while Neil Ten Kortenaar broods on Achebe's use of an omniscient narrator to hold the novel's center together.

Clayton G. MacKenzie and Joseph McClaren consider attitudes towards colonialism, and stress the dominance of religion by political considerations.

Ibo cosmology and its resultant kind of democracy are shown to figure in *Things Fall Apart* by Clement Okafor, after which Imafedia Okhamafe ascribes the true blame for the tragedy of Okonkwo not to colonialism but to Ibo genealogical over-determinism.

Eustace Palmer argues that Okonkwo's tragedy arises from his inca-pacity to accept societal change, while Richard K. Priebe sees the hero's downfall as his evasion of proverbial wisdom.

In this volume's final essay Joko Sengova compares *Things Fall Apart* to Richard Wright's *Native Son*, finding in them common elements of alien-ation, a conclusion that neglects the greatness of Okonkwo.

Introduction

Things Fall Apart is a historical novel, set in the British colony of Nigeria at about the turn from the nineteenth into the twentieth century. Since Chinua Achebe was born in 1930, he goes back a full generation, to the Nigeria of his parents. The story's famous opening establishes a characteristic tonality: simplification through intensity (a Yeatsian formula):

> Okonkwo was well known throughout the nine villages and even beyond. His fame rested on solid personal achievements. As a young man of eighteen he had brought honor to his village by throwing Amalinze the Cat. Amalinze was the great wrestler who for seven years was unbeaten, from Umuofia to Mbaino. He was called the Cat because his back would never touch the earth. It was this man that Okonkwo threw in a fight which the old men agreed was one of the fiercest since the founder of their town engaged a spirit of the wild for seven days and seven nights.
>
> The drums beat and the flutes sang and the spectators held their breath. Amalinze was a wily craftsman, but Okonkwo was as slippery as a fish in water. Every nerve and every muscle stood out on their arms, on their backs and their thighs, and one almost heard them stretching to breaking point. In the end Okonkwo threw the Cat.

Now in early middle age, Okonkwo is an angry man, a victim of his own impatient temperament, and of his sense that he had a bad father. His quite likeable father was a failure, in debt to everyone, and Okonkwo himself is enormously successful, driven by the fear that he also might fail, that he might be mistaken for his father. It would not be excessive to regard Okonkwo as a brutal person, judged pragmatically, but that would be misleading: he is not brutal by nature, but only by his compulsion *not* to

1

repeat his father's life. I may be a little premature in ruling all the critics (one or two excepted) reprinted here out of court, but I submit that Okonkwo's apparent tragedy is universal, despite its Nigerian circumstancing. It is—and this is Achebe's strength—a universal sorrow, and therefore can only be secondarily illuminated by all the ordinances of Multiculturalism, African consciousness-raising, and new-mode canonizers. This is a splendidly traditional book, Oedipal and proverbial, and owes nothing to the Four Horsemen of Resentment: Fanon, Foucault, Derrida, and Lacan. It is a timeless book: if the British Colonial regime had not driven Okonkwo to self-slaughter, then his own people would have done the job. But that, I would submit, most unfashionably, is the aesthetic value and spiritual meaning of *Things Fall Apart:* Okonkwo is an Ibo, and Achebe writes of what he knows. And yet Okonkwo could be a North American, a Spaniard, a Sicilian, an Eskimo. The end would be the same: he would kill and then take his own life.

I am aware that such a judgment would be repudiated by all of the essayists collected in this volume, but *Things Fall Apart* will survive its ideological admirers. Its firmly controlled prose, profound compassion, and loving insight into its people will not wear out. Whether the fate of Okonkwo constitutes authentic *literary* tragedy, I am uncertain. He returns, after a seven-year exile, to his own clan, and is fundamentally unchanged, but British supremacy has changed his people, particularly by conversion to Christianity. Grieved, the returning warrior mourns for his lost world, and then rejoices in the destruction of the Christian church. Humiliated by ill-treatment from the British regime's Ibo messengers, Okonkwo despairs of the clan's will to rise up against the British, and angrily beheads the most abusive of the messengers. The act is unreflecting, and inevitable, given Okonkwo's impulsive nature. Is it, or the hero's subsequent suicide, tragic?

You can argue that the Oedipus of Sophocles is also over-determined by his nature, so that his killing of his father at the crossroads is not primarily an act of the will. And yet Oedipus earns tragic stature by his unrelenting drive for the truth, his refusal to let anything block him from full knowledge. To be victimized by a blend of temperament and circumstance is also the situation of Okonkwo. Yet what destroys him is his inability to accept change. Since the change is ignoble, the tragic argument would be that the clan must fight, though pragmatically that would mean suicide for the community. Okonkwo, as the last warrior, hangs himself because there is no way out of his dilemma. He is not an intellectual quester, like Oedipus, and there is no enigma for him to solve.

It always hurts me, rereading the book, that Achebe cannot allow Okonkwo a heroic death. But aesthetically, that is another mark of Achebe's literary tact. There is no one to fight alongside of Okonkwo: he ends as isolated as Shakespeare's Coriolanus. If *Coriolanus* is a tragedy, then so is *Things Fall Apart*. Okonkwo, like the Roman hero, is essentially a solitary, and at heart a perpetual child. His tragedy stands apart from the condition of his people, even though it is generated by their pragmatic refusal of heroic death. Their refusal grants him only his final offence against the Earth, and denies him an Ibo burial. This may not be tragedy, but there is heroic pathos in it, as there is in the terrible death of Coriolanus, as he cries out for the Volscians to destroy him. Achebe's motto is from Yeats, but it could also have been from Shakespeare's Volumnia, the terrible mother of Coriolanus:

Anger's my meat. I sup upon myself
And so shall starve with feeding.

RICHARD BEGAM

Achebe's Sense of an Ending: History and Tragedy in Things Fall Apart

One of the more notable consequences of cultural globalization has been the exchange that has occurred over the last decade or so between what we have come to call postmodernism and postcolonialism. This meeting of First World and Third World has inspired more controversy than consensus, but on one point there seems to have been wide agreement: if we want to understand colonialism, then we must understand how it is represented. As Hayden White has argued, speaking of historiography in general, the "form" is the "content," and this means that the language, vocabulary, and conceptual framework in which the experience of colonialism is produced inevitably determine what can and cannot be said about it. To borrow Homi K. Bhabha's formulation, "nation" and "narration" are not easily separated—the one implies the other.

The present paper explores the intersection between narrative construction and colonial representation by focusing on an aspect of literary form that has received little attention in postcolonial studies—namely, the question of closure or ending. It is puzzling that this subject, which has generated so much commentary in modern and postmodern studies, has gone virtually unexamined in the area of postcolonial literature. Yet it is certainly reasonable to assume that a literature that identifies itself as *post*colonial and defines itself in terms of the aftermath of colonialism, will have a passing interest in the

From *Studies in the Novel 29*, no. 3 (Fall 1997). © 1997 by University of North Texas.

way endings are narratively achieved, in what they mean and how they are fashioned. Of particular interest in this regard is the highly problematic relation that postcolonial literature has to its own past and, more specifically, to the writing of its own history.

We may begin to appreciate some of the difficulties entailed in this relation by considering a number of connected questions. First, where do postcolonial writers locate their past? Is it to be found in the colonial, precolonial, or postcolonial period? Second, can we neatly separate the different historical strands that traverse and intersect these various epochs? Can we confidently assign to them decisive beginnings and conclusive endings? Third, what historical stance should postcolonial writers assume toward their own history, especially if they wish to forge a sense of national identity after colonization? To what extent does "critical history," of the sort described by Nietzsche, become a luxury that the postcolonial writer cannot afford?

In examining these questions, I want to take up the case of Chinua Achebe's *Things Fall Apart* because, as an exercise in historical recuperation, it is necessarily concerned with issues of formal shaping and narrative closure. Of course, at first glance, the novel appears to have a perfectly transparent narrative line: it tells the tragic story of Okonkwo's rise and fall among the Igbo people, concluding with that least ambiguous of all endings, the death of the hero. With only a few exceptions, critics have understood the novel in precisely these terms, seeing its closing pages as entirely unproblematic. Yet any straightforward reading of Achebe's ending must reconcile itself with the fact that the novel describes a situation of profound cultural entropy, a society in which the norms of conduct and institutions of governance are in the process of "falling apart." What is more, while Achebe's novel movingly elegizes the passing away of traditional Igbo culture, the long view it adopts—looking ahead to the future establishment of Nigeria—suggests that Achebe's own position on the modernization of Africa is, at the very least, complicated. Given the subject of Achebe's novel and his own divided response to it, we would expect a fairly open-ended conclusion, one that acknowledges its own closure as tentative, even contingent.

In what follows, I will argue that *Things Fall Apart* resists the idea of a single or simple resolution by providing three distinct endings, three different ways of reading the events that conclude the novel. At the same time, I will relate these endings to three different conceptions of history, especially as it is produced within a postcolonial context. First, Achebe writes a form of nationalist history. Here the interest is essentially reconstructive and centers on recovering an Igbo past that has been neglected or suppressed by historians who would not or could not write from an African perspective.

As Achebe observed in 1964, four years after Nigerian independence: "Historians everywhere are re-writing the stories of the new nations—replacing short, garbled, despised history with a more sympathetic account." Nationalist history tends to emphasize what other histories have either glossed over or flatly denied—namely that "African people did not hear of culture for the first time from Europeans; that their societies were not mindless but frequently had a philosophy of great depth and value and beauty, that they had poetry and, above all, they had dignity." Second, Achebe writes a form of adversarial history. Here the emphasis falls not on the reconstruction of an authentic past that has been lost, but on the deconstruction of a counterfeit past that has been imposed. Adversarial history enables Achebe to write against what he himself has called "colonialist" discourse, against the attitudes and assumptions, the language and rhetoric that characterized British colonial rule in Nigeria. Third, Achebe writes a form of metahistory. This kind of history calls attention to itself as a piece of writing, a narrative construction that depends on principles of selection (what material will be included?), emphasis (what importance will be attached to it?) and shaping (how will it be organized and arranged?).

Yet *Things Fall Apart* is concerned not only with writing history, but also with fashioning tragedy. Achebe himself made this point in an interview with Robert Serumaga, in which he discussed the political implications of tragedy and explicitly referred to his novel as an example of that genre. A good deal of the critical literature has focused on this issue, addressing the question of whether the novel is indeed a tragedy and, if so, what kind of tragedy. Thus, Bruce Macdonald and Margaret Turner maintain that *Things Fall Apart* fails as an Aristotelian tragedy; Alastair Niven asserts that it succeeds as "modern" tragedy; while Afam Ebeogu treats it as an example of Igbo tragedy, and Abiola Irele considers it more generally as an instance of cultural and historical tragedy. It will be my contention that much of the disagreement over generic classification has resulted from a failure to identify Achebe's multi-perspectival approach to the problem—a failure to recognize that he has written three distinct endings. Hence, I also want to argue that the novel offers us a variety of responses to tragedy, as well as history. According to the model I shall develop, nationalist history is associated with classical or Aristotelian tragedy; adversarial history is associated with modern or ironic tragedy; and metahistory is associated with critical discourse. My larger purpose in pursuing this line of analysis is to suggest that *Things Fall Apart* demands what is, in effect, a palimpsestic reading, a kind of historical and generic archaeology, which is designed to uncover, layer by layer, those experiences that have accreted around colonialism and its protracted aftermath.

* * *

The first of the novel's three endings centers on Okonkwo's killing of the messenger, his failed attempt to rouse his people to action, and his subsequent suicide. This ending presents the events of the novel largely from an African perspective, equating Okonkwo's demise with the collapse of Igbo culture. The idea that Okonkwo is a great man whose destiny is linked with that of his people is immediately established in the novel's celebrated opening:

> Okonkwo was well known throughout the nine villages and even beyond. His fame rested on solid personal achievements. As a young man of eighteen he had brought honor to his village by throwing Amalinze the Cat. Amalinze was the great wrestler who for seven years was unbeaten, from Umuofia to Mbaino. He was called the Cat because his back would never touch the earth. It was this man that Okonkwo threw in a fight which the old men agreed was one of the fiercest since the founder of their town engaged a spirit of the wild for seven days and seven nights.

In this passage history recedes into myth, as the narrator presents the seven-year reign of Amalinze and the seven-day struggle of the founder of the village in epic terms (here seven obviously functions as a conventional rather than a naturalistic number). The passage also serves both to connect Okonkwo with the beginnings of Umuofia (through his wrestling exploits he is compared with the village's symbolic progenitor) and to look forward to his own and his people's end (the "spirit of the wild," representing Nature, will be replaced by the more powerful alien force of British imperialism). In a few deft strokes, Achebe illustrates how Okonkwo has come to personify the destiny of his community, extending from its earliest origins to its final destruction.

The larger effect of Achebe's opening is to establish Okonkwo as a particular kind of tragic protagonist: the great warrior who carries with him the fate of his people. Seen from the standpoint of the first ending, he is, as Michael Valdez Moses has argued, a Homeric hero cast in a distinctly Achillean mold:

> Like Achilles, Okonkwo is "a man of action, a man of war." His "fame" among the Igbo rests "on solid personal achievements," foremost of which are his exploits as the greatest wrestler and most accomplished warrior of the nine villages. He is a man renowned and respected for having brought home from battle

five human heads; and on feast days and important public occasions, he drinks his palm wine from the skull of the first warrior
he killed.

Okonkwo is, in other words, identified with his community to the extent that
it esteems the martial ethos he embodies, and while his village certainly does
more than make war, it especially prizes those men who win distinction on
the battlefield ("in Umuofia . . . men were bold and warlike").

This is not to say, however, that Okonkwo epitomizes all the virtues of
Igbo culture, or that he is himself without fault. On the contrary, Achebe
himself understands that, within an Aristotelian framework, his hero is
necessarily a flawed character, guilty of errors in judgement—guilty, to use
the Greek term, of *hamartia*. As Achebe has observed in an interview with
Charles Rowell: "[The tragic protagonist is] the man who's larger than life,
who exemplifies virtues that are admired by the community, but also a man
who for all that is still human. He can have flaws, you see; all that seems to
me to be very elegantly underlined in Aristotle's work." Obviously Okonkwo
is "larger than life" ("He was tall and huge, and his bushy eyebrows and wide
nose gave him a very severe look") yet his epic proportions carry a figurative
as well as a literal significance: they indicate the difficulty he experiences
fitting within the boundaries of any social order. So it is that as a "man of
action," a great athlete and warrior, he is excessive both in his high-spirited-
ness, what the Greeks called *thymos* ("whenever he was angry and could not
get his words out quickly enough, he would use his fists"), and in his prideful
arrogance, what the Greeks called *hybris* ("The oldest man present said
sternly [to Okonkwo] that those whose palm-kernels were cracked for them
by a benevolent spirit should not forget to be humble"). Indeed, like many of
the heroes of classical tragedy, Okonkwo's immoderate behavior consistently
places him at cross-purposes not merely with his fellow Umuofians, but with
the gods themselves ("Okonkwo was not the man to stop beating somebody
half-way through, not even for fear of a goddess"), and it comes as no
surprise when, in the second part of the novel, he is sent into temporary exile
for offending Ani, the Earth deity. Nevertheless, if we are to appreciate the
tragedy of the first ending—something that Achebe clearly intends—then we
must recognize that Okonkwo's faults are essentially virtues carried to an
extreme, and that while he is obviously not perfect, he nevertheless represents some of the best qualities of his culture. As Obierika remarks near the
novel's end, "That man was one of the greatest men in Umuofia."

The crisis of the novel comes in the penultimate chapter when an
impudent messenger, sent by the colonial authorities, orders a tribal meeting
to disband. Okonkwo the warrior is moved to action:

In a flash Okonkwo drew his machete. The messenger crouched to avoid the blow. It was useless. Okonkwo's machete descended twice and the man's head lay beside his uniformed body.

The waiting backcloth jumped into tumultuous life and the meeting was stopped. Okonkwo stood looking at the dead man. He knew that Umuofia would not go to war. He knew because they had let the other messengers escape. They had broken into tumult instead of action. He discerned fright in that tumult. He heard voices asking: "Why did he do it?"

He wiped his machete on the sand and went away.

The scene is presented with a devastating simplicity. From the perspective of the first ending, the people of Umuofia have deserted Okonkwo and in the process betrayed themselves, but the wiping of the machete is the only eloquence he permits himself. It is an ordinary and everyday gesture, yet in the present context it acquires special significance: Okonkwo remains true to the martial ethos that his people have abandoned, here represented by the warrior's care of his weapon; at the same time, he symbolically dissolves his connection with his people, wiping away the blood bond that has joined them. This gesture is especially resonant because, as critics have pointed out, in killing the messenger he is shedding the blood of a fellow Igbo.

The suicide that follows is itself a profound violation of Igbo law, which strictly prohibits acts of self-destruction. The question of how we should respond to Okonkwo's final deed has been examined in detail by Kalu Ogbaa and Damian Opata, but with strikingly different results. For Ogbaa the suicide grows out of Okonkwo's failure to act with sufficient piety toward the Igbo gods and traditions, while for Opata it is a consequence of the Igbos' refusal to rally around Okonkwo and join him in resisting the British. As was the case with discussions of the novel's tragedy, the disagreement arises in the first place because the reader has difficulty establishing Achebe's position on a number of issues—difficulty knowing, for example, where he stands on the question of violent resistance to the British. Of course, this interpretive problem largely disappears once we begin to read the novel palimpsestically as a layering of diverse perspectives on history and tragedy. Hence, understood within the terms of the novel's first ending, Okonkwo's suicide is the logical and necessary consequence of an idealistic and absolutist position. Both nationalist history and heroic tragedy demand that he remain unyielding and that the Igbos honor their cultural heritage by refusing assimilation. Even in this final gesture, then, Okonkwo functions as the true representative of his people. For, as he sees it, Igbo culture has willingly succumbed to its own annihilation, committing what is a form of collective suicide by submitting to the British. In taking his own life, Okonkwo has simply preceded his people in their communal destruction. Once again he has led the way.

* * *

The novel's second ending, which I associate with adversarial history, views events from the heavily ironized perspective of the District Commissioner. Igbo culture is now presented not from the inside as vital and autonomous, but from the outside as an object of anthropological curiosity, and its collapse is understood not as an African tragedy but as a European triumph. As the final scene of the novel unfolds, the Igbos take the District Commissioner to the place where the suicide was committed:

> Then they came to the tree from which Okonkwo's body was dangling, and they stopped dead.
>
> "Perhaps your men can help us bring him down and bury him," said Obierika. "We have sent for strangers from another village to do it for us, but they may be a long time coming."
>
> The District Commissioner changed instantaneously. The resolute administrator in him gave way to the student of primitive customs.
>
> "Why can't you take him down yourselves?" he asked.
>
> "It is against our custom," said one of the men. "It is an abomination for a man to take his own life."

What is particularly noteworthy in this episode is the way the District Commissioner effortlessly shifts from the "resolute administrator" to the "student of primitive customs." Here Achebe demonstrates that, within a colonial context, the Foucauldian power-knowledge nexus is much more than a speculative theory—it is an inescapable and omnipresent reality. Thus, those who wrote historical and anthropological accounts of the Igbos were typically either representatives of the British government or their semi-official guests, and the colonial administration not only helped to enable such research by "opening up" various regions, but also relied upon it in determining local policy. In the case of Igboland, the earliest anthropological studies were written by P. Amaury Talbot, himself a District Commissioner, and G. T. Basden, a missionary whose safety and well-being literally depended on the colonial office. As Robert M. Wren has shown, both Talbot and Basden were, by the standards of the day, sympathetic observers of the Igbos—indeed, the latter was a personal friend of Achebe's father—but this did not prevent them from expressing in their published writings typically European attitudes towards the Africans. By way of illustration we might consider how the scene with the District Commissioner continues:

> "Take down the body," the Commissioner ordered his chief messenger, "and bring it and all these people to the court."
>
> "Yes, sah," the messenger said, saluting.
>
> The Commissioner went away, taking three or four of the soldiers with him. In the many years in which he had toiled to bring civilization to different parts of Africa he had learned a number of things. One of them was that a District Commissioner must never attend to such undignified details as cutting a hanged man from the tree. Such attention would give the natives a poor opinion of him. In the book which he planned to write he would stress that point.

Achebe makes much the same point himself, though obviously to very different effect, in his essay, "Colonialist Criticism":

> To the colonialist mind it was always of the utmost importance to be able to say: "I know my natives," a claim which implied two things at once: (a) that the native was really quite simple and (b) that understanding him and controlling him went hand in hand—understanding being a pre-condition for control and control constituting adequate proof of understanding.

Yet notice how carefully Achebe has chosen his words: it is important for the colonialist mind not to know the natives but to be able to say "I know my natives." What the District Commissioner ultimately achieves is not genuine understanding but the illusion of understanding that comes with the power to control:

> Every day brought him some new material. The story of this man who had killed a messenger and hanged himself would make interesting reading. One could almost write a whole chapter on him. Perhaps not a whole chapter but a reasonable paragraph, at any rate. There was so much else to include, and one must be firm in cutting out details. He had already chosen the title of the

book, after much thought: *The Pacification of the Primitive Tribes of the Lower Niger.*

With these words, *Things Fall Apart* completes its passage from the heroic tragedy of the first ending to the biting irony of the second ending. In his well-known essay on *Heart of Darkness*, Achebe argues against European accounts of Africa that have reduced its people to—I quote Achebe quoting Conrad—"rudimentary souls" capable only of "a violent babble of uncouth sounds." In presenting Okonkwo's epic story, epitomized by the first ending, Achebe offers a powerful counter-statement to the "dark continent" idea of Africa. But with the second ending he does something more. By ironically undermining the perspective of the District Commissioner, by exposing the latter's personal ignorance (not a "whole chapter" but a "reasonable paragraph") and political interests (the "pacification" of the Lower Niger), Achebe seeks to confront and finally to discredit the entire discourse of colonialism, those quasi-historical, quasi-anthropological writings that have treated Africa as nothing more than—again I quote Achebe—"a foil to Europe, a place of negations."

At the same time, the second ending begins to redefine our point of view on the tragic events of the novel. Although this ending is clearly meant to undermine the District Commissioner's position, indeed to portray him as a fool, it nevertheless substantially alters the tone and mood of Achebe's resolution. Obviously the novel would read very differently—and its tragedy function very differently—if it concluded with, say, a heroic recitation of Okonkwo's suicide by Obeirika. In other words, the final chapter of *Things Fall Apart* serves not as a simple denouement—one that helps us sort out a rather messy climax—but as a significant qualification of what has gone before, a distinctly new ending that complicates our sense of Achebe's approach to both history and tragedy. In this regard, it is important to remember what Achebe himself has observed in interviews and essays: that while the passing away of traditional Igbo culture involved profound loss, it also held out the possibility of substantial gain. Thus, when he was asked about returning to pre-colonial society, the kind of world Okonkwo inhabited before "things fell apart," Achebe responded, "It's not really a question of going back. I think if one goes back, there's something wrong somewhere, or else a misunderstanding." In another interview, he pushed this position further, arguing that colonization was a multi-faceted phenomenon, which had produced benefits as well as burdens: "I am not one of those who would say that Africa has gained nothing at all during the colonial period, I mean this is ridiculous—we gained a lot." Finally and most tellingly, he has insisted that, despite his own ambivalence on the subject, modernization is a necessary and essential part of Africa's future: "The comprehensive goal of a developing nation like Nigeria is, of course, development, or its somewhat better variant, modernization. I don't see much argument about that."

What all of this means is that Achebe's response to colonization is far more nuanced, far more complex, than most critics have recognized or been willing to acknowledge. How such complexity expresses itself, and how it modifies Achebe's sense of tragedy, is further explored in the third ending.

* * *

What I shall identify as the third ending is located in *No Longer At Ease*, the sequel to *Things Fall Apart*. No doubt, the assertion that one text contains the ending of another will immediately strike some readers as dubious. Such a claim begins to gain credibility, however, when we remember that Achebe originally conceived of his two novels as the first and third sections of a single work. In other words, the compositional history of *Things Fall Apart* and *No Longer At Ease* provides some justification for treating the latter as a continuation of the former, an extension that qualifies Okonkwo's story, even redirects its course. Indeed, there is good reason to argue that *No Longer At Ease* is not only a continuation of *Things Fall Apart* but also a rewriting of it, one that essentially recapitulates the action of the earlier novel, though in a markedly different setting. Hence, both novels tell the story of a representative of the Igbo people who takes a stand on a question of principle and is destroyed in the ensuing collision between African and European values. To paraphrase one critic, the fall of Okonkwo's machete is replaced by the fall of the judge's gavel, as we are transported from a heroic to a legalistic world, but the narrative outline remains essentially the same. The very structure of *No Longer At Ease* indicates, then, that Okonkwo's story has not reached its end, that the tragic destiny it implies continues to be lived out.

This does not mean, however, that in writing *Things Fall Apart* and *No Longer At Ease* as independent works Achebe somehow betrayed the internal logic of his own narrative. On the contrary, the decision to treat Okonkwo's and Obi Okonkwo's stories separately contributes to what I have called Achebe's palimpsestic effect, the sense that the same or similar events acquire new meanings in different contexts. It is therefore not surprising that in moving from the first novel to the second, we observe Okonkwo's traditional tragedy transform itself into Obi's modern tragedy, as the heroic gives way to the ironic.

The point of intersection between the two novels, the scene in which I locate the third ending of *Things Fall Apart*, occurs when Okonkwo's grandson,

Obi, a university-educated civil servant, finds himself discussing tragedy with a British colonial officer. Obi advances the opinion—of special interest given the first ending of *Things Fall Apart*—that suicide ruins a tragedy:

> Real tragedy is never resolved. It goes on hopelessly forever. Conventional tragedy is too easy. The hero dies and we feel a purging of the emotions. A real tragedy takes place in a corner, in an untidy spot, to quote W. H. Auden. The rest of the world is unaware of it. Like that man in *A Handful of Dust* who reads Dickens to Mr. Todd. There is no release for him. When the story ends he is still reading. There is no purging of the emotions for us because *we are not there.*

Obi draws a distinction in this passage between two kinds of tragedy. In traditional or Aristotelian tragedy, there is a clear resolution, an aesthetic pay-off that comes in the form of *catharsis;* but in modern or ironic tragedy, the tragedy described in Auden's "Musée des Beaux Arts," the fall from a high place is likened to Brueghel's famous painting of Icarus. In the foreground the ploughman ploughs his field; in the background a ship sails on its way. And it is only after careful inspection that we are able to discover the place of tragedy: there in the corner, barely perceptible, we see Icarus's two legs breaking the surface of the water, sole testimony of his personal catastrophe.

While the point of departure for Obi's discussion of tragedy is Graham Greene's *The Heart of the Matter,* his observations have an obvious application to *Things Fall Apart.* Okonkwo's story as viewed from the Igbo perspective presents history in the form of classical or heroic tragedy. Okonkwo's story as viewed from the District Commissioner's perspective presents history in the form of modern or ironic tragedy. One of Obi's remarks is particularly apposite: there is no purging of the emotions in modern tragedy, because "we are not there." These words perfectly describe the situation of the District Commissioner. He "was not there" in the sense that he was never in a position genuinely to understand Okonkwo, to appreciate who he was and what he represented.

It is important to stress, however, that the novel's first ending is not in some way compromised because it is associated with the "conventional," while the novel's second ending is in some way enhanced because it is associated with the "real." Indeed, if Achebe provides us with any controlling point of view, it comes with the third ending, which illustrates the vexed and ambiguous relation in which the postcolonial stands to its own past. For with his remarks on tragedy, Obi is offering a narrative analysis of what is *literally* his own past. In describing a tragedy that ends in suicide, he is describing his grandfather's tragic fall and its significance for Igbo culture after it was lost, after "things fell apart."

What the novel's third ending illustrates, then, is that the boundaries between the "conventional" and the "real," the heroic and the ironic, are not clearly or cleanly drawn. From Obi's perspective—and, for that matter, the reader's—Okonkwo functions both as a literary persona and a living person, an epic hero and an historical anachronism. Yet the novel does not invite us to select one of these alternatives so much as to understand the various, though decidedly distinctive, truths they articulate. In other words, we are not meant to choose from among three possible endings, but to read all of them, as it were, simultaneously and palimpsestically. If we are able to do this, we shall see how Achebe's sense of an ending is intimately bound up with his sense of cultural loss; how the tragedy of the past necessarily depends on the perspective of the present; and how history is inevitably written for both the "they who were there" and the "we who are not there."

* * *

At the beginning of this paper I asked three questions about the relation of postcolonial literature to the writing of history. I would now like to propose, however provisionally, some answers to these questions. First, where do postcolonial writers locate their past? There is certainly no single or definitive response to this question, but a writer like Achebe is acutely aware of how problematic are the issues it raises. For this reason *Things Fall Apart* and *No Longer at Ease* not only situate themselves in periods of historical transition (Nigeria at the turn of the century and in the late 1950s) but also superimpose these periods on each other through a series of intertextual connections, suggesting that postcolonial writers are the products of all the historical periods through which their cultures have lived. Second, can we confidently assign decisive beginnings and conclusive endings to the various epochs of colonial and postcolonial history? It is not immediately apparent how Achebe would answer this question, but his experiment in extended closure reminds us that the narrative shaping that necessarily comes with beginnings and endings is a human creation—a product of what Richard Rorty calls "contingency"—rather than a naturally occurring or divinely given reality. So it is that each of the three endings with which Achebe concludes *Things Fall Apart* grows out of different interests, different assumptions, different intentions, and none of these is, ultimately, true in itself. Finally, what historical stance should postcolonial writers assume toward their own history? This is a particularly difficult problem and one that cannot be fully treated in the space that remains. Still, it is worth observing that Achebe has not only qualified the kind of nationalist history with which his work is so often associated, but also that he has shown a willingness to criticize traditional Igbo culture. While Achebe urgently feels the need to recuperate an African past that has been lost or overlooked, to tell the story that has not been told, he nevertheless recognizes the importance of maintaining a sense of intellectual and historical integrity:

> The question is how does a writer re-create this past? Quite clearly there is a strong temptation to idealize it—to extol its good points and pretend that the bad never existed . . . [But] The credibility of the world [the writer] is attempting to re-create will be called into question and he will defeat his own purpose if he is suspected of glossing over inconvenient facts. We cannot pretend that our past was one long technicolour idyll. We have to admit that like other people's pasts ours had its good as well as its bad sides.

The last general point I would like to make touches upon methodology. Too often the literature we call postcolonial has been read as little more than an exercise in political thematics. Such an approach is not surprising, given the enormous historical pressure out of which this literature was born, but it has led many critics to ignore crucial issues of form and technique. Yet, as I have sought to show, we can only begin to appreciate how a writer like Achebe envisions his past, both as history and tragedy, if we understand how he narratively shapes his material, how he achieves his sense of an ending. Attention to formal organization is particularly important in the case of Achebe, because he conceives of history neither in teleological nor positivistic terms, but as something human beings create, a series of stories built around beginnings and endings, a narrative construction. This is not to say that Achebe is fundamentally a postmodern writer, but neither is he exclusively a postcolonial writer. Or rather, to put the matter more precisely, he is a postcolonial writer insofar as he is a product of cultural globalization, insofar as he is an African who has grown up and continues to live at "the crossroads of cultures."

Obviously, life at the crossroads is not easy. As a student of classical tragedy—not to mention a sometime rebellious son—he is aware of the perils, as well as the possibilities, that await us at those places of Oedipal intersection: "the crossroads does have a certain dangerous potency; dangerous because a man can perish there wrestling with multiple-headed spirits, but also because he might be lucky and return to his people with the boon of prophetic vision." But if forebears like Okonkwo, and alter egos like Obi, have been vanquished wrestling the demons of multiplicity, Achebe has emerged from these spiritual contests with a deeper and more comprehensive sense of what it means to inhabit the alternate worlds of postcolonialism, worlds that are at once aristocratic and democratic, heroic and ironic, ancient and contemporary. We are all of us the heirs of Achebe's prophetic vision, grappling with the problems and promises of a globalized modernity, working our way through its diverse scenarios, its different endings.

RHONDA COBHAM

Problems of Gender and History in the Teaching of Things Fall Apart

"This is a sexist novel!" the (female) (white) student declared. Her ethnic earrings jangled in angry assent as she stabbed the pages of her Heinemann paperback for emphasis. As if to distance itself from the offending object, her red checked imitation PLO scarf slipped backwards off her shoulders. It was clear that she spoke on behalf of all oppressed humanity.

In a voice tinged with longsuffering, her teacher (also white, but male) attempted to explain that not to write about wife beating in a story about a society where it was practiced would be aesthetically inauthentic. He tried to shift the discussion back to an appreciation of the critical distance between the author and his main character before the jocks at the back of the class got wind of what was going on, but it was too late. Within seconds the high school class had degenerated into a slanging match between those who felt texts like *Things Fall Apart* should be expurgated from the syllabus and those who wanted to tell the censorship group what they would like Okonkwo to do to them if he were a member of the class. The teacher held his head in his hands and fantasized about reintroducing corporal punishment.

Change the bracketed terms of ascription and this in modified form becomes a scenario that all teachers of Achebe's novel must recognize. I encountered it in a more subtle, inverted form when a Nigerian university student (female) during a discussion of Buchi Emecheta's *Joys of Motherhood*

From *Canonization and Teaching of African Literatures*, Raoul Granqvist, ed. © 1990 by Editions Rodopi B.V.

suggested tentatively that though she could appreciate how Nnu Ego felt about her husband in the Emecheta novel, she thought that the writer was being polemical because "traditional Igbo women did not feel that way about these kinds of things," and it became apparent that her point of reference for the psychological responses appropriate for traditional Igbo women was the vision of early Igbo society presented in *Things Fall Apart*.

In an age where violence and the demand for women's rights are constant features of our public rhetoric, there may be something instructive about the way in which these representative student responses insist on conflating all kinds of textual and political issues. In the response of the wearer of ethnic earrings several issues have been conflated. In the first place, there is no concept of historical time in her reading of the novel. For all she probably knew, the Igbo society Achebe was describing was contemporaneous with both the author and herself. Achebe, through his pseudo autobiographical character, Okonkwo, was merely describing and rationalizing the attitude to women which he himself shared with the contemporary Igbo society. For her, this (mis)reading is borne out by Obierika's closing eulogy for his dishonoured friend which she reads simplistically as overt endorsement of all that Okonkwo stood for. Her sense of dis-ease is compounded by the total identification of the most brutal elements within her own society with Okonkwo's attitudes and actions. PLO scarf notwithstanding, she cannot imagine what it must feel like for an entire culture to have its customs, values and idiosyncrasies not merely challenged but made totally irrelevant by a simple equation of moral authority with superior military strength.

Where Western student readers of *Things Fall Apart* complain that the novel is "sexist", meaning usually that they find Okonkwo misogynist, African student readers are more likely to praise Achebe and chastise a writer like Buchi Emecheta for not being as authentic as Achebe in portraying traditional Igbo women. Okonkwo's physical abuse of his wives is evaluated precisely within the novel on a scale of values that has at its highest point the devotion of the old couple Ndulue and Ozoemena who remain devoted to each other even in death, and at its lowest point the cruelty of wife batterer, Uzowulu, whom the Egwugwu themselves must discipline. But for the student reader in a Western culture, Okonkwo's petty viciousness remains a more vivid travesty of human rights than the action of the District Commissioner in the novel, when he enjoins the goalers to treat with dignity the elders whom he has just tricked, humiliated and imprisoned!

In the case of the African student reader, the issues that are conflated are somewhat different. Speaking from within modern Nigerian society, she cannot help but be aware of the differences between the world she inhabits and the one Achebe describes. She is a product of the Africanized Nigerian education system and has been taught to respect the world of tradition by her parents as well as by set books like *Things Fall Apart* on her school examination syllabus. She fully expects to be married in church as well as within some modified form of a traditional ceremony and to be the only legal wife of her modern educated husband. The polygamously married senior sisters of her father belong to a world to which she pays her respects but which she assumes is as remote to her reality as the Igbo village Achebe describes at the turn of the century—at least for the present. Because her interaction with traditional culture is indirect, and because she considers her emancipated notions of a woman's role a product of her westernized/nigerianized education, she cannot conceive of women in traditional Igbo society sharing her notions of selfhood. For her, the world that Achebe brings to life is a beautiful tableau that exists to reinforce her sense of belonging to a noble tradition. And this is true, whether her ethnic origins are Igbo, Yoruba or East African Kikuyu.

Both the readers of the novel described above imply by their conflation of lived and imagined realities that there is some truly objective, unbiased version of traditional life which it is the writer's duty to deliver to the reader in such a way that our sympathies are engaged for the "right" causes and our imaginations are stimulated in the "right" directions. Neither seems concerned that the imaginative point of departure for the writer could have incorporated different preoccupations and perspectives from the ones they bring to their reading of his work.

Achebe probably had an agenda in writing his novel quite different from either of these readers in studying it. As the son of a village catechist and a scholarship winner, first to secondary school and then to the newly established Ibadan College, Achebe was one of the first generation of African writers to be familiar from early childhood with Western and indigenous traditions. Both the eloquent oral traditions of the Igbo community and the compelling prose of the King James Bible would have imbued him with a love of beautiful language and an appreciation of the timing and perfect cadence of a well wrought sentence. The texts which formed his vision of Africa, however, were novels like Joyce Cary's *Mr. Johnson* and Conrad's *Heart of Darkness*, texts in relation to which Achebe has described himself as a resisting reader. Like his modern African readers, he would have been aware of the ways in which the values of his Christian family differed from or coincided with those of more traditional Igbo families. Like his Western readers, he must have been uncomfortably aware that many of the traditions which still influenced his life would have been considered brutal or misogynist from the perspective of the fictive author of *The Pacification of the Primitive Tribes of the Lower Niger.*

Unlike both groups of readers, however, and indeed, unlike either of the cultures to which they had access, Achebe's generation of African intellectuals had no readily available symbolic discourse through which they could represent and ascribe value simultaneously to the various cultural influences that had formed them. To be sure they could quote Yeats and Eliot at will to each other in one breath and spar with traditional proverbs in the next, but who besides them would "get" the joke? Who in their community who had come before them or was likely to come after them would understand and give full value to all aspects of their accomplishments and ways of seeing? Okonkwo voices a similar *angst* in a rare moment of filial solidarity with his father in *Things Fall Apart* as he contemplates the defection of his eldest son Nwoye to join the Christians:

> Suppose when he died all his male children decided to follow Nwoye's steps and abandon their ancestors? Okonkwo felt a cold shudder run through him at the terrible prospect, like the prospect of annihilation. He saw himself and his father crowding round their ancestral shrine waiting in vain for worship and sacrifice and finding nothing but ashes of bygone days and his children the while praying to the white man's god.

In the rhetoric of our age we would say that both Okonkwo and his creator are concerned with the construction of a personal, in this case masculine, identity through which to mediate their connections to past, present and future communities. Okonkwo's quest is easily charted. Deprived by his father's anomalous lifestyle of an inheritance of land, yam seed or junior wives, he has access to no material objects that can provide him with a reference for who he is or what he may become. In fact his most immediate point of male reference, his father, is described by the society *asagbala*, a word that "could . . . mean a man who had taken no title," but which also meant "woman." Like Shelley's monster in *Frankenstein*, Okonkwo must fabricate a social context for his identity and values rather than simply assuming a system of references in relation to which he can define himself. He does so by isolating and responding to specific symbols of masculinity within his culture as if they, in the abstract, could constitute all that a man needed to construct his social self.

The pivotal example of this process in the novel is Okonkwo's understanding of the concept of courage. At the outset it is the masculine attribute most immediately accessible to him, as it seems wholly contingent upon his performance as an individual. In the opening paragraphs of the novel Okonkwo is defined for us in terms of his courage when he throws Amalinze the Cat in wrestling. Later we discover that Okonkwo's courage on this occasion is immediately translated into affirmation of his social identity since it wins him the love of a woman whom, in terms of material wealth, he is not yet "man enough" to marry.

Such early instances of social recognition for his courage are compounded over the years as Okonkwo struggles manfully against bad weather and harvests to acquire his own yam seed and as he takes lives in battle. Gradually, for Okonkwo prestige and manliness become synonymous with the ability to do difficult, even distasteful jobs without flinching. When the Oracle demands the life of his ward, Ikemefuna, Okonkwo finds himself without access to a system of values which would allow him to distance himself from the killing of the child who "calls [him] father" and remain a man. He strikes the blow that kills the child, offending the earth goddess, Ala, and setting in motion a chain of events which ultimately lead to his downfall.

Okonkwo's limited personal understanding of physical ascendancy as courage and his equation of courage with masculinity are set against a much richer and more complex set of values available to his clan as a whole. In the novel Okonkwo's friend, Obierika, is the main spokesman for this greater tradition. His words are reinforced structurally by the narrative's juxtaposition of Okonkwo's actions and those of other members of the society in a way which invites us to consider the complexity of the clan's values. Thus, Okonkwo sees tenderness as incompatible with masculinity, viewing marriage as yet another social situation in which a man's worth is measured by his ability to control others through superior physical strength. Yet the reader is made aware of the ways in which such notions of male prerogative are qualified by the community. Okonkwo's response to the almost simultaneous deaths of Ndulue and his wife Ozoemena dramatizes the gap between his personal code and that of the clan as a whole:

> "It was always said that Ndulue and Ozoemena had one mind," said Obierika. "I remember when I was a young boy there was a song about them. He could not do anything without telling her."
> "I did not know that," said Okonkwo. "I thought he was a strong man in his youth." "He was indeed," said Ofoedu. Okonkwo shook his head doubtfully. "He led Umuofia to war in those days," said Obierika.

Okonkwo himself is punished when he breaks the Week of Peace and beats his wife, a judgement which reflects a symbolic recognition of wifebeating as violence even though it may also be associated with legitimate masculine privilege. Finally there is the unequivocal censure of the *egwugwu* who are called forth to reprimand the chronic batterer, Uzowulu. Their judgement shows where the community draws the line between physical prowess and bullying; courage and cowardice.

Okonkwo's most complex conflation of brute force with the "masculine" virtue of courage occurs in the final pages of the story where he cuts off the head of the court messenger and then hangs himself. Here courage is dissociated from those other manly attributes: caution, diplomacy, and the ability to weigh both sides of an argument. The irony is that none of these "higher" values in his society will have any effect on the superior military might of the colonizers. Thus, in a twisted sense, Okonkwo and the District Commissioner share the same world view: that ultimately physical strength and the ability to inflict one's will on another human being, be it one's wife, one's son or one's natives are the only significant forms of social differentiation in establishing a masculine identity.

The act of suicide marks symbolically the parting of the ways between Okonkwo and his clan. Until now he has accepted the censure of his community for his unpremeditated acts of violence, because at heart he accepts that their universe encompasses his. Faced now with the whispered comment "why did he do it" after he kills the messenger, Okonkwo finally decides that his clansmen no longer share his values and that to be a man on their terms would be a form of living death. His community reciprocates his final act of distancing, to the extent that it denies him a man's burial. And yet, ultimately, Okonkwo characteristically underestimates the flexibility and comprehensiveness of the clan's values. When Obierika declares "[t]hat man was one of the greatest men in Umuofia" he extends to Okonkwo the same complex and qualified acceptance accorded to Ndulue who was great and/but who could not do anything without telling his wife. Thus the accolade of manhood is conferred on Okonkwo even in default, both in the words of his friend and in the act of narration which constitutes Achebe's novel.

Okonkwo's final solution brings us back full circle to the dilemma of his creator. Like Okonkwo, who attempts to carve out a relationship with his clan in the absence of an inherited sense of identity, Achebe must renegotiate a relationship to traditional Igbo society, which his education, religious training and internalized moral standards have made tenuous. Like Okonkwo he often proceeds by isolating specific aspects of the societies to which he has access, and allowing these to stand for many other possible readings of a given social situation. Achebe has described his mission in writing *Things Fall Apart* as being to teach other Africans that their past was neither so savage or benighted as the colonizers have represented it to be. Another way of stating this goal could conceivably be that Achebe needed to prove to himself that the best of the values he associated with his Christian upbringing were compatible with the values of traditional Igbo society.

There are many examples of selective incorporation of supposedly Western/Christian values into the celebration of the traditional way of life in *Things Fall Apart*. I would like to discuss briefly three: the killing of Ikemefuna, the presentation of marriage, and the selective elaboration of women's roles within traditional Igbo society.

In presenting Ikemefuna's death, Achebe, like Okonkwo, must find a way of synchronizing the qualities he wishes to represent with the values he has internalized. While sharing the mission school horror at the idea of human sacrifice that he attributes to the converts in *Things Fall Apart*, Achebe must find ways of addressing this issue while keeping the reader's sympathy for the community as a whole. He does so by structuring the story of Ikemefuna's death so that it parallels the biblical story of Abraham's near sacrifice of his son, Isaac. The journey out of the confines of the village, the boy's carrying of the vessels associated with the sacrifice and his last disarming words, "[m]y father, they have killed me" all resonate with the bible story. Isaac performs each of the roles attributed to Ikemefuna, including the utterance of a last disarming remark: "My father . . . behold the fire and the wood: but where is the lamb . . ." (Genesis 22: 7). The major difference, of course, is that no ram is provided to be a substitute for Ikemefuna. Yet we feel sure that, just as Abraham would have killed his son, had the ram not been caught in the thicket, Okonkwo would have spared his, had a ram materialized for him. Both fathers act in strict obedience to their Gods, and both contemplate the deed they must perform with horror as well as fortitude.

There are further parallels between Okonkwo's situation and the New Testament story about God's sacrifice of his son Jesus for the greater good of all humanity (itself a version of the Abraham/Isaac motif). What is important here, however, is that Achebe has picked the form of human sacrifice most compatible with Judaeo-Christian myth as the centerpiece of his examination of human sacrifice in Igbo culture. The more ubiquitous forms, such as the "throwing away" of twins in the bad bush or the killing of slaves on the death of their masters, are mentioned only in passing, as evils already under fire within traditional society, whose eradication is hastened by the coming of the missionaries. For the tragedy of Ikemefuna's death to be shared by his readers as a moment of pathos rather than one of revulsion, the parallel with Abraham must function as a shared archetype. The object of sacrifice must be a sentient individual, bound to the person who makes the sacrifice by bonds of affection. In this way the act of sacrifice becomes a symbol of devotion to a principle higher than earthly love, rather than the brute machinations of a culture incapable of elevated sentiments. Though Okonkwo's personal intervention in Ikemefuna's death remains tragically wrongheaded, the context in which he acts retains its dignity.

Achebe's technical manipulation of such parallels within his story are reinforced as thematic strategies in the conversations between the enlightened missionary Mr. Brown and the enlightened Igbo, Akunna. Their conversations may be read as a metaphor for Achebe's own search for a point of convergence between the two codes which have informed his ethics. Similarly, his description of what it is that attracts Nwoye to the Christians mirrors his own strategies with the reader in using biblical myth to reinforce Igbo values. As he points out: "It was not the mad logic of the Trinity that captivated [Nwoye]. He did not understand it. It was the poetry of the new religion, something felt in the marrow."

On the personal and political levels, Achebe's presentation of women within Igbo society can be seen to follow a similar pattern. Although we are told of Okonkwo's many wives and children, the male-female relationships in Okonkwo's family which Achebe isolates for our scrutiny are almost indistinguishable from those of monogamous couples within Western tradition. Okonkwo has three wives but we come to know only one: Ekwefi, the mother of Enzinma. She has married Okonkwo for love, having run away from her first husband. Her relationship with her husband, for better or worse, has all the passion, violence and shared trauma we associate with the Western romantic tradition. Achebe's point clearly is that all these emotions existed in traditional Igbo society but, as with his choice of situation in dealing with the issue of human sacrifice, the relationship he describes between Okonkwo and Ekwefi is by no means normative. We never really see the wives in Okonkwo's compound interacting with each other the way we are shown the men interacting among themselves or even Okonkwo interacting with his children. From a Western perspective the omission is hardly experienced as a loss, as the reader can identify effortlessly with the structure if not the content of the relationship described between Okonkwo and Ekwefi. Indeed, its similarity to versions of marriage with which Western students are familiar may help explain why empathy with Ekwefi's mistreatment is so spontaneous and a reading of the text as misogynist can take place so easily. By contrast students seem to have much more difficulty dealing with friendly alliances between senior and junior wives in the work of other African writers. Many of them reject outright the idea in Ama Ata Aidoo's *Anowa* that a wife could actively seek out a junior wife for her husband as a way of marking her own material consequence; of asserting her own identity. Such relationships are important in the constructing of female identity, and that is clearly not what Achebe's novel is about.

A similar selective process occurs in the presentation of women's public roles. Achebe names one of the two groupings within the clan which endowed women with specific political authority: the *umuada*, or daughters of the clan. Since Igbo marriage ties were usually exogamous a woman also belonged to another group in her husband's village consisting of the wives of the clan. Directly or indirectly, these groups controlled between them many aspects of civic and familial spheres of influence. In *Things Fall Apart* these range from the policing of stray animals to the solemnizing of certain stages within marriage and betrothal rituals and the preservation of a maternal line of land entitlement. Indeed, Okonkwo's survival in exile hinges on his right to exercise his entitlement to land in his mother's village via the connections vested in her as a wife in Okonkwo's father's clan and a daughter in her father's clan.

Achebe does not tell us, however, that the *umuada* also regulated the markets in each town and that their intervention or threatened intervention was crucial in civic as well as marital disputes. When Uzowulu is brought to judgement for chronic abuse of his wife, one of the elders asks why such a minor matter has been brought to the attention of the *egwugwu* and is told: "Don't you know what kind of man Uzowulu is? He will not listen to any other decision." It is clear that Achebe introduces the *egwugwu* here to underline for his audience in terms they can appreciate how seriously the community looks upon violence against women. But in fact it would seem from the anthropological accounts that a more likely scenario in a case such as this would have been the intervention of the wives of the clan, who would have enforced the judgement by "sitting" on the man in question: that is by so shaming him publicly through rude songs and obscene gestures that he would be forced to mend his ways. Alternatively, the female kinswomen of the battered women who had married into the clan of the offending male could have threatened to enforce a sexual strike if their husbands did not see to it that Uzowulu mended his ways.

Clearly Achebe would have been hard put to imbue such scenarios with the decorum expected of women within Western tradition. And indeed, he may have internalized a Western view of legal authority, defining male courts of law as the ultimate seat of power in any society, to such an extent that alternative ways of dramatizing Uzowulu's ostracism through female intervention may have seemed ineffective by comparison. In any event, their omission from the narrative leaves us with no example of female authority within the Igbo social structure that is not compatible with traditional Western ideals of femininity as nurturing, ornamental or in need of protection. Indeed, a truly jaundiced eye would have also to note that the women in the novel are described cooking, plaiting their hair, decorating their bodies, dancing, running from *egwugwu* and being given in marriage. We do not see them planting in their farms, bartering their goods in the market place, sitting in judgement on members of their community or taking action alongside or against their men. The only woman we see acting with any authority is the priestess of Chielo, and she is presented, in terms consistent with Western practice, as a witch—a force for good or evil separated from the regular run of womenfolk rather than part of a chain of ritual and social female authority.

Such omissions become all the more difficult to reconcile when one remembers that it was precisely the outbreak of the Women's War in Aba in 1929, organized by the wives and daughters of a number of clans that had delivered one of the most sweeping challenges to colonial authority in living memory among the Igbo at the time when Achebe was writing. In fact, it was this event which motivated the British government to give research grants to several "amateur" colonial anthropologists to study Igbo society specifically. These studies produced the spate of early anthropological accounts Achebe satirizes in his references to the District Commissioner's projected book on *The Pacification of the Primitive Tribes of the Lower Niger.*

One sees the consequence of this selective process in one situation in the novel which in my opinion would have been richer had Achebe paid closer attention to women's political structures within Igbo society. When Okonkwo is forced to flee to his motherland after committing the female crime of manslaughter he is given a lecture by his maternal uncle on the importance of the feminine principle in Igbo culture. Okonkwo, who can only define masculinity in relation to what his father was not, is understandably out of his depth when asked to accept a notion that his identity may also be formed by qualities represented by his mother. But because we as readers have no sense of the full range of qualities both protective and assertive that are associated with the feminine principle in Igbo society we are given as few options as Okonkwo in interpreting the scene. We know that he should be patient and dependent and grateful for the protection of his motherland. We also know that in spiritual terms the earth goddess Ala is the deity Okonkwo has most often offended and that she is responsible for his exile. However, we have no way of knowing that female power symbolized by Ala is represented in the clan by a system of legal codes and practices controlled by the women in Okonkwo's society . . . that in a sense Okonkwo's refusal to be comforted by his motherland is also a rejection of aspects of the very civic culture by which his access to the privileges of manhood is partially regulated. Much of this would seem to be implied in Achebe's presentation of this scene but there is none of the rich working out of all the implications that occurs elsewhere in the unfolding of masculine systems of values and authority.

Achebe's selective use of those aspects of Igbo traditional society which best coincide with Western/Christian social values, speak ably to his own need to establish a view of a world, both modern and traditional of which he can be a part. To call this treatment of the formation of a masculine sense of identity sexist is a facile and not very accurate reading of a gendered response to a specific cultural dilemma. That Achebe's narrative is indeed a selective, gendered one which partakes of both traditional and Judaeo-Christian patriarchal values only becomes a problem in the light of the history of *Things Fall Apart*'s reception as the definitive, "objective" account of the Igbo, not to say African, traditional past. In expanding a hypothetical paragraph in a district commissioner's text into the saga of a lost civilization, Achebe was able to address imaginatively the nostalgia, social insecurity and nationalist sentiments of an entire continent. The problem is that he succeeded so well that his representation of the past has become a substitute for the reality which, inevitably, is far more complex than one novel could hope to make it. The result is that, like the institutions it helped debunk, Achebe's text has itself become the object of deconstructive exercises in the work of more recent Nigerian writers. In the work of Buchi Emecheta, Achebe's chapters, (or perhaps extended paragraphs?) on the position of women in Igbo society have been revised to offer a complete alternative vision of the attitudes of traditional women to their status in the society. It is a partisan and revisionist picture, committed to challenging Igbo and Judaeo-Christian values from the perspective of an upwardly mobile fellow traveller in the women's movement. However it, too, must resist the temptation to limit the roles it ascribes to women in traditional society to those "invented" by Achebe. Indeed, for the modern woman writer in Africa, Achebe's authority must seem as compelling and as difficult to challenge as the district commissioner's voice must have been for Achebe in his time.

This irony serves to remind us that literature, like anthropology or history, is a form of selective representation, replete with its inherent assumptions about authenticity and "objectivity". For those of us who teach *Things Fall Apart* as an appendix to anthropological and sociological documents, or as a way of bringing history to life, it is important to keep in mind that this particular fiction is a response to history which mimics the structure and claims to objectivity of "science" without for a moment abdicating its right as fiction to be selective, subjective or unrealistic. Those of us who teach *Things Fall Apart* as literature in the hope of reaffirming traditional values may do well to bear in mind that the values we discover in the text will be most likely our own. Achebe's novel is a brilliant resolution of the conflict experienced by his generation between traditional and Western notions of manhood, courage and the construction of communal values.

Such resolution is seldom if ever about choosing between two clearly defined alternatives and inevitably involves a process of selection. When our students accuse Achebe of sexism or Emecheta of historical inaccuracy, what their statements really attest is the creation for better or worse of an African literary canon, based on a highly selective system of values shared by Achebe and his cohort of African intellectuals that has come to be used as a way of reading history: a touchstone for the literature as well as for the society of the postcolonial age. Time, perhaps, to rename *Things Fall Apart—*
Things Are Consolidated?

EMMANUEL EDAME EGAR

Rhetorical Implications of the Theme in
Things Fall Apart

*T*hings Fall Apart takes its title from W. B. Yeats' poem, *The Second Coming*, which opens with:

> Turning and turning in the widening gyre
> The falcon cannot hear the falconer
> Things fall apart, the center cannot hold
> Mere anarchy is loosened upon the world."

Allen Tate, in his *Romanticism: Twentieth Century Views* (1963), considered this poem a symbol of disunity: "The gyre here can be visualized as the circling flight of the bird constantly widening until it lost contact with the point, the center, to which it ought to be able to return." Tate did not see the negation in repetition and redundancy which seems to anticipate its own death. However, disunity is only one aspect of the poem. Tate did not see the sense of chaos and anarchy which incite evil and override goodness. The poem evokes a sense of gloomy mystery. There is the sense of fear intensified by the shadows of grim desert birds. There is also a lingering sense of doom and catastrophe. There is the vision of the beast, mysterious and dreadful, but which, nevertheless, seems to provoke admiration and fear. There is also a twisted irony about this beast, which is half human and half

From *The Rhetorical Implications of Chinua Achebe's* Things Fall Apart. © 2000 by University Press of America.

animal, slouching strenuously towards Bethlehem to be born—a symbol of confusion, myth and wonder.

The poem works through a reader's sensory organs, stimulating his/her sensibilities through symbols, the cadence of its rhythm, the lingering sense of spiritual mystery, and the sense of disaster which threatens to explode but which closes up at the critical point of explosion. In this poem, all the sense of gloom, disaster, and fear move rapidly into a condensed image of a struggling beast slouching towards Bethlehem to be born. This mysterious beast epitomizes Okonkwo in *Things Fall Apart*, around whom Achebe welds a powerful history of Ibo culture using Ibo rhetorical forms expressed in English.

Things Fall Apart depicts a unified society nurtured and sustained by a complexity of relationships. This society maintained its tenuous unity through the exclusion of women, children, slaves, and foreigners. It was a society ruled by powerful men who made sure that the weak felt the force of this power. Okonkwo was the executor of this power, until he confronted Western culture, was defeated, and caused his culture to fall with him. With the summary of the novel comes the critical questions: Is it possible to accurately translate Ibo rhetorical form into English? Will the English language be able to catch the "thingly" character of the thing which is in Ibo rhetorical form? For Heidegger, in his *Poetry, Language, Thought* (1975), the "thingly" character of the thing can be captured through symbols and allegories, but he also expressed doubt about the authenticity of Latin translation of the Greek language:

> Beneath the seemingly literal and thus faithful translation there is a concealed, rather, a translation of Greek experience into a different way of thinking. Roman thought takes over the Greek words without a corresponding, equally authentic experience of what they say, without the Greek word. The rootlessness of Western thought begins with this translation.

Heidegger here is expressing doubt regarding the authenticity of translations. But Heidegger is not alone. African poets, writers, and critics have expressed this doubt in the ambivalence of admission and rejection associated with writing in a foreign language. Some of the writers include Simon Mpondo, Obi Wali, Albert Girard, C. S. Izevbaye, Ayo Banjo, Peter Young, Chinua Achebe, Wole Soyinka, and Leopold Senghor.

Nevertheless, the expression of doubts and the associated problems with translation have never stopped writers from producing masterpieces in foreign languages. It stopped neither Joseph Conrad nor Wole Soyinka, a

Nigerian writer, from winning Nobel prizes in literature. Achebe wrote out of a compulsion to capture and preserve the Ibo rhetorical form, the art of conversation, the use of proverbs, and the use of the wooden gong, the *Ogenne*. He therefore listened to Freud who claimed that "one writes because one hears a request (demand) and in order to answer it. . . ." To answer this request, Achebe was able to domesticate and appropriate the English language through the art of conversation, the use of proverbs, the use of the wooden gong (the *Ogenne*), and the earthy nature of his diction.

The pattern of change that Yeats sees in this poem, "The Second Coming," is an instrument of prophecy. He looks at a long tradition of Western civilization crumbling before a nameless something. Achebe, however, is interested not only in prophecy but in the interpretation of that prophecy. That is why the first part of the novel depicts that ceremony of innocence, peace, piety, and blissful communal life. In this part of the novel, one sees rituals of man and nature, of man and the spirit, the supernatural. The spirits help man to solve his problems in the tribe, problems that could have destroyed the clan.

In the novel, every rule is created and every religious ritual conducted by wise and respected counselors. A man may speak and judge from a mask, but the man who wears the mask is a symbol of the living embodiment of the clan. His role is like that of the Catholic priest, who, in saying mass, ceases to be himself and becomes a channel for the divine.

But how does one explain this custom, this culture, this way of life, to an unenlightened British administrator who believes that military power equals wisdom in tribal affairs? This naivete is demonstrated in the treatment of village chiefs by the British Commissioner. The Commissioner claims: "We have brought a peaceful administration to you and your people so that you may be happy. If anyone ill-treats you, we shall come to your rescue" (Achebe 1995).

This statement is bold and overbearing, because it induces a sense of the master and servant syndrome, a sense of superiority, a lordship, and a painful sense of domination. It makes the chiefs seem feeble, weak, vulnerable, helpless and incapable of defending themselves. This was an appalling degradation to a community that had run its affairs smoothly for generations. This is the kind of statement that would arouse the gods of the land, the ancestral spirits and the children of the clan to rise and fight. Why do these people need protection from a complete stranger in their own land? The coming of the white man to Umuafia was really mere anarchy let loose on the land. Yeats may have had the same vision: "How twenty centuries of stormy sleep were vexed to nightmare by a rocking cradle." Christianity, to Yeats, seemed to be a nightmare to a sleeping Europe. But the nightmare was even greater among the converts who had lost what they had, because they succumbed to divided loyalties. Chinua Achebe is therefore able to interpret and incorporate the abstract prophecies and visions of Yeats into his novel. It is of interest to note that Yeats was not bound to experience the frustration, anxieties, doubts, pains, mutilations and desires of his visions. But, for Achebe, the vision was not just a prophecy, it was real life. Thus, Kerenyi and Jung, in their *Essays on the Science of Mythology*, may be right in thinking that the primitive man does not invent myth, he experiences it.

Achebe seems to have an obsession with the secular vision of the artist, the writer as a teacher, a seer, a prophet and diviner of his society, whose voice should be obeyed. This obsession with the secular vision of the artist is demonstrated in Achebe's other novels such as, *No Longer at Ease* (1960), *A Man of the People* (1966), and *Arrow of God* (1969). *No Longer at Ease* takes its title from T. S. Eliot's poem, *The Journey of the Magi*. "We return to our places, these kingdoms, but no longer at ease here, in this old dispensation with an alien people clutching their Gods. Should be glad of another death" (1936).

Eliot's concern here seems to be the relation between the converted Christian and his friends who still hold on to their immoral ways of life. The fate of the new Christian converts here is similar to those of three wise men who went to see the child Jesus. These men, because of their contact and association with Jesus, became purged of their sins, purified, cleansed and born again as Christians. But their real problem was that this very act of purification became a tragedy because they could no longer accept the old ways of their friends, nor could their friends accept the converts. The critical question here became: How did Christianity help the Magi, the individual, and his community? A possible answer could be that Christianity did not help; instead, it became a plague that would either destroy the Magi or be destroyed in the interest of a peaceful communal living.

In *No Longer at Ease* (1960), Achebe translates this tragedy of the Magi into the tragedy of Obi, the protagonist, educated in England, in the platonic tradition that made him conscious of truth, philosophy and morality. Obi now returns from England with his new knowledge and tries to inflict this knowledge on his society, Nigeria. He fails, is rejected and punished. The critical question of the novel becomes: What good is a Western-educated Nigerian to his country if he cannot use his knowledge when he returns home? The tragedy for Obi and others is that their Western education itself becomes the burden that will either make them or break them.

In *A Man of the People* (1966), Achebe writes a satire on greed and corruption. It is a dog-eats-dog morality that is particularly disturbing because the wealth of the nation is being ravaged by a few. The poignancy of this corruption is that the leaders of the nation drive Jaguars and splash filthy street water onto the throngs of beggars who line the streets. Achebe's outcry here is: When is enough really enough?

In *Arrow of God* (1969), Achebe struggles to combine his secular vision with a religious factor. To understand his vision in this novel calls for a summary of the novel. A summary of the novel reveals that, in Ibo society, a Chief Priest has to eat one sacred yam for each of the twelve months of the year. He must eat the twelfth yam on the twelfth month before the villagers can celebrate their new yam festival and taste the crops of their harvest. But complications could occur if, for some reason, the priest is prevented from eating these yams as expected, and so he has to carry some yams forward into the new year. Second, the moon must shine brightly as a sign of acceptance of the ritual by the supreme deity. But, sometimes in the rainy season, the moon hides under thick clouds for weeks and months. This means that the appearance of the moon may not synchronize with geometric time. The problem here is that whoever made the rules for the New Yam Festival did not anticipate these problems. The rules were then tested when the Chief Priest was arrested and detained for two months. This means that while time progressed, two yams were not eaten. It is at this point that the role of the priest as the arrow of his god is tested. To compound things for the priest, his son died a mysterious death during these tensions. Was this a warning from his god? Ezeulu's obedience to his deity, which became a form of insensitivity to his community, raises fundamental questions: Is Ezeulu the arrow, the mouthpiece of his god, or has he become the god himself? Second, does a God who is insensitive to human suffering deserve the service and obedience of free men? Third, how could a community be committed to an insensitive god in the midst of severe human suffering? Fourth, if the people abandon this god, does he continue to exist and sustain himself? The issue here was that, according to geometric time, it was the twelfth month of the year and time for the New Yam Festival, the yearly harvest and feast. The question then was: Would Ezeulu, the Chief Priest, eat the two yams and let the ceremony go on? Or will he carry on with the demands of his god for the next two months, while people die of starvation during that time? In rage, the villagers demanded that he eat the yams and let the wrath of the god fall upon them. Ezeulu still did not move. He must obey the wishes of Ulu and wait for two months.

Answering any of the questions concerning Ezeulu, his god and community, requires sober thought and meditation, particularly since the first question has troubled man from Abraham to Agamemnon. Ezeulu, for not listening to the sufferings of his people, may have become the god, the judge and the jury of spiritual and cultural rituals. He took over the role of the god, but he was supposed to be only the messenger. The next question to ask is: Could Noah have asked Jehovah to stop the flood? The answer to this question is that the Ibos really do not believe in permanent gods. A god is dispensable. If one god behaves badly, another replaces him. To answer the second question calls for a comparison of the relationship between the children of Israel and their God, Jehovah. It will appear that the Israelites stood by their God because he supplied them manna, food from heaven. To answer the fourth question, it would seem that only the Judaic God has the capacity to sustain Himself, because He is omnipotent and omniscient. But the Ibo god survives based on the wishes of the people. He does not have the luxury of the Judaic God, which is a terrible handicap to a god. It was this handicap that Soyinka remarked about in his "dialogue and outrage."

Wole Soyinka, a master of dramatic ritual, has written a treatise on Chinua Achebe's *Arrow of God*. Soyinka's treatise pertains to the demise of the deity, Ulu, and his priest:

> In Achebe's work, the gods are made an expression of political unity (dis-unity) of the people. Their history or measure testifies to their subjection to secular consciousness. However generously the element of the inexplicable is introduced into the lives of the community, it is not possible ultimately for the gods to overcome their beginnings. The deity Ulu came into being as a result of a security decision, an expression of survivalist will of the community. . . . How could such people disregard a god who founded their city and protected them, muses his priest. They could although a new existence was brought into being through the agency of the god, it was a purely political existence. . . . The will of this creative relationship remained with the human side of the partnership. (Soyinka 1992)

The human side of the relationship that Soyinka refers to is that the Ibo create their gods to serve them. If he fails to do their will, they abandon him and his priest. The rhetorical implication of the role of the god is that the Ibos respect the community more than the individual, and even god. The power that the Ibo god carries is quite different from that of the Judeo-Christian Jehovah. The behavior of the Ibos to the gods shows that they really believe that, without man, there would be no god.

Chinua Achebe, in his secular vision, raises this apocalyptic view for his community, first with the British intrusion in *Things Fall Apart*. However, despite the negative portrayal of British intrusion, the British intrusion had many benefits. First, the British introduced Western education, trade, Christianity and stability to the diverse tribes. It was this British education that produced characters like Obi, in *No Longer at Ease* (Achebe, 1960). Obi, a protagonist, was educated in England, in the Socratic dialectic, in the Platonic admiration of morality, truth and beauty. This British education also produced greedy leaders who gave rise to the novel, *A Man of the People* (1966). If the British intrusion destabilized the fabric of the traditional culture, the last sector of this culture that remained stable was the religious one. But this religious sector, as one witnesses in *Arrow of God* (1969) was not destabilized by the British, but by the communal will of the people. The will of the people dethroned a god that was no longer sensitive to the needs of the community. The critical question for Achebe becomes, if the will of the people was stable enough to dethrone a god, how could the British have succeeded in destroying the culture that Achebe writes about in *Things Fall Apart*? Maybe Achebe had other reasons for highlighting this tension, this secular vision, of the terrible wrongs that the Western European is accused of inflicting on the African.

Achebe is concerned that the artist act as an educator, a teacher, a prophet and a diviner. In *Things Fall Apart*, Achebe wanted his society to know that: "What we need to do is to look back and try and find out where we went wrong, where the rain began to beat us (Achebe 1995)."

In *Things Fall Apart*, one doesn't need to look too far to ascertain what went wrong. By allowing the white man to land on African shores, Africans allowed the white man to impose Christianity, Western European education, trade, monetary economy, and Socratic dialectic—with its craving for right and wrong, its love of truth and beauty—on the African social system. Achebe continues to pound on this theme, but nowhere else has he openly espoused this secular vision of the writer than in his essay, *The Novelist as Teacher* (1989).

In this essay, Achebe expounds the notion that racism is essentially a lie. Racism lied about African culture, morals and mores. He urges the artist to reinforce the self-dignity, self-worth and self-actualization of his or her society, and to impart the realization that Africa did not suffer through one long night of savagery before being liberated by the Western European intrusion. In an exasperated tone of indignation and concern, Achebe (1989) claims:

> Here then is an adequate revolution for me to espouse to help my society regain belief in itself and put away the complexes of years of denigration and self abasement. And it is essentially, a question of education in the best sense of the word. Here I think my aims and deepest aspirations of my society meet. For no

thinking African can escape the pain of the wound in the soul.
. . . But, for the moment it is in the nature of things that we may
need to counter racism with what Jean-Paul Sartre has called an
anti-racist racism, to announce not just that we are as good as
the next man, but that we are much better.

A careful examination of this passage should raise some concerns. First,
the world "revolution," as used in this passage, is too violent, too aggressive
and too abrasive and is therefore intolerable for a man who calls himself a
teacher. This dissertation writer is concerned that a revolutionary can
encourage and explode problems that he/she does not intend to solve, nor
know how to solve. Africa, this dissertation author believes, is tired of revo-
lutionaries. Africa needs people who can supply answers and solutions to the
problems of the continent. Africa needs individuals who will set up mecha-
nisms to improve agriculture and curb starvation. Africa needs people to
provide a clean water supply which will reduce the transmission of water-
born fatalities. Africa needs people to set up hospitals and build safe and
sturdy roads in order to minimize needless fatalities. Writing a novel may
produce readers, but how do you produce people who become readers? How
do you provide good schools, nutritious diets, adequate health care, and the
tools for basic hygiene that will produce healthy, educated people who can
read and understand a novel? Achebe does not consider these questions
because it is easier to write and start a revolution than to supply solutions to
pressing problems.

Achebe also claims in this article that Africans need education "in the
best sense of the word" (1989). His phrase, "in the best sense" is meaningless
because the word "best" is a relative term that depends on the user to make
sense. It may be reasonable to argue that the writer was unable to define his
brand of education, and that is why his meaning is silent in his text. He also
claims that the aims and aspirations of his society meet in education. But the
education that aims at flaming negative aspects of Africa's association with
the West does nothing for Africa. His call seems to be directed at disorder
without providing a solution for the real problems. Perhaps, the most
disturbing part of his article is the claim that "No thinking African can
escape the pain of the wound in the soul" (1989). This is a blatant universal
statement which seems to provoke the master/servant syndrome. From this
statement, Achebe unilaterally makes himself the god of and spokesperson
for Africa, who thinks for the rest of Africa, who knows the soul and the
minds of all Africans. He seems to indicate that an African is "non thinking"
if he/she does think and feel as he does. That statement takes the majority of
Africans for granted; it suppresses dissident and minority voices and thereby

injects feelings of inferiority into the society. It is important to remember that inferiority is the very attitude that Achebe seems to be fighting against. For instance, since this dissertation writer does not think that Africa's association with the West was all bad, despite the subtle negations which were not inflicted internationally, does it mean that this writer is "non thinking?" The "pain of the wound in the soul" is not that of social or historical evils on Africa; the pain is how to take care of the environment and the African cosmos. Consequently, Achebe's anti-racist racism can be turned against him because all he is doing is drumming up trouble and tension in order to create an interest and a market for his novels. It is of interest to note that not one hospital or clinic has been built in Nigeria from the proceeds of Achebe's book royalties. This is where this dissertation author thinks the real concern should be for a social revolutionary.

Perhaps equally disturbing is his claim that his reason to write was to "announce not just that we are as good as the next man, but much better" (1989). This sentence evokes the same superiority complex, the same anti-racist racism, that he claims to be fighting. How did Africa become better than Europe? The white man did not create the rain or the fatalities that came with the rain. Hence, if Africa had taken care of its own rain and fatalities, the coming of the white man would have been irrelevant.

This dissertation author's greatest concern regarding Achebe's secular vision is the lack of explanation regarding how Africans can escape this ugly association with the West. How can Africans escape this negation when even Achebe's voice, the song and dance of his revolution, are all tainted with the master's voice, the Socratic dialectic? How can he free the African from his master's voice when his very own voice expresses the master's voice and song? Is he really sincere in writing as if Africa's association with the Western European did not produce any form of good? The good of the association, despite some subtle frustrations, was quite profound. African contact with Europe provides most of the continent with a common language of communication, freeing the continent from the confusion of many tribal languages. Contact with Europe brought education, hospitals, improved roads, monetary economy, and improved hygiene. Again, Achebe's revolutionary writing will not balance a national budget, nor will it increase Nigeria's foreign reserves in the international world bank. His novels will, however, increase his personal wealth, a wealth that he can sustain so long as he is able to keep pounding on the theme of hostility to the West. As Barthes claims, "So long as there is no bet, there is a game" (1994).

Achebe has an obsession with this game. His understanding of the role of the artist in his society seems to be an imitation of the poet, Imlac, who, in Johnson's *Rasselas*, claims that the poet must write: "as the interpreter of nature and the legislature of mankind, and consider himself as presiding over the thoughts and meanings of future generations; as a being superior to time and place."

The above statement is an awful presumption for the poet who becomes the god, the judge, and the fury for all mankind. But one must not forget that before the poet Imlac came to this conclusion, he had first expressed surprise at the unusually high social recognition that the poet received. This is a recognition that placed the poet on the hierarchy almost equal to the angels. One must not forget that the implication of Imlac's statement was that the society of antiquity depended upon superstition and not on rational reasoning and quickly placed any blame upon the gods. Imlac was particularly surprised that poetic art, a gift of inspiration that comes at the spur of the moment, should carry such resounding honor. It was due to this seemingly innocent nature of poetic inspiration that Imlac decided that the real poet must have a deeply-seated learning that is diversified and broad. The rhetorical implication of Achebe's secular vision is to foment a perpetual tension between Africa and the West so as to create a market for his theme and his books.

If the theme of the novel provides Achebe the means to propagate his ideas and sell his novel, it is in the character of Okonkwo that Achebe unleashes his greatest pitch. In Okonkwo, Achebe is able to persuade the Western European reader that an African writer could create a hero with characteristics comparable to the heroes in the Greek and Shakespearean tragedies. In ancient Greek tragedies, before the transformation in Orestes, the fate of the hero depended upon the gods. The gods were to blame for their fall. In Shakespearean tragedy, the fall of the hero depends on his character flaws. This is why Shakespeare believed that character equals fate. The character of Okonkwo combines that frail human dependence on the wishes of the gods with a fatal individual character flaw.

ABDUL JANMOHAMED

Sophisticated Primitivism: The Syncretism of Oral and Literate Modes in Achebe's Things Fall Apart

I

The use of the English language and literary forms by African (and other Third World) writers must be understood in the context of a larger social, political, and ideological dialogue between British, and particularly colonialist, literature on the one hand and the ex-colonized writers of the Third World on the other. Faced by the colonialist denigration of his past and present culture and consequently motivated by a desire to negate the prior European negation of indigenous society, the African writer embarks on a program of regaining the dignity of self and society by representing them, in the best instances, in a manner that he considers unidealized but more authentic. This negative dialogue transcends the literary polemic about authentic "images" of Africans and manifests itself in an opposition of forms as well: thus, for instance, Chinua Achebe is drawn to realism partly in order to counter the "racial romances" of Joyce Cary.

However, some critics have argued that the African end of this dialogue is unable to negate colonialist literature totally precisely because it relies on the English language to do so. The question that underlies this criticism is indeed an important one: can African experience be adequately represented through the alien media (ones that were fashioned to codify an entirely different encounter with reality) of the colonizers' language and literary forms or will these media inevitably alter the nature of African experience in

From *Ariel* 15, no.4 (October 1984). © 1984 by The Board of Governors University of Calgary.

significant ways? But the question cannot be answered very easily. While the ideological sentiment behind this criticism is perfectly understandable and laudable, the critics who want Third World writers to abandon European languages and forms have not concretely examined the results of the contemporary syncretic literatures of the Third World. Whatever answers are ultimately given to the underlying question, the concrete evidence must be scrutinized first. Thus I would like to bracket temporarily the controversy about English in order to examine, in this essay, an issue that, one can argue, has causal priority: how is the encounter between the predominantly *oral* cultures of Africa and the *literate* cultures of the colonizer represented and mediated by anglophone African fiction? Is such fiction, which, to stress the obvious, is *literate* and written in *English*, able to do justice to the phenomenology of oral/mythic cultures, which is radically different from that of chirographic cultures? From an ideological viewpoint we must also inquire whether or not the adoption of the alien language makes a significant contribution to the negative dialogic relation between African and English literatures.

The African writer's very decision to use English as his medium is engulfed by ironies, paradoxes, and contradictions. He writes in English because he was born in a British colony and can receive formal education only in English. More significantly, however, he is compelled to master and use English because of the prevailing ideological pressures within the colonial system. At the surface level these manifest themselves through the ethnocentric narcissism of the European colonialists who will only recognize the other as a "civilized" human being if he recreates himself in their image by adopting the appropriate European language as well as literary forms. This applies to all aspects of culture and politics: for instance, the granting of "independence" itself is contingent upon the adoption of some version of Western parliamentary democracy. At a deeper level the insistence that the colonies accept European forms, values, and beliefs represents a deliberate, if subconscious, strategy to ensure an unproblematic change from dominant to hegemonic colonialism. "Independence" marks the transition from the dominant phase, where "consent" of the dominated is obtained by direct coersion, to the hegemonic phase, where "consent" is procured through the ideological formation of the dominated subject. Thus the adoption of European languages, and subsequently European values, beliefs, etc., by the native remains crucial to the hegemonic transfer, which generates, as by-products, anglophone, francophone, etc., Third World writers who may or may not be involved in a negative dialogue with European literature. (Some writers, such as V. S. Naipaul, who has clearly adopted the "author function" of the colonizer, are more inclined to represent a version of the colonialist viewpoint.)

Finally, a potential writer from a British colony is induced to use English because it is an intimate part of a powerful society that will control all technological and cultural development in the foreseeable future.

Yet the decision to use English produces a contradiction between, on the one hand, the unconscious and subconscious phychic formations of most Third World writers, determined by the indigenous languages, and, on the other hand, the more superficial, conscious formation, determined by the formal, public function of English in most colonies. The problem is compounded by the fact that, unlike English, most African languages were non-literate and that the noetic structures of these oral cultures are significantly different from those of chirographic ones. The African writer who uses English, then, is faced at some level with the paradox of representing the experience of oral cultures through literate language and forms. Chinua Achebe, on whose first novel I shall concentrate, is subconsciously aware of this problem and has depicted in his fiction not only the material, political, and social destruction of indigenous societies caused by colonization but also the subtle annihilation of the conservative, homeostatic oral culture by the colonialists' introduction of literacy. Thus his novels not only depict the materiality of the destroyed and destroying worlds, but as chirographic representations of oral cultures they also become simultaneous agents of the preservation and destruction of the oral world. The style and structure of *Things Fall Apart*, I shall argue, do encode the phenomenology of oral cultures and thereby create a new syncretic form and contribute to the negative dialectics by deterritorializing, to some extent, the English language and the novelistic form.

II

The differences between oral and chirographic cultures have been articulated most thoroughly and systematically by Jack Goody and Walter J. Ong, and the following, somewhat schematic summary of these differences is based on their modulated analyses. Goody correctly emphasizes the fact that traditional anthropological formulations of the differences between these kinds of cultures through the binary and ethnocentric categories such as civilized/savage, rational/irrational, scientific/mythic, hot/cold, etc., are essentially manichean, that is, they tend to valorize morally one term at the expense of the other and to characterize the differences as being qualitative, categorical, and ontological rather than quantitative, material, and technological. Both Goody and Ong insist that the essential differences between these cultures can be explained through a scrutiny of literacy and its effects.

The point, as Goody puts it, is that the "relationship between modes of thought and the modes for the production and reproduction of thought . . . [lies] at the heart of the unexplained but not inexplicable differences that so many writers have noted," that changes in the modes of production and reproduction of thought, i.e., (alphabetic) literacy and later printing, are bound to affect the very content and modes of thought.

Literacy, by isolating thought on a written surface, tends to alienate language, knowledge, and world in positive and productive ways. When an utterance "is put in writing it can be inspected in much greater detail, in its parts as well as in its whole, backwards as well as forwards, out of context as well as in its setting; in other words, it can be subjected to a quite different type of scrutiny and critique than is possible with purely verbal communication. Speech is no longer tied to an 'occasion'; it becomes timeless. Nor is it attached to a person; on paper, it becomes more abstract, more depersonalized." This kind of scrutiny eventually leads to the development of syllogistic and other forms of analysis. By allowing one to record events as they occur, to store them for long periods of time, and to recall them in their original forms, literacy eventually builds up a dense representation of the past and thus leads to the development of historical consciousness and secular teleology. The availability of a dense past and more sophisticated analytic tools in turn encourages greater reflexivity and self-scrutiny. One must emphasize again that oral cultures are unable to develop these characteristics not because of some genetic racial or cultural inferiority but simply because they lack the proper tool, namely literacy. Yet in the absence of these essential features of chirographic societies, the phenomenology of oral cultures tends to be characterized by the following traits: it defines meaning and value contextually rather than abstractly; it is conservative and homeostatic; its universe is defined by mythic rather than historical consciousness; it valorizes collectivity rather than individuality; and it is dominated by a totalizing imperative.

Oral cultures tend to define concepts through situational, operational frames of reference that are minimally abstract. Ideas are comprehended either through their concrete manifestations or through their context, but rarely in terms of other abstract ideas; lexis is controlled through direct semantic ratification, through experience rather than logical definition. Writing, on the other hand, creates a context-free or "autonomous" discourse. Written words are no longer directly bound up with reality; they become separate "things," abstracted from the flow of speech, shedding their close entailment with action and context.

Since the conservation of conceptualized knowledge in oral cultures depends on memory, that which is not memorized through repetition soon disappears. This mnemonic need establishes a highly traditionalist or conservative set of mind that tends to inhibit experimentation and innovation. On the other hand, the mind in chirographic cultures, freed from this mnemonic constraint, is not only able to experiment but, perhaps more significantly, to record and build on innovations and changes. Consequently, oral societies tend to adopt a protective attitude towards their epistemological and phenomenological categories and established theories and practices, whereas literate societies, particularly after they have embarked on a program of "scientific" inquiry, are more sceptical, critical, and analytic. The former tend to systematize and valorize belief, the latter, doubt. A corollary of the conserving function of the oral community is its homeostatic imperative, that is, its decision to maintain the equilibrium of the present by sloughing off memories which no longer have present relevance. The present needs of oral societies constantly impose their economy on past remembrances, and past events that are released from memory can never be recuperated in non-literate cultures.

The inability of oral cultures to document this past in a systematic and detailed manner, of course, means that they are dominated not by a historical but a mythic consciousness. As an account of origins, myth differs from history in that its claims cannot be verified with anything like the kind of accuracy available to literate societies. Based on this fundamental difference, Ernst Cassirer makes further distinctions between oral/mythic and scientific/historical consciousness that seem to be accurate but that are unfortunately formulated in fundamentally ethnocentric, manichean terms. However, at the very least, one can say that because the noetic economy of oral/mythic consciousness is not burdened by the needs of ratification it is able to develop a more fluid symbolic exchange system. This fluidity not only facilitates the enactment of the central teleological imperative of oral cultures, i.e., to maintain a constant homeostatic balance, but also permits the development of a specific relation between collectivity and individuality (weighted towards the former) and the economy and configuration of its totalizing imperative.

Communication in oral societies necessarily takes place in "primary group" relationships, that is, through intimate face-to-face contact. The result of this "intimate association, psychologically, is a certain fusion of individualities in a common whole, so that one's very self, for many purposes at least, is the common life and purpose of the group." Thus oral cultures tend to valorize collectivity over individuality and to create "individual" personality structures that are in fact communal and externalized, not inclined towards introspection. The externalized individual, then, is easily managed through the symbolic exchanges involved in communal ritual and practices. Writing and reading, on the other hand, are solitary achievements that tend, at least momentarily, to throw the psyche back on itself, and the knowledge that one's thoughts, when they are committed to writing, can endure in time encourages the emergence and recognition of individuality.

According to Ong, sight (and hence writing) isolates, while sound (and hence speech) incorporates. Whereas sight situates the observer outside what he views, at a distance, sound pours into the hearer; while sight is unidirectional, sound is enveloping. The centring action of sound affects man's sense of the cosmos. For oral cultures, the cosmos is an ongoing event with man at its centre. Man is the *umbilicus mundi.* In such societies, where the word has its existence only in sound, the phenomenology of sound enters deeply into a human being's feel for existence. All the characteristics of oral cultures discussed above relate intimately to the unifying and centralizing effect of sound. If we add to this tendency the fact that, in the absence of the analytic categories that are predicated on writing, oral cultures must conceptualize and verbalize all their knowledge with more or less close reference to the human lifeworld, assimilating the alien, objective world to the more immediate, familiar interaction of human beings, then we begin to glimpse the totalizing imperative of oral cultures. In such societies words, ideas, and reality are intrinsically bound; they are part of the same continuum. There is little distinction made between the pragmatic and non-pragmatic, the phenomenal and the numenal. All mundane reality is impregnated with spiritual significance, and the entire cosmos inheres in the most insignificant object; metonymy and metaphor, as essential phenomenological and epistemological structures, are more deeply integral to the oral consciousness than they are to the chirographic mind. If man is the centre of the fluid symbolic economy of such a society and if such a universe is conceptualized through its humanization, then potentially man has total control of it if only he knows the correct formulas and practices. In such a culture an "individual" can easily become the emblem of the desires and conflicts of the entire society, and this characteristic is, of course, important for the production of heroic, epic narratives.

Narrative is more functional in oral cultures than in others for two reasons. Since oral cultures cannot generate abstract or scientific categories for coding experience, they use stories of human (or anthropomorphized animal) action to organize, store, and communicate knowledge and experience. Second, such societies use narratives to bind a great deal of cultural signification that exists in less durable verbal forms. Thus, for example, oral narratives will often incorporate folktales, orations, genealogies, proverbs, etc. Unlike the linear or pyramidal plots of chirographic narratives, which are predicated on careful written revision, the plots of oral narratives are episodic and non-sequential: the narrator will report a situation and only much later explain, often in great detail, how it came to be. Yet, as Ong insists, this is not due to the narrator's desire to hasten into the midst of action. Such an interpretation is a product of literate cultures which assume that a linear plot has been deliberately scrambled. The episodic oral "plot" is really a product of the narrator *remembering* the story in a curious public way—remembering not a memorized "text" or a verbatim succession of words but themes, episodes, and formulae, which, along with the entire story, are *already known* by the audience as part of the culture's myths.

The narrative thus simultaneously exists as a public and private event: "as a traditional and external fact, the oral tale is foreseeable; as a literary fact (poetic, individual experience, etc.), the produced oral text has an internal finality that finds support in the foreseeable." The relation between the public (already known) and private (a specific retelling) version of a narrative is dialectical. The narrative is a potentiality that exists prior to the productive act of the narrator, while a specific performance of the story is a variation and an innovation that refers to the potentiality just as *parole* refers to *langue*. Thus creativity as well as aesthetic appositeness lie in choosing a formal element (proverb, folktale, etc.) and in (re)arranging of episodes in a plot sequence in ways that are appropriate to the specific narrative context. The oral narrative, then, is "situational" in a double sense: it proceeds episodically, that is, it reports a situation that is modified or explained much later and apparently at random; and the specific performance is partly determined by the narrative situation, that is, by the interaction between audience and narrator. The "scrambled" sequence of an oral narrative, with its necessary recapitulations and postponed amplifications and explanations, results in repetition or copia as one of its characteristic features. Yet repetition must not be mistaken for redundancy (a term that Ong uses as a synonym). As Harold Scheub has shown, it has an aesthetic function; oral narratives deliberately cultivate and intensify repetitions in order to realize their cumulative effects. We may add to this the possibility that the neotic function of repetition may be to reinforce the homeostatic imperative of oral cultures because well-modulated repetition would have the effect of recreating the balance of an already known, ordered, controlled, and rhythmically harmonious universe. A specific aesthetic corollary of copia that also characterizes oral narrative is the predominance of parataxis, both at the level of syntax and that of larger narrative units—formulas, episodes, etc.

The noetic economy of oral narratives also tends to generate heroic figures, not for romantic or deliberately didactic reasons but for more basic ones. In the first place, outsized characters are more memorable than the "ordinary" individuals of literate texts, and this is, of course, an important consideration for cultures without texts. In addition to encouraging triumphalism this economy also prefers heroic "flat characters" because around them can be organized the most significant elements of the culture: in fact these characters serve as the emblems of the culture and can be used to manage all kinds of non-narrative elements embedded in the story. Psychic and social interiority, the "roundedness" of well-developed chirographic characters, is rarely a significant concern of these narratives. Since such narratives emblemize, through the heroic figure, the totality of the culture and since the formal features of such stories evoke the noetic structures of a oral universe, the very performance of an oral narrative is itself a profoundly totalizing act. As Ngal insists, such narratives incorporate and commune with the core of the culture and evoke a "sense of belonging to a common history." I think it might be more accurate to say that such narratives allow the narrator and the audience to (re)integrate themselves with the totality and the totalizing imperative of their culture. As Goody points out and as Ruth Finnegan's study illustrates, while the content of these narratives can vary widely, the formal characteristics invariably remain constant.

III

Chinua Achebe's style in *Things Fall Apart* is consonant with the oral culture that he represents. In fact, the congruence between the style, elements of the narrative structure, and characterization, on the one hand, and the nature of the culture represented, on the other, account for the success of the novel: because Achebe is able to capture the flavour of an oral society in his style and narrative organization, *Things Fall Apart* is able to represent successfully the specificity of a culture alien to most Western readers.

His sentence structure is on the whole paratactic; it achieves its effect largely through juxtaposition, addition, and aggregation. Consider the opening paragraph of the novel:

> Okonkwo was well known throughout the nine villages and even beyond. His fame rested on solid personal achievements. As a young man of eighteen he had brought honor to his village by throwing Amalinze the Cat. Amalinze was the great wrestler who for seven years was unbeaten, from Umuofia to Mbaino. He was called the Cat because his back would never touch the earth. It was this man that Okonkwo threw in a fight . . .

In spite of the glaring opportunities for consolidating the short, simple sentences and subordinating some of them as modifying clauses, thereby emphasizing the more important elements, Achebe refuses to do so precisely because syntactic subordination is more characteristic of chirographic representation than it is of oral speech. The desired effect of this parataxis, which, as we will see, is echoed in the narrative organization of the novel, is the creation of a flat surface: since one fact is not subordinated to another more important one, everything exists on the same plane and is equally important. Of course, as one proceeds through the novel one begins to see that all the details coalesce around the heroic figure of Okonkwo, but while reading any one paragraph or chapter the initial effect is one of equivalence. This style and its effects, it must be emphasized, are deliberate. As Achebe himself has shown by comparing a more abstract and hypotactic version of a paragraph from *Arrow of God* with the concrete and paratactic original, the former is inappropriate for the protagonist of the novel and his context. The deliberateness of this style is also emphasized by its contrast with passages of oratory at political gatherings, funerals, and other formal occasions when the language, though still paratactic, is characterized by greater rhetorical formality. For instance, Uchendu's avuncular advice to Okonkwo is not only very dramatic and punctuated effectively with rhetorical questions but is also tightly structured according to the demands of the logic of his argument.

The effect of parataxis, however, is modulated by the repetition of various kinds of details. Significant facts keep resurfacing like a leimotif: for example, Okonkwo's achievement of fame through wrestling is introduced in the first paragraph on page seven, then repeated again on pages eleven and twenty-nine, and finally the narrator devotes an entire chapter to the importance of this sport in Igbo culture. At times virtually identical statements are repeated. Chapter three begins with the following statement: "Okonkwo did not have the start in life which many young men usually had. He did not inherit a barn from his father. There was no barn to inherit." This is followed by a two-page depiction of his father's laziness, which ends with "With a father like Unoka, Okonkwo did not have the start in life which many young men had. He neither inherited a barn nor a tile, nor even a young wife." Playing against the flat surface of the paratactic prose, such repetitions create a sense of rhythm and valorize some facts above others. This does produce a kind of subordination, but the fact that these repetitions are embedded in a flat narrative surface implies that they must be understood in terms of the overall situation; without the context these facts lose their value. In this novel significance is a function of recurrence, not of logical analytic valorization. The importance of context is illustrated by the fact that meaning of complex concepts is defined by reference to concrete situations rather than abstract elaboration. Thus, for example, *efulefu*, a worthless individual, is defined as follows: "The imagery of an *efulefu* in the language of the clan was a man who sold his machete and wore the sheath to battle." Or the apparent contradiction between the two definitions of *chi* as they appear on pages twenty-nine and thirty-three is explained by the context, which makes it clear that the *chi* is in agreement with the self when one is in harmony with oneself and the entire culture but that it becomes antagonistic when one is alienated from self and society. Though repetition and contextual definition modify the flat surface of the narrative, they do not, as we shall see later, create a distinction between background and foreground. Rather their function is to create a series of patterns on that surface.

Elements of the narrative structure and organization repeat and amplify, on a different register, the same effects. Yet the narrative, like the style, is a product of a double consciousness, of a syncretic combination of chirographic and oral techniques. Just as the style represents in writing the syntax and thought patterns of oral cultures, so the narrative operates on two levels: in its novelistic form the story of Okonkwo is unique and historical, yet it is told as if it were a well-known myth. The narrative acknowledges the latter fact in its opening sentence: "Okonkwo was well known throughout the nine villages and even beyond." The story of his poverty "was told in Umuofia," and that of Ikemefuna's sacrifice "is still told to this day." Similarly other aspects of this narrative manifest themselves as circulating oral tales, and the white colonizers first appear to the hero in the form of stories. The reader is left with an impression that these tales are loosely connected but that the narrator of *Things Fall Apart* will (re)stitch them in his own unique order. However, even though the "myth" about Okonkwo and his family is common knowledge it has to be told (and heard) as if for the first time. Thus, for example, after introducing the fact of Nwoye's apostasy and after depicting for several pages the first encounter between the Christian missionaries and the Igbos, Achebe returns to Nwoye's conversion with the following sentences: "But there was a young lad who had been captivated [by Christianity]. His name was Nwoye, Okonkwo's first son." This presentation of the apostasy, the name of the character, and his parentage as if for the first time is not due, we must assume, to narrative amnesia. Rather it is a part of the process of remembering in a public way, a product of returning, after a "digression" and in the absence of a text, to the facts. This technique of public remembrance, which seems to annoy many "literate" readers, accounts for the pervasive pattern wherein Achebe introduces a topic and then repeatedly returns to it in order to explain it piecemeal (see, for example, the series of reversions to the story of Ikemefuna until he is finally executed in chapter seven). Aspects of this pattern can be accounted for by the need to foreshadow, which is common to both chirographic and oral narratives. The overall effect of this pattern of postponements and reversions, of the juxtapositions of central themes and "digressions" is to create an interlocking mosaic of episodes out of which the significance of the story gradually emerges.

By proceeding through public remembrance the narrative makes ample use of periphrasis, which, according to Achebe, is a highly prized technique of Igbo conversation: "Among the Igbo the act of conversation is regarded very highly, and proverbs are the palm-oil with which words are eaten. Okoye was a great talker and he spoke for a long time, skirting round the subject and then hitting it finally." Like Okoye, the narrater skirts around his subject but carefully maintains certain ambiguities (which we shall examine later). The first chapter provides a good example of this narrative circularity. It covers the following subjects in that order: Okonkwo's fame, wrestling ability, personality, his father's character and indebtedness, Okonkwo's shame, his struggle for recognition and wealth, and his consequent custody of Ikemefuna, and the latter's destiny. In this spiral the chapter encapsulates the entire plot of part one of *Things Fall Apart.* The other twelve chapters of part one explore all of these issues in much greater detail, but not in the same order. In fact, the topics are thoroughly scrambled and a great deal of space is devoted to the depiction of the central events in the life of an agrarian community—planting, harvesting, etc., and the various festivals that accompany them—as well as rituals such as marriages, funerals, convening of the legal-spiritual court of the *egwugwus,* etc. Out of the one-hundred-and-eighteen pages that comprise part one of the novel only about eight are devoted, strictly speaking, to the development of the plot. The narrator is therefore anxious to represent the cultural "background" as much as the heroic figure, and in doing so he is able to depict the core of his culture and show that Okonkwo is one of its heroic representatives. Having thus depicted the interconnected totality of the culture and having established Okonkwo as its emblem in part one of the novel, the narrator, who in keeping with the already known narrative, is sensitively aware of the arrival of the destructive colonialists and their chirographic culture, changes the organization and the pace of the second and third parts of the novel: the plot now follows a more rigorous and increasingly urgent chronological and causal pattern until it ends suddenly with Okonkwo fixed as a minor detail in a minor book of a vast chirographic culture. The elaborate oral narrative that has been sustained throughout the novel is startlingly displaced by a causal, "objective" paragraph about Okonkwo in the District Officer's book.

However, the narrative principle that leads to this dramatic end is not causality but contiguity. As the outline of the first chapter illustrates, most often the narrative proceeds through association of subject matter. At times, however, the association focuses explicitly on a word, such as "household" which provides the link between the three parts of the second chapter. Achebe's studied avoidance of causality as an organizational principle is consonant with the epistemology of oral cultures, which have not developed their analytic capacities because they do not have access to literacy. The subsequent dependence of the plot on contiguity results in parataxis at the narrative level, which in turn reinforces the flat surface of the novel.

Nowhere is the decision to preserve this flatness, the refusal to emphasize the divisions between foreground and background, between the phenomenal and the numenal more apparent than in the narrator's management of the border between the secular and the sacred. In pure oral cultures such a distinction does not exist, but Achebe and his novel both exist in the margins of chirographic and oral cultures. The author is thus challenged with the unenviable task of ensuring that his characters do not seem foolish because they believe in the absence of that border while he is obliged to acknowledge it for the same reason. Achebe meets this challenge by endowing his characters and narrator with a double consciousness. At the beginning of the legal-spiritual court where *egwugwus* first appear, the narrator tells us that "Okonkwo's wives, and perhaps other women as well, might have noticed that the second *egwugwu* had the springy walk of Okonkwo. And they might also have noticed that Okonkwo was not among the titled men and elders who sat behind the row of *egwugwu*. But if they thought these things they kept them within themselves. The *egwugwu* with the springy walk was one of the dead fathers of the clan. He looked terrible. . . ." Thus the narrator demonstrates for us the double consciousness—the awareness of the border and its deep repression—of the characters, while admitting to the reader that Okonkwo is "dressed up" as an *egwugwu* and then proceeding to deny that admission (i.e., Okonkwo "*was* one of the dead fathers . . .", italics added). By maintaining a deliberate ambiguity, a double consciousness in keeping with the syncretism of a written narrative about an oral culture, the narrator refuses to emphasize either the chirographic/scientific or the oral/mythic viewpoint, thereby once again reinforcing the flat surface.

The same effect is obtained through the monotony of the narrative voice and the timeless aura of the story. The voice remains unchanged even when it is retelling a folktale recounted by one of the characters. The chronology is extremely vague; temporal locations are designated only by phases such as "many years ago," "years ago," "as old as the clan itself," "the worst year in living memory," and so on. The only specific periods in the novel are associated with ritual punishment: Ikemefuna's three years in Okonkwo's custody and Okonkwo's seven years in exile. Otherwise the novel is as timeless as one with a historical setting (indicated most obviously by the arrival of English colonialists to this area, around 1905) can be: the narrative, as an aggregation of an already known, circulating stories, exist in seamless mythic time rather than segmented historical time.

Characterization too is a product of the oral aesthetic economy; it is, however, more clearly modified by the historicizing demands of the (chirographic) novelistic imperatives. As Bakhtin points out, in the historicizing move from the epic to the novel, it is "precisely the zone of contact with an inconclusive present (and consequently with the future) that creates the necessity of [the] incongruity of man with himself. There always remains in him unrealized potential and unrealized demands." Unlike the tragic or epic hero, who can be incarnated quite satisfactorily within the existing sociohistorical categories, the "individual" in the novel invariably raises the issue of his inadequacy to his fate and situation, and thereby calls into question the efficacy of the existing sociohistorical categories. The movement from the monochronic and totalized world of the epic to the historicized and dialogic world of the novel also leads to the disintegration of the individual in other ways: "A crucial tension develops between the external and the internal man, and as a result the subjectivity of the individual becomes an object of experimentation and representation. . . ." *Things Fall Apart* is delicately poised at the transition from the epic (oral) to the novel (chirographic). In keeping with its oral origins, Achebe's novel entirely lacks the tension between internal and external man. Although Okonkwo's repression of the "feminine" emotions and Nwoyo's revulsion towards the discarding of twins and the execution of Ikemefuna are so crucial to the plot and the meaning of the novel, Achebe never explores them as dense interiorities (as a contemporary western writer would have). Rather he stays on the flat surface and represents the emotions through concrete metaphors. Consider, for example, Okonkwo's "meditation" of his son's apostasy. As he contemplates the incredulity of his son's action, Okonkwo, whose nickname is "Roaring Flame," gazes into the fire in his hut. The narrator finally presents the results of the ruminations as follows: "[Okonkwo] sighed heavily, and as if in sympathy the smoldering log also sighed. And immediately Okonkwo's eyes were opened and he saw the whole matter clearly. Living fire begets cold, impotent ash. He sighed again, deeply." From our viewpoint, the crucial aspect of this procedure is that Achebe chooses to represent interiority only through its concrete, material manifestation or reflection. Similarly, Nwoye's revulsion is represented through metaphors of physical sensation: when confronted with Ikemefuna's death "something seemed to give way inside him, like the snapping of a tightened bow." Thus, unlike Wole Soyinka's *The Interpreters*,

Things Fall Apart refuses to "experiment" with the representation of subjectivity in a way that is familiar to contemporary Western readers.

However, the externality of representation does not mean that Okonkwo
lacks subjectivity. The reader is made fully aware of the pride and anger with
which the hero attempts to mask his shame and fear. In fact, the narrative
focuses on the binary relationship of these emotions to the point where other
aspects of the hero's psyche are ignored. Thus in keeping with the tradition of
oral narrative Okonkwo remains a relatively flat character, whose efficacy must
be judged not according to the criteria of some vague realistic notion of
"roundedness" but rather in terms of his twofold narrative function. First, he
is an emblem of his culture. Through his mundane preoccupations and tribu-
lations—his involvement in harvesting, planting, building houses, weddings,
funerals, legal and spiritual rituals, etc.—we are allowed to penetrate the interiority of the Igbo culture before the arrival of British colonizers. Consequently when he commits suicide—which not only cuts him off from his
ancestors but which is also the product of a complicated alienation from the
principle of the continuity of ancestral lineage (he rejects his father, kills his
foster son, and drives away his real son)—his death leaves us with the feeling
of massive cultural destruction, of an end of traditional Igbo culture. His
second, ideological function is tied to the first; his shame and pride are also
emblematic: the former represents the shame produced among the colonized
by the colonizers' rhetoric about savagery and the latter reflects the resurgence
in the African's pride in the moral efficacy of his culture as he understands it.
For if Achebe introduces us to traditional Igbo culture through Okonkwo, he
is doing so in order to show that it was civilized and, by extension, that the
colonized individual need not be ashamed of his past. Yet in the process of
using Okonkwo as an emblem Achebe also accedes to novelistic pressures. The
transformation of Okonkwo from a heroic figure to an insignificant detail in a
paragraph about savage custom is clearly a deflationary movement that raises
questions about his potentiality and his adequacy to his situation. The novel is
content neither with leaving Okonkwo as a completely stylized heroic figure
nor with the impulse to idealize traditional Igbo culture. The reflexivity of the
novel manifests itself through the dialogic relation between Okonkwo and his
friend Obierika. While the former, driven by his fear, voices a simplified
version of his culture's values, the latter voices its doubts. Obierika briefly but
significantly questions general practices such as the discarding of twins and
Okonkwo's participation in the execution of Ikemefuna, and at the end of the
novel he is left contemplating the transition of Okonkwo from hero to pariah.
Similarly, Nwoye's apostasy opens up another horizon: by espousing the new
chirographic culture he creates the potential for one of his descendents to
write a novel like *Things Fall Apart*.

Achebe's first novel, then, can be seen as a unique totalizing and syncretic achievement. Its totalizing ability is most clearly visible in its syncretism. While rescuing oral cultures from their inevitable transitoriness, writing also alienates the objects as well as the unreflexive (or rather less reflexive) subject of that world by allowing one to examine them at a distance. In turn the fixity, distance, and scrutiny permitted by writing facilitate greater familiarity with and understanding of self and the world. This dialectic of distance and proximity, of alienation and understanding is inevitably involved in the configuration of Achebe's novel. *Things Fall Apart* documents, among other things, the destruction of oral culture by a chirographic one. However, Achebe uses that very process of chirographic documentation in order to recreate and preserve a symbolic version of the destroyed culture; in recording the oral culture's preoccupation with the present, Achebe historicizes its evanescence. The novel incorporates its own condition and occasion into itself. However, the most fascinating aspect of this totalization is that while *Things Fall Apart* depicts the mutual misunderstanding and antagonism of the colonizing and colonized worlds, the very process of this depiction, in its capacity as a *written oral* narrative, transcends the manichean relations by a brilliant synthesis of oral and chirographic cultures. By deliberately adhering to a flat surface Achebe obtains a result curiously similar to the effect obtained by one of Picasso's paintings: the illusion of depth and perspective, of the third dimension in symbolic representation, is deliberately wrenched and displaced in order to create a two-dimensional representation that includes within it an abstract reminder about the third dimension. While Picasso drew his inspiration from West African art, Achebe draws his from West European fiction. Like Picasso's paintings, Achebe's novel presents us with sophisticated primitivism, with a deliberate return to an innocence re-presented.

IV

The syncretism of Achebe's fiction, most clearly evident in *Things Fall Apart* and *Arrow of God*, has two important ideological consequences. As we saw at the beginning of this essay, the Third World writer uses European languages because of certain ideological and technological pressures. In Achebe's case there is an additional compulsion to write about his culture in English because not to do so would leave the definition and representation of his society at the mercy of (usually) racist colonial writers. However, under these constraints he uses English in a way that deterritorializes it. By deliberately simplifying and willing a certain kind of poverty he pushes the English language to its limits: the rhythm of the endless paratactic sentences negates the diversity and complexity of which the language is capable. The deliberate simplicity is combined with a dryness and sobriety of voice to create a new register. Achebe develops a mythic voice that can evoke sympathy and concern while remaining entirely neutral. This neutral, mythic voice, which is entirely new in modern English literature, is able to recuperate a vanishing cultural experience without lapsing into sentimentality or spitefulness. In addition to this innovative deterritorialization, Achebe is able to expand the English language through the transfusion of Igbo material. For example, the transliterated proverbs reintroduce into the language a kind of figurative, analogical element that has gradually been displaced by the scientific-empiric consciousness that favours precision based on literalness. Finally, as we have seen, Achebe also expands the form of the novel through his sophisticated primitivism. Thus we must conclude that *Things Fall Apart* is able to do justice to the phenomenology of oral cultures and that by deterritorializing the English language and the novelistic form, Achebe's novel also contributes to the negative dialogic relations between African and English literatures. Achebe takes the English language and the novelistic form and creates a unique African form with them. Of course, this does not mean that African fiction cannot be written in African languages, but it also does not mean that English can be excluded as a language of African fiction on purely ideological grounds.

The second ideological implication of the syncretism is a less happy one. Both the synthesis of oral and chirographic cultures enacted by the form of *Things Fall Apart* and its deterritorialization of English contradict the substance of the novel and thereby reveal the major ideological implication embedded in the contradiction. The content creates a longing for a vanished heroic culture, but the linguistic and cultural syntheses within the form of the novel point to future syncretic possibilities. While the content laments a loss and points an accusing finger at colonialist destruction, the form glories in the pleasures of a new formal synthesis and transcends the manichean antagonisms of the colonizer and the colonized. Thus while the initial layer of the emotive intentionality coincides with the traditional ideology of colonized resentment and bitterness and reveals the ideological bondage of the colonized man who is caught between historical catalepsy and cultural petrification, the deeper layer of emotive intentionality which finds pleasure in linguistic and formal syncretism implies a freedom from that ideological double-bind. Achebe's long silence in the field of fiction is probably due to his preoccupation with catalepsy and petrification and perhaps to the ideological pressure to discard the use of English as creative medium.

ANTHONIA C. KALU

Achebe and Duality in Igbo Thought

Achebe's interpretations of Igbo life place him among the artists and philosophers of Igbo tradition. Claiming to be an ancestor worshiper, he uses aspects of Igbo religious life and practice to delineate the importance of traditional Igbo religious objects as artifacts. In his *African Oral Literature: Backgrounds, Character, and Continuity* (1992), Okpewho, in discussing the reevaluation of the relationship between African oral and contemporary written literatures asserts:

> There has, indeed, been an increasing tendency on the part of modern African writers to identify with the literary traditions of their people in terms both of content and technique. When these African nations won their independence from foreign domination, they undertook to reexamine and overhaul not only the institutions by which they had been governed but also the image of their culture that had long been advertised by outsiders. The aim was to demonstrate that Africa has had, since time immemorial, traditions that should be respected and a culture to be proud of . . . [t]hat African culture is not obsolete but relevant for the articulation of contemporary needs and goals.

From *The Literary Griot* 10, no.2 (Fall 1998). ©1998 by *The Literary Griot*.

Although most of the work done since independence has focused on the question of image retrieval, the effort that has gone into the exploration of content has been largely ignored. Consequently, it has been difficult for contemporary African communities to find "a culture to be proud of," as Okpewho puts it, in these retrievals. This essay posits that although the level of cultural pride that African nationalists envisioned at independence is possible, it can only be achieved through a conscious reexamination and application of African cultural content.

But, such reexamination must move beyond the structural, engaging cultural content by searching for meanings in ways that will shape that immanent "expression-continuum" that African scholars recognized long before independence. In his discussion of a "Theory of Codes," Umberto Eco looks at the extent to which early linguistics research simplified and rigidified the relationships between reference, symbol and referent. He reaches the conclusion that,

> Within the framework of a theory of codes it is unnecessary to resort to the notion of extension, nor to that of possible words; the codes, insofar as they are accepted by a society, set up a "cultural" world which is neither actual nor possible in the ontological sense; its existence is linked to a cultural order, which is the way in which a society thinks, speaks and, while speaking, explains the "purport" of its thought through other thoughts. Since it is through thinking and speaking that a society develops, expands or collapses, even when dealing with "impossible" worlds (i.e. aesthetic texts, ideological statements), a theory of codes is very much concerned with the format of such "cultural" worlds, and faces the basic problem of how *to touch* contents.

In light of the above, the use of semantics to touch content, as opposed to focusing on the referent, is crucial to this essay's project of excavating relevant meaning from contemporary African literature. Here, the main assumption is that a significant number of African writers work from an African oral narrative base, whose framework is constructed from a recognizable "cultural" world.

Achebe's understanding of Igbo society and thought places him on a plane parallel to that of the traditional elders of the land in their capacity to (re)create order from familiar cultural worlds in conflict and transition. The relationships between these worlds constitute the explanatory bases for significant aspects of the Igbo worldview. The explanations emphasize the transitional/reference points that Igbo thought provides for the emergence of a viable future.

As with the traditional priest/artist's religious objects, Achebe's works demonstrate the contemporary artist's commitment to the well being of Igbo (African) society and its dynamic role in the contemporary discourse on political and socio-economic development. By extending the boundaries of Igbo cultural practice through the form of the novel, the contemporary Igbo writer acknowledges similarities and differences between the Igbo and the vast terrain of African thought. So far, the degree of congruence has shown that Africans have a great deal in common beyond the oppressive impact of colonialism and western domination.

Focusing on selected works by Achebe, it is possible to begin to understand how he uses cultural references to evoke an Igbo (African) epistemological congruity that traverses all aspects of social and political interaction. The role of the scholar/activist is, therefore, to articulate the path toward an African Renaissance, a reassertion of an intrinsic integrity predicated on a dynamic ancestral legacy. If, as most scholars of African literature have established, African arts have always been in the service of the people, then an African literary criticism should be able to reestablish those significant relationships that were obvious to traditional African artists. Given that one of the aims of Independence "was to demonstrate that Africa has had . . . traditions that should be respected and a culture to be proud of," the relevance of such relationships to contemporary African issues in the "expression-continuum" are self-evident.

Beginning with *Things Fall Apart* (1958) Achebe's works maintain a consciousness of duality, the relationship between the natural and the supernatural, the real and the metaphysical worlds, as manifested in all aspects of Igbo thought. An understanding of this relationship is critical to the study of Igbo arts. Briefly, one of the explanations based on the Igbo myth of the origin of yam asserts a relationship between the Igbo and the Nri people. The discussion between Eri and Chukwu culminated in Eri's and his children's mediation between the people and Chukwu on the one hand, and the people and Ani, the Earth Goddess, on the other. In executing their duties on behalf of their society, Eri's descendants became diviners of the wills of both Chukwu and Ani. This made them both priests in charge of the people's religion and medicine men who cleansed the land and people of abominations. This linkage between the physical and the spiritual persists in a majority of African socio-cultural relations.

Throughout Igboland, priests of other deities, oracles and nature spirits performed functions similar to those executed by the Nri priests. They all needed specific objects like carved figures and dishes made from

metal or clay for sacrifices and other religious activities. The people special-
ized in the making of these objects, which became important in the Igbo art
tradition. The priests themselves, adorned in their priestly regalia, were part
of this art tradition, which translated abstract Igbo thought into concrete
forms. Consequently, the priests bridging the two worlds became important
to the community because while they more perceptively interpreted the basis
for maintaining the harmonizing principles of the society, they became part
of those interpretations themselves. Contemporary examples include the
liberating roles of scholar/activists like Nigeria's Wole Soyinka and Flora
Nwapa; Senegalese poet/president Léopold Sédar Senghor; South Africa's
Bishop Desmond Tutu; Kenya's Ngugi wa Thiong'o; Egypt's Nawal el
Sadaawi; Ghana's Ama Ata Aidoo and others whose searches for collective
liberation and relevance reflect the dual functions embedded in traditional
concepts of service and community.

Erroneous interpretations resulted in chaos between the two worlds and
this was felt intensely by the community. In such a situation, an abomination
could be declared and the priests had to purify the people and/or the land. In
most parts of Igboland, Nri priests were called upon to perform such purification as part of the effort to maintain this relationship across Igboland. Some
Igbo groups saw them as blood relations while others looked on them as associates with the responsibilities to cleanse the land when crimes like homicide,
murder, suicide were committed. Thus, problems were perceived as the results
of disharmonious relationships between the community and the supernatural
realm. Equilibrium between the two worlds was established through sacrifices
and rituals, which aimed at warding off evil spirits that were believed to invade
the community during periods of disharmony. In essence, traditional priests or
contemporary scholar/activists serve as mediators between the masses and that
which stands between their communities and progress. The most recognizable
of these obstacles to progress in recent memory are colonial oppression and
the misguided leadership of the post-independence era.

On the individual level, priests were also required to offer sacrifices for
people who were experiencing imbalance in their lives. An extremely sick
person, for instance, would seek the help and intercession of priests or medicine men. Analogously, sick communities as is currently the case for many
African states, look to the scholar/activist for guidance toward progress.

In his role as mediator, the priest became both man and spirit. The
people (and he himself) perceived him as such when he performed the duties
of his office. The priestly duality is part of a broader Igbo concept of the existence of things in pairs. Other pairs are good and evil, earth and firmament,
and past and present. Balancing of such complementary opposites form the
basis for a continuous maintenance of harmony between two worlds.

[the] Igbo look forward to the next world as being the same as this . . . [and] picture life there to be exactly as it is in this world. The ground there is just the same as it is here; the earth is similar. There are forests and hills and valleys with rivers flowing and roads leading from one town to another. . . . [P]eople in Spirit-land have their ordinary occupations, the farmer his farm.

On the level of Igbo religious belief and spirituality,

> . . . Chukwu owns all
> And Sundry:
> He and Ana.
> Chukwu and Ana own all.

The relationship between Ana, the earth, and Ana, the Earth Goddess, and between them and Chukwu offer explanations that deal implicitly with duality. Out of Ana, the earth, on which the Igbo tread and from which they get life-giving food grew the venerated Ana, the Earth Goddess. The Igbo saw this as a closer relationship than the one maintained with Chukwu, who, though powerful, was more abstract and therefore distant, and was not as directly involved in the affairs of humans as Ana. In traditional Igbo life, these relationships gave rise to the pervasiveness of religion in other areas and from them emanated Igbo relationships with other gods and spirits. In Igbo thought, these parallel universes allow the careful observer to draw from one universe to enhance and/or complement the other.

On the individual level, Chukwu was seen as the creator in charge of all, but everyone had his or her own chi, personal god, which also had creative qualities and endowed each person with creative talent and skills. This created "a world order in which contrasting opposites within a unity len[t] harmonious creative tension to [Igbo] society and its culture." Individuals were encouraged to reconcile their creative talents to the community as this ensured conformity to society's standards. This need for conformity remains obvious in the Igbo art tradition which itself grows out of Igbo religion.

Originally, Igbo art is functional. However, the society also requires that beauty and elegance in art objects balance their utilitarian qualities. This balancing concept, although not always explicitly expressed among the Igbo, is still practiced with much vigor. It can be found in myths, poetry and other artistic modes of expression. It is a perception that holds as true for the carving of an Ikenga as it does for the performing of an oral narrative. In its implicit expression in oral narrative performance, the protagonist is portrayed as having to balance his personality and activities with that of the community. These narratives reflect part of this concept in their portrayals of the constant traffic between the natural and spirit worlds in which each protagonist searches for and finds personal wholeness.

Authors of early written Igbo narratives used the concept of duality in their works. In Achara's *Ala Bingo* (1954) the king, living one year on earth and the next year in the sky, reflects this dualism. Later in the story, he has to balance his arrogance with humility, his individualism with a sense of community and using an awareness of the worth of others. In Pita Nwanna's *Omenuko* (1933) the man, Omenuko, years after selling his apprentices, seeks the help of medicine men to mediate between him and the spirits and the whole community. Only after the reestablishment of harmony between Omenuko and these two groups can he return peacefully to his home of birth. The individual already aware of and practicing this concept in his life like Elelea in Achara's *Elelea Na Ihe O Mere* (1952) implicitly endorses individual and communal advancement and progress. Thus, Elelea reflects the ideals of traditional Igbo priesthood. Perceiving the priest as possessing this awareness of duality, the people vested in him the power to mediate the concept of duality in their lives. Thus, the figure of the halfman, halfspirit priest symbolized the extent to which the concept of duality was realizable in the real world.

In *Things Fall Apart*, this figure is concretely portrayed by the *egwugwu* and by the priestess Chielo, on a more abstract level. This last point remains one of the most difficult in the transition from an oral to a written African verbal art. The problem is this: while the *egwugwu* is a practical and visual part of Igbo life and art, Chielo is an inherent discourse celebrated on a metaphoric level. Although she does not appear in priestly regalia, she is cloaked by the night darkness, when she takes Ezinma to the Oracle of the Hills and Caves, and by the mystery of ordinariness by day. This mystery of the ordinary informs Achebe's exploration of women. Chielo, the priestess of Agbala, is introduced as one of the women in the crowd during the wrestling match that takes place on the second day of the New Year when she stands, "shoulder to shoulder" with Ekwefi. Achebe explores this relationship between the ordinary and the sacred further in *Arrow of God* (1964) when all the women of Umuaro (e)merge during the festival of the Pumpkin Leaves as dancers "stamping [their feet] together in unison . . . [until] the pumpkin leaves . . . had been smashed and trodden into the dust." Like Chielo, the women of Umuaro are ordinary women who, without visible priestly regalia, are co-participants with Ezeulu in his celebration of the annual cleansing ritual. This capacity of traditional African art to merge the concrete with the abstract remains problematic for contemporary African literature's efforts to transcend the colonial legacy of the Roman script.

Among Igbo authors writing in English about Igbo life and experiences, Achebe's portrayal of the priest figure as a major participant in Igbo ontology stands out. Achebe goes beyond other contemporary interpreters to explore Igbo social, political, economic and religious realities but stays within the Igbo art tradition by couching Igbo thought in the "metaphor of myth and poetry." Viewed against the Igbo art traditional background, his interpretations of traditional and contemporary Igbo life and experience are authentic in their reconciliation of personal creative talent to the society's concept of beauty and functionalism. Especially obvious in this regard is his art's reflection of the functionalism and aestheticism of the traditional mask carvings and Ikenga.

Achebe's early short stories reveal his first attempts to achieve this unity. "Dead Men's Path" *(Girls at War)* depicts the importance of the relationship between the natural and the supernatural, while "Akueke" *(Girls at War)* demonstrates the balance between traditional wisdom in the elderly and the ignorance of youth. The themes of these brief portrayals are developed in *Things Fall Apart*, which explores the complexities of the relationship between the male and female principles, among others. In *Arrow of God* (1969) the descriptions and interpretations are more explicit and intricate. Here, Achebe sets recognized pairs within the Igbo duality concept against each other and also looks at a new pair, the Igbo world and that of the British colonial administration. Where earlier Igbo authors focus on the second half of this new pair as an independent unit, Achebe works it into the tensions of Umuaro life. He compares Ezeulu to Winterbottom, and Ezeulu's intemperate son, Obika, to the adventurous Mr. Wright. Ezeulu's involvement in Umuaro's politics reflects the functions of the traditional priests and the *okpala*, the heads of families, whose duties were to maintain harmony between individual families and the society.

Achebe's interpretations mediate the priest and artist's functions, linking the past and the present and harmonizing contemporary Igbo existence. He achieves this by disposing of the wrong interpretations that characterized colonial perceptions about Igbo (African) life and experience. His basic premise hinges on the tensions between the axiomatic pair, the individual and the community. The relationship between the two and their significant references in Igbo life cannot be overstated. In precolonial Igbo life, an individual who sought harmonious relationships with the spirit world had to be in good moral standing with the whole community. Thus, an *ofo* (staff of justice) holder had to be upright in every sense of the word. A man's *Ikenga*, the symbol of the strength of his right hand, had to have the *aka ikenga*, right hand, thrust upwards. This upward thrust shows that the hands of *Ikenga* are clean and that one's thrusts in life are ethically sanctioned by society's codes of moral behavior: *Lee m! Akam di ocha* ["look at me! My hands are clean!"].

An individual's "clean hands" ensured his and the community's progress, good health and wealth. They indicated the maintenance of balance between the two worlds. In some areas, the upward thrust of the *Ikenga* was interpreted as a ram's horns, defining one's moral and physical strength. Whatever the interpretation, a viable *Ikenga* revealed an individual from whom his kin could expect fairness, justice and great achievements because of his awareness of the duality principle. When a man suffered regressions in life, his *Ikenga* was blamed and he could abandon it to make a new one. Traditional Igbo society disposed of fractious individuals, oracles or gods who threatened its well being, thereby creating new avenues for success and the maintenance of individual and societal harmony. But such disposal was only a last resort, because the perception that everything and everybody contributed in some way to the maintenance of balance ensured that individuals were aware early of a tightly knit system of relationships. All worked to keep their places in each system until they fulfilled the requirements for moving up to the next. Most of these systems, like title taking and marriage, became synonymous with stages of social achievement. Movements between stages were determined more by individual ability than age. However, people tended to move to successive stages or social ranks in groups which were directly proportional to their ages. For example, young men or women of a certain age group would get married within three years of each other. The same was true of title taking. This led to a situation in which the ruling elders of a given community belonged in a certain age range. In this way, consensus democracy among the elders was possible because members did not feel threatened by each other.

In addition to this working together of the elders, the leader of each household was responsible for the activities of its members, directing and guiding their social behavior. This meant that a person's behavior in a household was subject to appraisal by his family and the community. However, one was first accountable to the immediate and extended family, as this ensured allegiance to *ora* or *oha*, the general community. The supremacy of *ora* remains a strong force in contemporary Igbo life and is demonstrated in Achebe's novels. In *Things Fall Apart*, Okonkwo, as head of the family, is able to put Nwoye and Ikemefuna to work on the fence. Ezeulu, in *Arrow of God*, asks his sons to help him once every four-day market week. When he wants them to help complete the work on Obika's homestead and Oduche declines, offering the excuse of having been chosen by his Christian group to go to Okperi, Ezeulu intervenes:

> Listen to what I shall say now. . . . It is I who sent you to join those
> people because of my friendship to the white man, Wintabota. . . .

I did not send you so that you might leave your duty to my household. . . . Tomorrow is the day on which my sons and my wives and sons' wives work for me.

Group solidarity is implicitly maintained with the help of elders who check and balance the individual's participation within the group and his alliance to it. Individual involvement in family or village events emphasizes the role of the individual in the community. After the women who are cooking for Obierika's wife, in *Things Fall Apart* have fined the owner of the stray cow, for instance, there is a headcount to help them determine absentees. The women's actions demonstrate that one does not have to be invited to participate in issues that threaten community welfare. Achebe emphasizes this by commenting after the incident, "Those women whom Obierika's wife had not asked to help her with the cooking returned to their homes, and the rest went back in a body to Obierika's compound."

In his *Omenala Igbo* (1967) Ogbalu records many Igbo customs, telling when they take place, what and who are involved and what purposes they serve for the people. Although there are no detailed comments or explanations, the emphasis on the relationship between the individual and the group is obvious in the descriptions. Connections between the community and the supernatural world are also seen in the activities of the family. The heads of families are usually the eldest sons. These are called the *okpala* or *okpara*. Traditionally, they held the family *ofo*. Olisa refers to the *ofo* as "the physical medium for the invocation of the powers of Ala and the ancestors." The man who held it for the family had the right to carry out rituals or sacrificial rites that involved the family or its individual members. He also led the family in decision making. Since all such activities among the Igbo were in some way connected with their ancestors or gods, the *okpala* with the *ofo* were closer to both. Ezeulu, in *Arrow of God*, stood in such stead for his family as well as for the clan. Okonkwo's uncle, Uchendu, in *Things Fall Apart*, also had this role in his family.

The concept of maintaining a balanced relationship with the spirit world was more visible at the community level. The community's staff of justice, *nne ofo*, was held by chief priests like Ezeulu. Ulu is not, however, representative of the nature gods, the permanent, gods of Igboland. According to Nwoga, "Ulu, in many ways, is not a characteristic Igbo god" because he did not survive confrontation like the other gods of "unknown" origin. Achebe created Ulu for the purposes of his artistic vision much as the traditional oral performers created spirits and human characters from their narrative visions. However, both Achebe and the traditional artist build their characters from aspects of well-known and accepted Igbo thought and belief systems. In creating an Ulu who is known and yet unknown, Achebe works within the traditional oral narrative technique of creating stories whose nameless characters his audience can only partly identify in the sense that their behavioral characteristics are familiar but their physical features are not. This technique allows the audience to identify with the character, which in turn facilitates the major didactic function of oral narrative performance. Ulu has enough characteristics to identify him as one of the gods. Using this narrative technique frees Achebe from theological or mythical perspectives on religion. Ezeulu, therefore, holding the *Nne ofo*, the Mother of all the *ofo* in Umuaro, becomes the focus for the narrator's art which works on the assumption of shared experiences, including religious beliefs, between the narrator and the audience.

A juxtaposition of two incidents, one from *Things Fall Apart* and the other from *Arrow of God* clarifies this relationship between man and spirit at the community level. In the latter, when the elders meet to discuss issues there is no need for them to invoke the presence of the ancestors by the donning of ritual regalia. This is because, as titled men and elders, they understand more than the average Igbo the operating concepts and relationships in the society's life and culture. They are the initiated. In *Things Fall Apart*, the situation is portrayed differently. Here, the elders of Umuofia have to settle the problems of some members of the community in public. The elders, therefore, reinforce for the uninitiated the fact that they depend on the wisdom of the ancestors for the maintenance of community harmony. They must wear *egwugwu* regalia, symbolizing for them and the rest of the people the source that balances and upholds their decisions. These become ratified because the ancestors have a hand in their creation. This may be seen in the comment of one of the elders after Uzowulu's case has been settled:

> "I don't know why such a trifle should come before the *egwugwu*," said one elder to another.
> "Don't you know what kind of man Uzowulu is? He will not listen to any other decision," replied another.

Uzowulu's insistence on the participation of the ancestors in the form of the *egwugwu* stems from the people's belief that societal harmony emanates from their awareness and application of the concept of duality. He takes back his wife after both men and gods endorse the act. Individuals like Uzowulu who need constant, overt expression of the duality principle make institutions like the *egwugwu* necessary. Their aggressive insistence on the balancing of perceived pairs in the duality principle endorses societal maintenance of the system. Significant in this regard is the balancing of the male/female principle on which *Things Fall Apart* places much emphasis.

Harmonizing the male and female principle is reflected in the place and function of men and women in society. On the surface, Igbo society seems predominantly patriarchal; however, women wield a considerable amount of influence. The idea of woman as counterpart to man is strongly emphasized. The female principle is revered. In the Igbo pantheon, the most revered and feared deity is Ala, the Earth Goddess. Shrines are built for her, and special priests, the Ezeala, are in charge of these. In the Owerri area a special art event, the Mbari is declared in her honor during intensive shortage of food crops or infertility in women. This event is supposed to help enhance the goddess' goodwill and a showering of her blessings on the community thereafter. In *Things Fall Apart*, Achebe portrays how the Week of Peace is held to "honor our great goddess of the earth without whose blessing our crops will not grow." Oracles are referred to as *agbala*, another name for woman. Potent medicines are believed to be female, like the *agadi nwanyi*, old woman, Umuofia's potent war medicine, or the ancient deity, Nwanyieke, the mythical old woman who is said to be in charge of the great market at Okperi.

On the other hand, men who have not shown their valor in war or taken any titles, like Okonkwo's father, Unoka, are also called *agbala*. This is because they cannot demonstrate the existence of the male principle in their lives. However, mere demonstration is not enough. All individuals have to be able to balance both the male and female principles in themselves to maintain their positions in the society. As Achebe demonstrates in his works, men like Unoka fail because they manifest only the female principle, while the Okonkwo's fail because they cannot maintain the balance between the two principles. Achebe uses the characters of Ogbuefi Ndulue and Ozoemena, his wife, to emphasize this. Before his death, Ogbuefi Ndulue, the greatest warrior in his day and the oldest man in his village, had lived in such harmony with his wife that they were said to have one mind. The people acknowledged his greatness by letting him lead Umuofia in wars. He was a great man because in will and physical strength he could be depended on to maintain a balance between the two demonstrable aspects of human existence.

Another aspect of the participation and place of the female principle in Igbo life is portrayed in the festival of the First Pumpkin Leaves in Umuaro. This festival is not held in honor of Ala as that which is held during the Week of Peace in Umuofia. Umuaro's aim is to cleanse its people and ask Ulu for abundance in all aspects of their lives. It is significant that pumpkin leaves, "a woman's crop," is used and that women go to the village square carrying bunches of these leaves, symbolizing the sins of the people. The image of the women ritually throwing the leaves at the priest who later buries the sins of the people in the earth demonstrates the balance achieved when the male and female principles work together. The priest—philosopher, scapegoat and male—representing the male principle, works together here with the women, the female principle, to expiate ritually the evils, which have taken place in the community during the previous year. The leaves that the priest does not bury are stomped into the earth by the women. In this way, the people are able to crystallize the concepts, which they acknowledge and recognize in the abstract.

Although men are the major participants in the politics of the traditional Igbo community, women also wield considerable influence in this area. As Olisa says:

> The Umuada or Umuokpu (daughters of the family married outside, or, in some areas all the women of the kindred) are perhaps the most powerful of the organized women groups. . . . Occasionally the Umuada could step in to settle longstanding kindred disputes which the male members have been unable to settle. They could also compel them, for example, to conform to any measures decided on the town level which measures they might have opposed.

Achebe provides brief glimpses of the Umuada and their activities when the youngest son of Uchendu, Okonkwo's maternal uncle, gets married, and also when the women who had been making music at a funeral go into Obi Okonkwo's father's compound to sing their welcome to Obi in *No longer at Ease*. Women's involvement in such matters that concern the individual or group shows the various ways in which their participation maintains community harmony.

Maintenance of balance in the traditional Igbo concept of duality did not stop with the individual or with groups of people in a community. The entire community was subject to the operation of this concept. Like the individual, the community also had its male and female aspects, for instance, kinsmen of one's father and mother. Each checked and balanced the activities of the other. For the individual, this had notable advantages, especially in times of stress. One could always, as Okonkwo did, take refuge with one section if the other was wronged. In *Omenuko*, neighboring communities went out of their way to establish such relationships with each other to ensure that their members would have a place of refuge in times of conflict. However, if the threat were from the outside, the society would try to remain as one unit. This was one of the reasons why colonial occupations upset Igbo solidarity and rifts occurred first within the communities. The people found it difficult to fight the white man after their own people had joined the new religion. They could not fight them because that would have meant fighting and possibly killing their own. As Obierika observes to Okonkwo,

> Our own men and own sons have joined the ranks of the stranger. They have joined his religion and they help to uphold his government. If we should try to drive out the white men in Umuofia we should find it easy. There are only two of them. But what of our own people who are following their way and have been given power?

But Okonkwo, lacking full understanding of what maintained community balance and harmony, fought and resisted both the strangers and his people. He disowned Nwoye and killed the court messenger. Achebe's portrayal of Okonkwo's inability to advocate balance between the two principles demonstrates the necessity for the complex system that maintained societal order and harmony. Although a titled elder, his dependence on the external manifestations of the system is similar to Uzowulu's discussed above. Unlike Obierika who knows when it is appropriate to ask questions that will lead to consistent upholding of societal and individual harmony, Okonkwo kills Ikemefuna because the oracle orders his death. Having carefully considered potential sources for the excoriation of the things within the society itself, the people had devised a system to ensure that the Okonkwos, though capable of achieving the conspicuous requirements for admission into the group of elders, would not be allowed to lead them toward self-destruction.

Where the concept of duality could not be easily perceived, explained or implemented in Igbo society, the people consciously established new and concrete relationships. This is demonstrated in the creation of new village groups, like Umuaro in *Arrow of God*. In real life, initiated elders maintain this potential through the use of ritual language. For example, there was the normal, everyday language spoken by everybody, and the language of spirits, which only the ancestors or their representatives in the world of the living could use. Others only use the second kind of language in the context of artistic expression like oral narrative performances. Situations where people had to impersonate spirits, as in certain festivals requiring the display of masks, also provided further opportunities for the expansion of boundaries. Igbo thought and philosophy therefore had a built-in egalitarian outlook in terms of government, freedom of artistic expression and other freedoms. The elders who spoke in the language of the spirits when they assumed ancestral roles could not have easily or even willingly stopped their children from learning the ways of the strangers who came to live among them. In the new dispensation, the Igbo cultural world expanded to include the new worldview and its efforts to introduce ideas about Unfreedom incompatible with the society's socio-political and other realities.

Achebe's special use of the English language fits into traditional Igbo thought, which allowed the development of new solutions in times of conflict and transition. Such attitudes enabled the society to change without experiencing the kind of violence that Okonkwo demonstrates in *Things Fall Apart*. In his use of the Yeatsian metaphor, "Things fall apart, the center cannot hold," Achebe, the artist of the new dispensation foresees the imbalance in African communities, a consequence of the emerging postcolonial reality, independence and subsequent acceptance of alienating notions of individuality over community. When things fell apart, communities could no longer grant their staffs of justice to individuals because in the new dispensation, the main character is the individual who holds the staff rather than the characters of justice, harmony and peace as inviolable responsibilities of Community.

NEIL TEN KORTENAAR

How the Centre Is Made to Hold in Things Fall Apart

Awhole volume has been written by Emmanuel Meziemadu Okoye on the encounter between traditional Igbo religion and Christianity in the novels of Chinua Achebe, a volume which concludes that Achebe has done his research and that his depiction of the colonization of Igboland is historically accurate. Fiction, of course, cannot be judged by its verifiability; it expresses not what happened but what might have happened. Precisely because it must be plausible, however, fiction has to meet standards of correspondence and be adequate as an image of the human experience of the world. Okoye's desire to establish the accuracy of Achebe's fiction is not misplaced. However, if we consider the novels as historiography and judge how faithful they are to the past, it is not just the details of culture and of incident that must be considered. The writing of history has two components: it depends on verifiable facts and it arranges those facts in a narrative. How does Achebe establish his narrative authority when writing about a period more than fifty years in the past, and more particularly about a world-view that has lost its original integrity?

Things Fall Apart ends with the decision taken by a historian to recount the process whereby a whole world was overturned. The narrative this historian will write is not, however, the one the reader has just finished reading, but a less objective and necessarily less accurate narrative. In the final pages

From *English Studies in Canada* 28, no.3 (September 1991). © 1991 by Carleton University.

the new District Commissioner walks away from the site of Okonkwo's suicide and wonders whether to make Okonkwo's death a chapter or a paragraph in his projected book, *The Pacification of the Primitive Tribes of the Lower Niger.* This appeal to an obviously false authority deploys irony to establish Achebe's own credentials as a historian of Igboland. We do not ask why we should trust the narrative we have just read: the District Commissioner's projected history and by implication other texts on Africa stand condemned as manifestly untrustworthy, and that is enough. We deconstruct what is told us of the District Commissioner and reconstruct a higher level where we join the author in seeing around the Europeans. But where exactly is this higher level?

In *Things Fall Apart* the District Commissioner's false narrative assumes the otherness of the Africans. Humanity is not one. What the District Commissioner finds of interest in Okonkwo's suicide is its mystery: its impenetrability as an example of the foreignness, the difference of supposed primitives. By fitting Okonkwo into a comprehensible narrative, the Commissioner establishes both Okonkwo's essential otherness and his own heroic character—his narrative says in effect, "I have travelled through Africa and seen such things for myself"—thus eliminating the threat of that difference. To underline the falsity of this version of events Achebe must reestablish the humanity of his Africans, must insist that Africans live in the same world and are not absolutely other.

The effect of Achebe's plain style—in spite of what Weinstock and Ramadan argue, it is singularly stripped of symbol—is to stress the everyday ordinariness of Igbo life. This world is comprehensible. The transition in the book from pre-colonization Africa to an Africa that has felt the European presence is, in terms of style, unremarkable. Indeed, because the transition is so fluid, Achebe has to draw our attention to it by means of divisions: the encroachment of the European missionaries takes place while Okonkwo is in exile, during the division identified as Part Two.

C. L. Innes has pointed out how in *Things Fall Apart* when Mr. Brown the missionary and Akunna, one of the great men of the village of Umuofia, discuss God, they misunderstand each other. But more remarkable is how they can discuss and learn from each other at all, as clearly they do: their mutual tolerance and their open-mindedness are applauded by the author and contrasted with the fanaticism of Mr. Smith and of Okonkwo. The report of the discussion between Mr. Brown and Akunna sounds like the published proceedings of a modern conference on inter-faith dialogue, full of a confidence that beneath the differences of language and ritual there is a common quest for God and a common view of human nature. There can only be discussion where there is an agreement more fundamental than the subjects of dissension. Argument is only possible where there are common terms.

Mr. Brown does not speak of Christ; Akunna does not speak of Ani the goddess of the land. Instead they speak in much more general terms of God and sound like nothing so much as eighteenth-century deists.

Achebe goes further in making African and European the same in a later novel, *Arrow of God*, which is generally considered a more complex, satisfying novel, with richer characterization and greater unity of plot than *Things Fall Apart*, but which is for that very reason less interesting. In that novel the narrative moves freely and alternately into the minds of both Igbos and Englishmen. Their thoughts, their desires, and their strategies are remarkably similar. The ease with which the narrative moves between the two communities is matched by the ease with which characters travel from one world to another. They misunderstand each other to be sure, but Europe and Africa are contiguous in time and space. By implication the story of each fits metonymically into a larger narrative, the history of modern Africa generally. Rather than a conflict between two worlds, we have a conflict between individuals who are very similar but who cannot see into each other's hearts. The unforeseen results of this mutual blindness recall similar tragedies in novels by Hardy.

The problem with seeing two cultures as occupying the same world is that they can then be measured against each other and one preferred to another as a reflection of that world. To measure them is to assume a scientific objectivity that allows the observer to stand outside both. But in this case scientific objectivity is a mode of knowledge associated with one of the cultures to be measured. Achebe cannot appeal to the scientific model of knowledge and still be fair to the Igbos about whom he is writing. What Timothy Reiss calls the analytical-referential model of knowledge, the way of knowing associated with science and modern historiography, sees language as a tool that, placed between the observer and the world observed, allows the observer to know the world as it truly is and to manipulate it. It is inseparable from Europe's claim to know fully the world and other societies, in a way that other societies with other modes of knowing are never allowed to know Europe.

Achebe believes, with Reiss, Foucault, and Lévi-Strauss, that the West's knowledge of the world is as culture-based and time-bound as any other mode of knowledge. The title *Things Fall Apart* refers to the Yeatsian prophecy of the decline and fall of the current incarnation of the West. In using it to speak of the collapse of the Igbo world Achebe plays with cultural equivalence. One mode of knowledge is forced to give way before another, but not because the other has a stronger claim to be able to know the world. Both are time-bound, culture-bound; either may fall apart. At one moment of history the Igbo world-view gave way before the Western analytical-referential model. The

triumph of one world-view does not imply its greater fitness in an evolutionary sense; given different circumstances, the encounter could have had
other results. In Nadine Gordimer's *July's People*, for instance, it is the self-
assured, bourgeois world of white South Africa that is falling apart, giving
way before an African world it cannot comprehend.

To emphasize the exclusivity of the two worlds, Achebe often leaves
Igbo words untranslated. These foreign traces in an English text refer
metonymically to a whole world that cannot be adequately translated, a
world that Achebe implicitly shares with the characters he writes about. The
non-Igbo reader, by implication, can only achieve a mediated knowledge of
that world. There is no model that will contain both worlds.

However, there is in this glorious relativity an *aporia* that Foucault,
Lévi-Strauss, and Reiss only overcome by openly admitting. The analytical-
referential model continues at the present moment as the dominant mode of
knowledge: it includes us and we are unable to see around it. It is incontro-
vertible because we look at it only through the lenses that it provides. Achebe
is writing of a moment of epistemic rupture, when one mode of knowledge
gives way before another. But how can he do justice to both? Reiss believes
that we cannot understand Greek tragedy, for instance, because the Greek
epistemic mode within which the tragedies were written is not ours. How
then can the Igbo world be made intelligible once it has bowed before
another *episteme*?

The difficulty is signalled in chapter nine of *Things Fall Apart*, which
describes how a year before the present of the novel a medicine-man exor-
cised Ezinma, Okonkwo's daughter. Ezinma was an *ogbanje*, a malicious spirit
that had been born many times to the same earthly mother, only to die and
return to the world of the unborn each time the mother came to love it.
Ezinma was ordered to reveal where her *iyi-uwa* was buried, the stone representing her link to the world of the unborn. This she did and the medicine-
man dug it up: Ezinma would now stay in the land of the living. Achebe's
narration recounts what happened without comment or irony: the reader
must suspend disbelief and enter into the Igbo world-view. So too, later in the
book, a militant Christian who dared to kill a sacred python falls ill and dies.
The traditionalists accept that the gods were protecting their own, let the
reader think what he likes. However, although there is no rhetorical irony in
the presentation of the *ogbanje* scene, there is an irony implicit nonetheless.

In the present of the novel, a year after the exorcism, Ezinma's mother
wakes Okonkwo to tell him his daughter is suffering from *iba*. The glossary
at the end of the book tells the non-Igbo reader that *iba* is fever. The word
is presumably not translated because "fever" in English has the wrong
connotations: it would be thought of as something to be diagnosed, then

treated with medicine. Okonkwo's people see in *iba* a manifestation of a spiritual disorder: the mischief of an *ogbanje* or the perversity of one's *chi*. Ekwefi, Ezinma's mother, is terrified.

The chapter opens with the buzzing of a mosquito in the ear of Okonkwo, who recalls a story his mother told him about why Mosquito buzzes near Ear, who had once refused to marry him. The inclusion of this story can be ascribed to the encyclopedic thrust of the narrative: in *Things Fall Apart* details are relevant not because they further the plot or reveal character but because they contribute to the display of Igbo culture. However, the irrelevant on one plane may assume significance on another. Mosquitoes have a meaning for both Achebe and the reader that they do not have for Okonkwo. The chapter, by making mosquitoes and *iba* contiguous, even if not explicitly linking them as cause to effect, acknowledges a connection where the characters themselves do not see one. Achebe and his reader both know Ezinma's fever would be diagnosed as malaria by a doctor, and the recurring deaths of an *ogbanje* considered a superstitious explanation of a high infant mortality rate more appropriately responded to by modern medicine.

We cannot say Achebe is exchanging ironic glances with his reader over the heads of his characters. The reader, if at all involved in Okonkwo's world, is likely to miss the reference to malaria. Yet I believe my reader will agree that the mosquitoes are significant and point to a foreign *episteme* that is otherwise absent. In Wayne Booth's terms the irony is covert, but stable and finite. If reconstructed it constitutes an invitation to the reader to join the author at a level of understanding higher than that of the literal account. When later in the novel the killer of the python is himself killed the reader suspends disbelief: we are given only the Umuofia point of view, and though another explanation is conceivable, it is not suggested. But in the exorcism of the *ogbanje* a second, irreconcilable way of looking at things is offered and we are reminded that no reader of the novel, and not Achebe himself, believes entirely in the existence of *ogbanjes*. Achebe shows us Okagbue the medicine-man actually finding Ezinma's *iyi-uwa*, yet is careful to indicate that Okagbue is digging in the pit alone when he announces his find: the reader may think what he will.

The exorcism of the *ogbanje* is recalled in an explanatory retrospective; it is thus twice distant in time from the reader—it occurs before the present of the novel, which is already set in the past. In another novel such distancing might make it easier to accept the inexplicable and the uncanny without question. In the homeostatic world of Umuofia, however, where nothing seems ever to change, the distance is removed. The exorcism appears related synchronically to the events of the present of the novel: specifically to the execution of Ikemefuna, Okonkwo's adopted son. When Okonkwo is woken up to respond to Ezinma's *iba* it is the first time he has been able to fall asleep since his participation in Ikemefuna's death three nights before. It is not an *ogbanje* but guilt that haunts him.

There is, moreover, present in the account of Ezinma's exorcism a potential figure of doubt: Nwoye, Okonkwo's son. The reader has already seen Nwoye ill at ease with traditional metaphysics. When his friend was executed to fulfil the ordinance of the oracle, Nwoye felt something give way inside him "like the snapping of a tightened bow": he had experienced a similar chill when he heard the crying of infant twins abandoned in the evil forest. That was in chapter seven. In chapter nine we are told that one year earlier, at the time of the digging up of Ezinma's *iyi-uwa*, Nwoye "stood near the pit because he wanted to take in all that happened." Did he see Okagbue find the stone that had always been there or did he see him plant a stone? This is not an idle question. If Nwoye saw the stone found, then he would have had to deny much that he once knew when later he joined the Christians, who dismissed Igbo religion as so much superstition. If he saw the stone planted, then his crisis in faith over the death of Ikemefuna can be seen to have had its seeds in an earlier time.

In another chapter Achebe shows us the *egwugwu* judging a marital dispute: the glossary at the back defines these, with thorough-going unbelief, as masqueraders impersonating ancestral spirits. We are told that the women of Umuofia never asked questions about the *egwugwu* cult. They "might have noticed that the second *egwugwu* had the springly walk of Okonkwo," and they might have noticed "that Okonkwo was not among the titled men and elders," but if they did, they kept these thoughts to themselves. Perhaps it was never possible that any reader of the novel should believe that the *egwugwu* were ancestral spirits returned to earth, but it is clear that the narrative itself does not believe. The reference to a possible doubt among the women spectators advertises the distance of the narration from faith in the world it describes.

Abdul JanMohamed explains the ambivalence in this scene by invoking a "double-consciousness." Achebe's characters, says JanMohamed, like all people in an oral society, make no distinction between the worlds of the secular and the sacred. However, this lack of discrimination would make the Umuofians appear "foolish" to modern readers, so Achebe makes his characters aware of the border between secular and sacred, but quick to repress what they know. JanMohamed's implication is that modern Western-educated readers know more than did the traditional Umuofians, and so can judge the Umuofians as "foolish" or at least ignorant. JanMohamed is right about the "double-consciousness" in *Things Fall Apart*, but it is not limited to the characters; a double-consciousness characterizes the narrative as a whole. As we saw in the *ogbanje* episode, two world-views are present even when the characters are not aware of them. It is in the reader, rather than in the characters, that a double-consciousness is created.

This "double-consciousness" is perhaps inevitable when writing about a society that did not itself know writing, or when using English to describe an Igbo-speaking world. Achebe's solution, as Abdul JanMohamed has detailed, was to forge a written style that as much as possible echoed oral story-telling. The abundance of proverbs and the absence of original imagery are only the most obvious features. More significant is the flatness of the style: it is repetitive and additive, and it refuses to subordinate or privilege narrative elements. Everything is thus made equal and there is a seeming lack of direction. The flatness of character also echoes oral narration: Okonkwo's psychology goes largely unexamined and he is a type, both larger and flatter than life. Only thus, by telling Okonkwo's story as the kind of story Okonkwo himself knew, can Achebe be fair to an oral culture. To bring to bear on Umuofia the novelistic techniques of bourgeois Europe, designed to explore the interior individual, would be unjust, because they would suggest that writer and readers know more about Umuofians than the Umuofians know about themselves.

JanMohamed describes the syncretism that results from writing about an oral culture that did not know writing, but the asymmetry involved in writing the history of a society that did not conceive of itself historically has not been sufficiently explored. An example of this asymmetry is the following passage, in which Elizabeth Isichei in her *History of the Igbo People* explains the powers ascribed to the *dibia*, the Igbo priests:

> I think that it is possible that Igboland's *dibia* were developing real skills—or sciences—in the sphere of what we would now call extra-sensory perception. The imposition of colonial rule has basically put an end to these skills, and deflected Igbo intellectual energies into such "modern" spheres as medicine or physics. It is possible that in doing so it cut off a real and original advance of the human mind, and impoverished the total development of human knowledge.

Isichei is writing a history of the Igbo people in order to prove that they have a history. Igbo knowledge must therefore qualify as real knowledge by European definitions, meaning it must be a science, verifiable and replicable. Igbo science was advancing because, Isichei affirms, the human mind does not stand still but is engaged in a progressive evolution. In other words, a history could be written of Igbo experiments in extra-sensory perception if the records existed. However, in portraying the *dibia* as scientists Isichei is ignoring what the Igbos saw as true about themselves. She denies the reality of the Igbo gods and implies that while the *dibia* thought they were praying they were actually doing something else that only we moderns can appreciate.

The narrative voice in *Things Fall Apart*, too, occasionally lapses into the knowing tone of an anthropologist; for instance, he will explain, "Darkness held a vague terror for these people, even the bravest among them." The narrator and his modern audience, presumed to be unafraid of darkness, believe they can know "these people" more fully than these people know themselves.

Chinweizu, Jemie, and Madubuike argue that since most Africans believe in spirits and the efficacy of magic, one should expect to find magic in the African novel. They further argue that there is no shame in believing in magic: Westerners are just as fervent in their belief in favourable and unfavourable omens. The Nigerian critics may be right about Westerners, but by their reasoning one would expect to find magic occupying a large role in the Western tradition of the novel. One does not, and the reason is that the realistic novel as established in the nineteenth century appeals for its authority to history writing, and modern historiography is based on the analytical-referential model of knowing. In novels we are invited to judge characters who believe in omens or in magic as superstitious.

Of course, Africans need not write realistic novels in the Western tradition. The metamorphoses in Amos Tutuola's novels belong to another world-view altogether, one that eschews cause and effect and inner and outer as explanations of events. Achebe's problem is that he wants to show that Africa has a history, as Europe has a history, and so he does not want to insist on the difference of Umuofia. Instead he invokes a double-consciousness.

In the *ogbanje* episode that we looked at, the analytical-referential model underlies the traditional Igbo model. But the one is not allowed to contain the other. Achebe wants his readers both to remember what we know and to forget what we know; or rather he wants his readers to suspend disbelief, not as in a fantasy that is without implications for our life in the world, but to suspend disbelief and yet continue to judge.

How we are to suspend disbelief even as we judge can be seen in a short story entitled "The Madman," in which Achebe presents a series of disputes demanding adjudication. Where one can stand outside and survey the two sides of a dispute, judgment is easy. Nwibe, an upright citizen, puts an end to the quarrel between his two wives by labelling one mad, the other one foolish for arguing with a mad woman, and bidding them both be silent. A quarrel between the local madman and the market women over the rightful possession of the market stalls where the madman sleeps is judged without difficulty by the reader: the madman is in the wrong because he is mad. However, when the madman steals Nwibe's cloth while the latter is bathing and the naked citizen chases the now clothed madman, the townspeople judge incorrectly. They assume Nwibe, who is naked, is the mad one. The family consult two medicine-men: one says Nwibe cannot be treated; the other, less famous and less strict, agrees to attempt a cure. Nwibe is cured and the townspeople praise the successful medicine-man.

Most readers will be confident they share Achebe's own judgment on the story: Nwibe was not truly insane and the medicine-man who cured him was a lucky confidence-man. The humour of the story lies in the fact that while we see that Nwibe is a victim of circumstances—he is a modern figure in an absurd universe—the townspeople do not believe in chance but believe everything has significance. The author invites his readers to see around the characters.

However, as soon as we have seen around the townspeople, the validity of our stance is called into question. How can we judge sanity or insanity across cultures? The townspeople assume Nwibe was insane when he ran into the sacred precincts of the market; we attribute the sacrilege to Nwibe's uncontrolled rage. But if he was not insane when he ran naked into the market, the townsfolk reason, the gods would certainly have taken away his wits as a punishment. Nwibe himself accepts that he was insane. And it is quite possible that Nwibe really was insane, whether driven to insanity by the gods or by the horror of what he had done. Who is to stand outside the difference of opinion between the reader and the characters and to judge?

The definition of madness is culture-specific. The townspeople see a naked man and assume he is mad, nakedness being part of the code for madness. Nakedness itself is defined by cultural context. In the market Nwibe's wife hurriedly removes her topcloth to cover her husband: behaviour that would be mad in many a non-African context. One cannot stand outside and pontificate on differences between cultures; the best one can do is appreciate where the difference lies.

This double-consciousness, whereby we judge and suspend judgment at the same time, leads to a certain unease. One student of mine objected that she could not even be sure the original madman in the story was really mad. True he talked to the highway, but she could not be sure that kind of communication with the world outside himself did not indicate a poetic sensibility the Igbo townspeople lacked. How is one to judge? Her suggestion will be felt by most readers to be a misreading, but it is a useful one, because it challenges us to justify the judgments that we have been invited to make. Achebe intends for us to judge—or the story would lose its humour—but also to doubt our judgment.

This discussion of radical doubt sounds like many another contemporary critical celebration of a post-colonial text. Abdul JanMohamed praises

Achebe's "syncretism"; Homi Bhabha argues that the indeterminacy of the post-colonial text makes it more valuable than the European critical approaches that privilege representation. My discussion, however, is intended to show that this quality of instability is as much a fault as it is a virtue, and that it is neither virtue nor fault, but a necessary condition of Achebe's text.

Paul Ricoeur argues that the proper way to consider the past is not as the same nor as different, but first as the same, then as different, and then in terms of an analogy parallel to the past: as a narrative. *Things Fall Apart* is about epistemic rupture, but rupture threatens to make narrative, which implies continuity and development, impossible. Yet the novel insists that the Igbos have a story. This needs to be insisted on, for in the District Commissioner's eyes Okonkwo has no narrative of his own. The imperialists brought history to Africa, but, as Fanon observes of colonial settlers, it is not the history of the plundered country that they made, but the history of the mother country. They could not make African history, because Africa was a blankness in the imagination, a land without narrative. George Allen, as the author of *The Pacification of the Primitive Tribes* is identified in *Arrow of God*, sees in Africa an invitation to make history extended to all "who can deal with men as others deal with material." Narrative is thus a product of European agents acting on raw material extracted from Africa: a literary parallel to the processes of colonialism more generally.

Edward Said argues that if non-European peoples are to be written about with justice it must be in a narrative in which they are themselves the agents. They would then be seen as the makers of their own world. JanMohamed, however, following Jack Goody and Walter Ong, characterizes oral societies as homeostatic; that is, oral cultures without written records testifying to the past tend to ignore the ways in which the past was different from the present and conceive of the world as always the same. Of course, people who have not built empires and did not have written records have nevertheless a past that can be unearthed by archaeologists and ethnographers. But to tell their story as history is to describe them in a way they themselves would never have recognized.

The problem with writing Igbo history is not just that the records are missing. The records are missing because the Igbos did not have writing, and, if one follows Walter Ong, it is writing that produces the self-consciousness of historical agents. Hayden White, in agreement with Hegel, argues that some periods, however event-filled, lack objective history for the very reason that people in those periods lacked the self-consciousness to produce written history. Ahistorical peoples may accomplish much, but no narrative can be written about the unself-conscious.

The District Commissioner, George Allen, was making history. He acted always with an idea as to how he would narrate the story of his actions afterwards. And the narrative of his own actions he fitted into the larger narrative of the British involvement in Africa. That in turn he saw as part of the narrative of British history, which was part of a yet larger narrative project, the unfolding of human potential. Allen has an eye on this larger narrative and the contribution he can make to it, which will be rewarded with a place when the history of his epoch comes to be written. Allen's own narrative, it is plain, is blind to others and self-deluding. Even a fellow British colonialist, twenty years later, when *Arrow of God* is set, will find Allen's narrative insufferably smug. Where Allen saw glory Achebe and we see sordid conquest and imperialist greed. But the point is that because Allen and his contemporaries emplotted their own lives as narratives, it is possible for the historian who follows to emplot those lives as narratives. Where the Europeans in Africa saw epic, the modern historian sees irony, but that the historian's configuration of events is possible at all is only because the British prefigured their own lives in a narrative (Ricoeur).

Is Okonkwo the hero of his own life, to use David Copperfield's words? Okonkwo does emplot his life according to a certain narrative pattern. He designs his life according to the upward curve of a romance: the hero of lowly origins overcomes great obstacles to prove his nobility. He rejects one kind of tale—the stories of animals, told by women—and delights in tales of tribal wars and military prowess. His faith that this is the story he is intended to live out is the guiding principle of all his actions.

The notion of emplotting one's life as a narrative is expressed by the Igbos as wrestling with one's *chi*. The term *chi*, as Achebe points out in an article on the subject, is rich in suggestive meaning. One definition seems to be that the *chi* is the writer of one's life story, and one must wrestle with one's *chi* to give the story the shape one wants. A strong man emplots his own life—when he says yes, his *chi* says yes also. Yet the narrative of one's life may not be the narrative originally emplotted—one cannot wrestle with one's *chi* and hope to win, as Okonkwo finds out. The upward curve that Okonkwo emplots takes a sharp downward turn and becomes the inverted U of tragedy. However, the reason Okonkwo has a story at all, even though not the story he intended, is because he self-consciously thinks of his life in terms of a story.

But is Okonkwo's emplotted story an example of historical narrative? Is it not more accurately an example of mythic thinking? Peter Munz distinguishes between cyclical myth, that is, myths of eternal return, and linear myth (or history), narrative that incorporates a sense of uni-directional time. *Things Fall Apart* introduces Okonkwo by relating how he gained fame by wrestling Amalinze the Cat in one of the fiercest fights Umuofia had seen since "the founder of their town engaged a spirit of the wild for seven days and seven nights." Okonkwo lives in the same world as the mythical or semi-mythical founder of Umuofia, in the same space as spirits of the wild.

According to Lévi-Strauss, past and present are joined in myth, "because nothing has been going on since the appearance of the ancestors except events whose recurrence periodically effaces their particularity." Thus every wrestling match would be a ritual repetition of the original fight between man and nature, man and spirit. At the same time, in myth the past is disjoined from the present because the original ancestors were of a nature different from contemporary people: they were creators and their successors are imitators. The ancestors set the rules that moderns must follow. In *Things Fall Apart* the ancestors return in the shape of *egwugwu* to render judgment in modern disputes.

Ricoeur lists three instruments of thought that allow the writing of history. They are the calendar, the succession of generations, and, above all, the survival of archives, documents, and traces of the past. These make possible extrapolations from the individual's story to the story of the world, to history. At least two of these connectors are not present in the Umuofia consciousness.

References to time in *Things Fall Apart* are to seasons, to moons, to weeks, and to time that has passed since memorable events occurred. There is no calendar measuring an absolute scale, for such calendars are the product of literate societies. Instead, time is cyclical, observing the recurrence of the seasons and the market days. We can date *Things Fall Apart*, locate Okonkwo's story in relation to events happening elsewhere, because at the end of the book the Europeans appear. In the first two thirds of the book we are shown a society such as we suppose might have existed at any time in the last three hundred years (they have guns, but have not met Europeans). At the end of the novel, however, when the missionaries arrive, there are references to the queen of the English. Since Victoria died in 1901, the narrative must be set in the late nineteenth century. There is a slight contradiction here. Okoye establishes that the events on which *Things Fall Apart* is based, specifically the killing of a solitary white man on a bicycle and the retribution exacted by British forces, occurred in 1905. That is the year of the large-scale British expedition to subdue Igboland. JanMohamed too assumes the novel is set in 1905. Of course, what Achebe has written is fiction and does not have to be faithful to the calendar in the same way as history has to be. But in not being faithful to dates he suggests his narrative has come loose from history, as in a way it has. The time frame by which these events can be dated and related to other events—the scramble for Africa, the Boxer Rebellion in China, the Boer War in South Africa, or the discovery in 1899 by Sir Ronald Ross that the malaria parasite is transmitted by anopheles mosquitoes—is unknown to Okonkwo.

In Ricoeur's opinion the dominant connector between the individual and history is the *trace*. The French means "track" or "spoor," as well "trace"; synonyms include "vestiges" and "remains." The *trace* is something that exists here and now and yet points to something that exists no longer. There are traces in *Things Fall Apart* that indicate to the reader, but not to the Umuofians, that change has occurred in Umuofia. Okonkwo's gun—he points it at one of his wives in a moment of anger—indicates that European encroachment has begun. Firearms were introduced into Igboland by way of the coastal trade with Europeans only in the seventeenth century; not until the nineteenth century did they become widespread. Okonkwo takes snuff from a snuff bottle with a spoon, unaware that his ancestors did not always do so. The women in his community grow cassava and maize, products originally brought from the New World by the Portuguese. These traces signal to the reader, but not to Okonkwo, that the approach of the Europeans is inevitable, has indeed already begun.

The Igbos might still have a history even if they are not aware of making history. Hayden White argues that once one people has entered history, has learned to see itself historically, then mankind as a whole has entered history; a historical consciousness implies a progressive integration of the world. It cannot be otherwise if we are one species. Those who do not enter history as makers enter as the victims of the makers. Eric Wolf, in *Europe and the Peoples Without History*, has written of the integration of the world into a single history, not the history of progress postulated by Europe, but the history of makers and victims implied by the development of capitalism.

One could read the first two thirds of *Things Fall Apart* as a synchronic presentation of a whole society. References to past and present events are commingled because there has been no change and thus there is no significance to time passing. The novel takes on a diachronic presentation only when the missionaries appear, bringing change and, just as importantly, the notion of change. Such a reading implies that the Umuofia community was an ahistorical, organic whole disrupted and set upon the path of history by the brutal entry of the Europeans. According to this reading traditional Igbo society has an end, but no beginning or middle, and therefore cannot be fitted into a proper narrative. Indeed the end is better seen as the beginning, as the Igbos' entry into history.

This reading stresses that Umuofians are not proper individuals, not true narrative agents, but rather they fulfil defined roles in a community structure. James Olney finds in Okonkwo "the generalized portrait of a man whose character is deliberately and significantly without individualizing traits." He concludes, "Thus one must read Okonkwo's fate, he being representative and typical, as nothing less than the symbolic fate of the traditional Ibo society with the advent of the white man." Olney, eager to prove his thesis that African narrative stresses the type rather than the individual, summarizes Okonkwo as follows: "We learn of Okonkwo, and this is really about all, that he is physically powerful, ambitious, generous and honest, proud, quick to anger, hard-working, a great wrestler."

Okonkwo is all those things and not much more than those things. Nor, as Olney points out, does Okonkwo change in the course of the narrative. However, there is something that Olney leaves out because it does not fit his thesis, a detail that does not fit with Okonkwo's representative status and that makes him an individual in time, and that is his relationship with his father.

The succession of generations is the third of Ricoeur's connectors between the life of the individual and history. Okonkwo is not the quintessential African of Olney's and George Allen's imagination, fulfilling the role of dutiful son, honouring the ancestors and maintaining their common wisdom. It is true that Okonkwo identifies with the ancestors to the point of donning a masquerade costume and becoming one of the *egwugwu*. On the other hand, Okonkwo has made rejection of his father the principle of his life. He is a self-made man. Because Unoka, his father, was a failure, always in debt and without status, Okonkwo has had to forge his own career. Okonkwo, the mainstay of tradition, has inherited nothing, but has as it were engendered himself.

The contradiction is signalled in the text when Nwoye, Okonkwo's son, abandons the traditional ways and joins the Christians. Okonkwo is enraged: why, he cries in his heart, should he be cursed with such a son? If all male descendents were to follow Nwoye who would there be to offer sacrifices to the ancestors? "He saw himself and his fathers crowding round their ancestral shrine waiting in vain for worship and sacrifice and finding nothing but ashes of bygone days, and his children the while praying to the white man's god." Okonkwo forgets that, even if Nwoye were to prove completely loyal, Okonkwo would never join his father round an ancestral shrine. Unoka died of a noxious swelling disease that made it impossible for him to receive the necessary burial. Instead he was put out in the Evil Forest to die. Unoka's spirit cannot join the ancestors and cannot be reborn; he is doomed to wander the world as a ghost. Okonkwo, upstanding titled man that he is, has an altar to the ancestors in his compound, but his father is not among the ancestors worshipped there. Okonkwo, who imagines himself and his father haunting the cold ashes of an abandoned altar, is not really as concerned with the fate of tradition as he is with the flouting of his own will; it is not the rights of ancestors that he cares about, but his *own* rights as a father to dictate to his son.

Okonkwo the wrestler patterns his life on the model of the founder—he proves his own greatness by reenacting the achievements of the founder. We have here a notion of time that stresses repetition, the return of the same: wrestling is a ritual that repeats the founding of the village. But Okonkwo's motivation is not merely obedience to the universal law; it is the restoration of what has been lost and what in every generation has always been lost. He is himself a would-be founder. The established pattern has been flouted by Unoka and is only reasserted by Okonkwo. The narrative of his life both follows the model of the successful man laid down by tradition and establishes that model. It sets down the law: if Nwoye follows it, all shall be well; if he does not there will be trouble. To establish his own authority as lawmaker Okonkwo appeals to the divine origins of the law, declares he is merely following traditional custom. But in this case traditional custom is an assertion of Okonkwo's own will.

Okonkwo wants the narrative of his life to correspond to the truth of traditional wisdom and at the same time to guarantee that truth. But what his narrative shows is that the search for absolute and fixed truth is itself the product of Okonkwo's upbringing, and must be understood in its context. Okonkwo, who sets himself up as defender of community values, totalizes those values and in so doing betrays them. When Okonkwo's adopted son Ikemufuna is sentenced to death by the oracle, Okonkwo accompanies the executioners. He does this to prove his fidelity to the oracle. He sets divine authority above personal sentiment. But this is the loyalty of the doubter who must prove to himself his uncompromising faith. In participating in the execution Okonkwo flouts the advice of the elder Ezeudu. The law is not universal and absolute, but made by men operating in historical circumstances. This Ezeudu understands. The law will be obeyed, but it need not be carried out by Okonkwo personally. Okonkwo, however, misunderstands the law. He wants it to be universal and to govern all situations. It does not.

The oral world of Umuofia is not wholly based on repetition and stability; there is an instability implicit, the instability of narrative. The succession of generations marks change, and this is most evident in the rejection of Okonkwo's law by his son Nwoye, who converts to Christianity. Christianity is brought by the Europeans, as history itself appears to be. But Christianity is portrayed as a fulfilment of historic trends among the Igbos; Nwoye has sought something other and thinks he has found it in Christianity. He has had doubts about the religion of his fathers; the songs of the

Christians fill his soul with sweetness and peace; they answer a need in his soul. Similar doubts are expressed by Obierika, who comes to destroy Okonkwo's compound after his friend has been exiled for an offence that was purely accidental. Achebe is anxious to show that Igbos make their own choices, are not victims of history, but makers of history. There is continuity and development, not just repetition and rupture. The Igbos chose Christianity, as Nwoye did, or rejected it, as Okonkwo did, because they were aware of themselves making their own world in time.

The title of the novel establishes that Okonkwo's whole life will be seen from the perspective of his end. But that end is not gratuitous; it is of a piece with his life. To appropriate what Louis O. Mink has written of the narrative unity of Oedipus's life: Okonkwo who hangs from the tree at the end is the son of a man who could not be properly buried, the warrior who must forever prove his own courage, the wealthy man who has taken the second highest title in the land, the short-tempered husband quick to suspect insubordination and to beat his wives, the wearer of a spirit mask, the father who is rejected in his turn by his son, the man who wrestles with his *chi*, and the killer of the white man's messenger. He is alive and he is dead, and he could not be anywhere else than hanging on that tree.

The coming of the Europeans is not portrayed by Achebe as arbitrary, a *deus ex machina* dropped from another realm. It fulfils in inevitable fashion the tragic narrative he has been telling. The narrative of traditional Igbo society can only now be told with an eye to the end, the coming of the colonizers. But that does not mean Igbo history is derivative. It is no different from the history of eighteenth-century France, which is always written and can only be written with 1789 in mind, even though those who lived at the time may have not seen the revolution coming. Umuofia's responses to the coming of the Europeans are the responses of self-conscious narrative agents to the circumstances in which they find themselves.

Ricoeur makes a useful distinction between seeing history as a totality and seeing it as a totalization. We can no longer, with Hegel, see history as a totality that can be expressed as the development of the Spirit, or as any other single concept. Universal history can mean tyranny if it means the hegemony of a particular society, and that is what seeing history as a totality is likely to mean. Not only is it wrong to see history as a totality, but it is no longer even possible. We must make do, not with a totality, but with a totalization, an imperfect mediation of an horizon of expectation (the future) and an area of experience (the past and the present). It is with such a totalization that Achebe is concerned.

In *Things Fall Apart* the author disappears behind an omniscient narrator who claims to know all sides. We should be suspicious of such objectivity; suspicious but not wholly sceptical. The objectivity can be justified if we keep in mind the writer who writes about the past with one eye on the present. *Things Fall Apart* is the work of a young Igbo in pre-independence Nigeria who must establish the common humanity of Africans and the difference of traditional African culture, and who must show history made by Africans in order to inspire them to make history. The needs of the present determine how the history is written, but that does not make the history false. An aphorism of John William Miller puts it well:

> There can be only one point of view from which history can be written, and further, there is such a point of view. Obviously something of this sort is necessary if history is to avoid dogmatic assertions of what really happened or skeptical refusal to say what really happened. Whatever the one point of view may be through which history needs to be written if it is to escape subjectivity, it seems that it, too, is a historical resultant. Thus the one necessary point of view from which history is to be written is itself the outcome of history.

CLAYTON G. MACKENZIE

The Metamorphosis of Piety in Chinua Achebe's Things Fall Apart

Matters of religion are thematically central to *Things Fall Apart* and *Arrow of God*. Both novels reflect revisions in the nature of traditional worship, and both attest to the demise of traditional mores in the face of an aggressive and alien proselytizing religion. The disparities between the two novels are equally significant. Possibly for reasons of historical setting, *Things Fall Apart* differs from *Arrow of God* in its presentation of the status of indigenous beliefs and in its precise delineation of the evolutionary process of those beliefs—a process not articulated in any detail in the later novel. The shifts of belief in *Things Fall Apart* are marked by the pragmatic transference of old pieties for new, a metamorphosis demanded by the realities of a revised socio-economic hierarchy.

The first mention of the religious beliefs of Umuofia in *Things Fall Apart* is a reference to the Oracle of the Hills and the Caves. It is a decisive allusion, correlating the will of the Oracle with the life and direction of the clan, and leaving no doubt as to the significance of the divine agency and of the necessity of obedience to it:

> . . . in fairness to Umuofia it should be recorded that it never went to war unless its case was clear and just and was accepted as

From *Research in African Literatures* 27, no.2 (Summer 1996). © 1996 by Indiana University Press.

such by its Oracle—the Oracle of the Hills and the Caves. And there were indeed occasions when the Oracle had forbidden Umuofia to wage a war. If the clan had disobeyed the Oracle they would surely have been beaten, because their dreaded *agadi-nwayi* would never fight what the Ibo call *a fight of blame.*

That the Oracle is perceived as supreme there can be no doubt. The sacrifice of the boy Ikemefuna is undertaken expressly because the "Oracle of the Hills and the Caves has pronounced it." Though the execution may run counter to clan feelings of attachment to the youngster, a profound sense of individual and collective religious belief lends to the sacrifice an inexorable determination. It is a mysterious decision but the Umuofia, for the maintenance of the universal well-being, must comply with it. Not even the most powerful paternal feelings of Okonkwo can stand in the way of the expression of religious duty and faith.

Opposition of a sort comes only from Obierika who asserts a defiant passivity in response to Okonkwo's charge that he appeared to be questioning the authority of the Oracle: ". . . [I]f the Oracle said that my son should be killed I would neither dispute it nor be the one to do it." Lekan Oyeleye suggests this indicates that "Obierika's loyalty to the community gods is not as over-zealous and thoughtless as Okonkwo's brand of loyalty." But the issue of Obierika's exceptionalism is stronger than this. Achebe's narrative characterizes Obierika's inaction as being not only at variance with Okonkwo's view of things but with the received canon of traditional deific lore. Obierika claims that "the Oracle did not ask me to carry out its decision," but this is a spurious absolution since, as a member of the clan, he is as responsible as the next clansperson for the execution of the Oracle's instructions.

His impiety is further censured by the source of the rebuke, since even the iron-willed Okonkwo, who has by this time himself transgressed against the earth goddess Ani in the beating of his wife, has duly and humbly atoned for his crime. Had Obierika's unapologetic misgivings found any sympathetic ear one might have thought it would have been that of his friend—but not so. True, part of Okonkwo's interrogative tone stems from his own inner turmoil about the death of Ikemefuna but, on a more significant level, as a penitent transgressor he speaks for the devotional mores of the clan in asserting the preeminence of collective obedience and action.

Okonkwo has been mentioned and, since he tends to dominate most critical deliberations on *Things Fall Apart,* it is worth offering an explanation of his diminished role here. Undoubtedly, Okonkwo's relation to the deific system is important, but it may not be as pivotal as some critics have contended. Bonnie Barthold, for example, believes that the "narrative structure of *Things Fall Apart* is defined by Okonkwo's relationship with the earth goddess, Ani, and the ever-increasing seriousness of the offenses he commits against her." The Ani-Okonkwo colloquy is intriguing but in fact most of the novel's allusions to deities come from persons other than Okonkwo and, as shall be argued, Achebe goes to some lengths to construct a religious pantheon that ranges beyond any single god or goddess. It is significant, too, that the initial religious allusions of the novel locate themselves firmly in the territory of an Oracle-clan discourse, and that, subsequently, the spiritual experiences of individuals are repeatedly referenced to that all-pervading dialogue.

Elsewhere in the novel, the strength of other oracles is attested. A group of fugitives who have found sanctuary in Umuofia recount the story of the arrival of the first white man in their village. The elders of the village consulted their Oracle. It foretold the demise of the clan and the arrival of more strangers: "It said that other white men were on their way. They were locusts, it said, and that first man was their harbinger sent to explore the terrain. And so they killed him." All true, of course, and all the more reason for the clan to believe in the efficacy of oracular worship and counsel. The role of the Oracle in Umuofia at the outset of *Things Fall Apart* is unambiguous, unequivocal, certain.

In Achebe's other novels there is little reference to oracles. *Arrow of God*, the most religious of these, is steeped in traditional belief but focuses essentially on the Chief Priest, Ezeulu. He is given some oracular functions: for instance, it is for him to name the day of the Festival of Pumpkin Leaves—but for the most part, there is articulated no elaborate ritual of oracular consultation. The world of *Arrow of God* has the feel of a monotheistic world, as its title suggests. Personal "chi" are mentioned, but Ulu stands firmly as the tutelary god; and Ezeulu is, essentially, the agent of Ulu rather than an intermediary priest who brings back divine messages from places of holy conference.

This may seem a minor, even insignificant, distinction between the two novels but it is important. After all, it is made clear in *Things Fall Apart* that Chielo, who at first dominates belief and worship in Umuofia, is the priestess of Agbala. Yet, the religious pantheon of *Things Fall Apart* is essentially polytheistic. Agbala is divine, but the novel explicitly styles him as only one of many divinities who are material to the life of the clan. Achebe, in fact, goes to some lengths to reveal a cosmology of deities in the novel. The notion of personal gods, or "chi," is established early; the narrator offers an account of the dispute between the sky and earth; their presence and that of Amadiora, the divine thunderbolt, is forcefully reiterated; the gods and goddesses of the traditional system are a source of disparagement on the part of the Christian intruders; a group of converts derisively repudiates the clan's worship of more than one god; the clansman Okika reminds the clan of their constellation of gods and goddesses: Idemili, Ogwugwu, Agbala, "and all the others."

This is not necessarily to infer that the setting of *Things Fall Apart* is a more "traditional" setting or a more authentic religious setting than that of *Arrow of God*. But it does indicate differences in the indigenous theistic designs of the two works. These may be traced further. In *Arrow of God*, the powers of the Chief Priest of Ulu, Ezeulu, are considerably less than his equivalent in *Things Fall Apart*—the priestess of Agbala, Chielo. On the question of going to war, an option expressly raised in both novels, oracular authority of the priest in *Arrow of God* is notably less secure than it is in the earlier work. Here, for example, is how Nwaka advocates war against the Okperi (a course of action opposed by Ezeulu):

> Nwaka began by telling the assembly that Umuaro must not allow itself to be led by the Chief Priest of Ulu. 'My father did not tell me that before Umuaro went to war it took leave from the priest of Ulu,' he said. 'The man who carries a deity is not a king. He is there to perform his god's ritual and to carry sacrifice to him. . . .'

In *Things Fall Apart* we are told that there can be no war without validation from the Oracle of the Hills and the Caves. This, as Cook rightly maintains, "is not a rationalisation of weakness but takes its stand from a position of strength." In *Arrow of God*, the oracular right of Ezeulu to forbid war is diminished by personal slanders as to his true earthly intentions. Obligations of divine belief have been weakened by the doubts and meanderings of mortal integrity. That Nwaka is at least partially successful in his argument is evidenced by the narrator's assertion that "Umuaro was divided in two" on the matter.

The disparities between the two novels may be partially explained by the variant time frame that separates the events they describe. *Things Fall Apart* is located at points immediately before and after the arrival of the colonialists. The work is a third over before white people are even mentioned, and even there the allusion is merely a trivial speculation about whether they have toes or not. The novel is more than two-thirds over before a white person actually appears in Umuofia—an occasion that brings out every man and woman in the village. *Arrow of God*, on the other hand, presents not simply a single white missionary but an entire colonial community within the opening three chapters. Here, white people are not fantastical rumors but a familiar and integral part of the social landscape. Their leader, Captain T. K. Winterbottom, has already spent fifteen years in the African colonial service and is now firmly entrenched in his bungalow atop "Government Hill."

Clan attitudes towards the indigenous religion in *Arrow of God* have been tempered, before the novel has even started, by contact with a dominant, monotheistic creed—and one which, though regarded with hostility by many clanspeople, has not yet seriously challenged the supposedly inviolate nature of indigenous belief and worship. By way of contrast, *Things Fall Apart* presents the process of attitudinal beliefs in relation to the indigenous religion prior to the socio-historical point at which *Arrow of God* begins. It appears that the arrival of Christianity not only secures native converts but also distorts, even among hostile clan non-converts, responses to and perceptions of indigenous beliefs. This goes beyond what some critics have called a simple "hybridization of culture." Hybridization implies a compromise of differences, a common meeting ground. It cannot of itself encapsulate the spirit and movement of Achebe's representation. Homi Bhabha has written incisively of "the cultural and historical hybridity of the postcolonial world . . . as the paradigmatic *place of departure*" (emphasis added). It is that point of "departure" in which Achebe seems acutely interested. He seeks to move beyond espousal of a dualist model of cultural attrition and inter-adaptation, to a delineation of the metamorphosis of faith-oriented traditional pieties into economically-driven "new world" pieties.

Once the first white person has arrived in Umuofia, a repudiation of indigenous clan religious beliefs follows almost immediately:

> At this point an old man said he had a question [for the white man]. 'Which is this god of yours,' he asked, 'the goddess of the earth, the god of the sky, Amadiora of the thunderbolt, or what?'. . . .
>
> 'All the gods you have named are not gods at all. They are gods of deceit who tell you to kill your fellows and destroy innocent children. There is only one true God and He has the earth, the sky, you and me and all of us.'

After this, the notion of the traditional "Oracle," so strong hitherto, disappears without a trace from the novel. It is never again mentioned, or even intimated. There are many opportunities when it could have been. The killing of the royal python is one. Achebe makes clear to us that the python is "the emanation of the god of water" and therefore sacred. Accidental killing of such an animal could be atoned through sacrifices and an expensive burial ceremony. But because no one has ever imagined that someone would knowingly kill a python, there is no statutory sanction for the crime. A decision about action, even if it is to be that no action should be taken, is required by the clan. What is interesting is the nature of the consultative process leading to that decision, and what does not happen rather than what does.

Chielo, the priestess, is not consulted. In fact, after she has called the clan's Christian converts "the excrement of the clan," we hear nothing more from or about her in the novel. A priestess, the high priestess of Agbala, who has hitherto played a central role in the process of traditional life, takes no further part in the story or the events it describes. Certainly no one suggests that the Oracle of the Hills and the Caves should be consulted over the killing of the python. The clan's first instinct is to resolve the issue through human discussion:

> . . . the rulers and elders of Mbanta assembled to decide on their action. Many of them spoke at great length and in fury. The spirit of war was upon them. . . .

We know from the first chapter of the novel that the clan never went to war unless its cause was confirmed as just by the Oracle. Why is it that consultation of the Oracle is now not even mooted as an option? Indeed, divine conference with the Oracle, once so integral a part of clan life, is suddenly abandoned to a new order of things—to a secular consultative context in which those wishing to go to war are opposed by those who do not wish to go to war. The reasons put forward by the latter are interesting:

> 'It is not our custom to fight for our gods,' said one of them. 'Let us not presume to do so now. If a man kills the sacred python in the secrecy of his hut, the matter lies between him and the god. We did not see it. . . .'

In other words, the gods can look after themselves, why should we do their fighting for them? A fascinating modification of devotion has occurred here. The cosmology of deities, the very cornerstone of clan being, has suddenly become distanced from the actuality of the existence of Umuofia. At one time an integral weave in the fabric of clan life, the indigenous religious order has abruptly become remote and distant. It is now located in a schemata of parallel activities in which the divinities of an ordered universe and the mortals of an ordered world function independently, avoiding interference in each other's affairs and linked only by a respectful cordiality of verbal oblation on the part of the traditional worshipper.

The transformation is dramatic and arresting. But is the new equation of relation plausible? In a sense and for a time, yes. It looks as if it is working in the case of the slaying of the royal python, an act which has apparently precipitate consequences. Okoli, a prime suspect in the crime, falls ill and dies: "His death showed that the gods were still able to fight their own battles. The clan saw no reason then for molesting the Christians." Perhaps Obierika's thesis of godly acceptance and human inertia, of belief and oblation without enactment, was a credible modus vivendi after all?

The assumption is false. The narrative rapidly and subtly undermines any thoughts that divine sanction comes without a reciprocation of mortal action. Okoli had, in fact, denied the crime and Achebe is careful to present no evidence against him. Not long after, we learn that Enoch was most likely the real offender. What is significant is not whether Okoli is guilty or innocent but that his death enables the clanspeople to seize upon a bogus exemplar of divine self-help in order to reassert the new order of things—to withdraw to the sanctuary of a piety that is passive, undemanding and removed, one which places no burden of sacrifice or atonement or forceful action upon the celebrant.

To the chagrin of Okonkwo, the spokesperson of the old faith now as he had been earlier in the face of Obierika's heretical passivity, the most the clan can offer against the Christians for the slaying of the emanation of the god of water is ostracization. It is an action calculated not to avenge the outrage against the god, but rather to distance the village from the crime that has been committed: "We should do something. But let us ostracise these men. We would then not be held accountable for their abominations." And the death of Okoli, be it fortuitous or not, removes from a grateful clan even that necessity.

This sense of wily self-preservation which now characterizes the clan may be usefully compared, for example, to their response earlier in the novel to Okonkwo's beating of his youngest wife. During the beating, his first two wives and a host of neighbors beg him to stop since this is a sacred week— and "it was unheard of to beat somebody during the sacred week." Ezeani, the priest of the earth goddess, Ani, visits Okonkwo to rebuke him, and refuses to eat "in the house of a man who has no respect for our gods and ancestors." His is not a humanitarian concern but a religious one:

> 'The evil you have done can ruin the whole clan. The earth goddess whom you have insulted may refuse to give us her increase, and we shall all perish.' His tone now changed from anger to command. 'You will bring to the shrine of Ani tomorrow one she-goat, one hen, a length of cloth and a hundred cowries.'

The whole episode is marked by certainties of transgression, of censure, of atonement. At the center of this process stands the priest, the intermediary between deity and mortal. There is no questioning of his position, no doubt about his authority, no possibility of his denial. Just as in the killing of Ikemefuna, there is no ambiguity or blurring of responsibilities and significances. The progress of the clan, divinely guided and humanly effected through the collective obedience of the clanspeople, is distinct and emphatic.

How rapidly things change. The only decisive communal action that occurs in the last third of the book is the burning of Mr. Smith's church. This act, in revenge for the unmasking of an egwugwu, an ancestral spirit and therefore part of the indigenous religious cosmology, fills Okonkwo with something approaching happiness. We are told:

> When the egwugwu went away the red-earth church which Mr Brown had built was a pile of earth and ashes. And for the moment the spirit of the clan was pacified.

The destruction of the church is framed in terms of a human victory. Immediately after the burning of the building, we learn that Okonkwo's clan "which had turned false on him appeared to be making amends"; Okonkwo himself rejoices that it was "like the good old days again, when a warrior was a warrior"; and a few lines later we learn that "[e]very man in Umuofia went about armed with a gun or a matchet." There is a sense of the clan's human destiny having been reasserted as the prerogative of the clan itself. No one thanks the gods for the building's destruction; no one even credits them with a hand in it.

Yet, why should this be? It is, after all, the egwugwu who have burned down the church. The egwugwu are explicitly linked, through their patronizing deity, with the world of the godly immortals:

> 'All our gods are weeping. Idemili is weeping. Ogwugwu is weeping, Agbala is weeping, and all the others. . . .'

Technically, it is not the living clanspeople at all who have been responsible for the action. Though the egwugwu masks are worn by living beings, according to traditional doctrine a transmigration of flesh and spirit occurs in which the human impersonators become unearthly spirits. If the victory over the church is a victory of the deific world (and we are told, after all, that "the spirit of the clan was pacified") how is it that the clan itself interprets the destruction of the church as a human act and never alludes to it in terms of divine intervention?

One explanation may be that they are no longer convinced of the divinity of the egwugwu, regarding the ritual of the nine spirits as no more than an historic re-enactment of people and actions from times past. Whether this is the case or not, the clanspeople appear not to covet further the idea that the path to community survival is traceable irrevocably to the cosmology of indigenous gods. If they did they would surely have left the issue of the egwugwu unmasking to the gods. Instead, they take up arms, apparently without any kind of oracular consultation, and steel themselves for the worst.

Adewale Maja-Pearce has speculated that one of Achebe's purposes in *Things Fall Apart* is to assert that "the spiritual values of pre-colonial Africa were in no way inferior to those of Europe, merely different." That difference became a source of vulnerability. The religious codes and practices of Umuofia, unchallenged for centuries and perhaps millennia, had not evolved strategies for adaptation or confrontation. Like the sacred python, no one ever thought their sacredness would or could ever be challenged. The real power of missionary proselytization lay in the breaking down of community norms. The evil forest became no longer evil; the outcasts became no longer outcasts; the objects and rituals of traditional sacrament were destroyed.

Despite this, some Umuofians yet seek an accommodation, a hybridization perhaps, with the new theology. As he struggles to find a compromise between the religion he has always known and that which has suddenly arrived, the village elder Akunna debates the issue of the gods with the missionary Mr. Brown:

> 'You say that there is one supreme God who made heaven and earth,' said Akunna on one of Mr Brown's visits. 'We also believe in Him and call Him Chukwu. He made all the world and the other gods.'
>   'There are no other gods,' said Mr Brown. 'Chukwu is the only God and all others are false. . . .'

Mr. Brown is no intercessor, no hybridizer. He spurns the idea that he is the earthly representative of his God, leading Akunna to exclaim, aghast, "but there must be a head in this world among men." There is no compromise on offer. Mr. Brown rejects not only the central indigenous notion of a multi-deity system, but also the pivotal function of a high priest or priestess within a religious framework.

It may be possible to see in *Arrow of God* how both of these crucial tenets of traditional worship—polytheism and priestly intercession—have been corrupted in the revised perception of traditional lore. As noted earlier, not only is Ulu a rather "singularized" god, but his earthly messenger, Ezeulu, is emphatically disrobed of the trappings of infallible or absolute authority by the clanspeople. Further, the clan's attitude towards Ulu becomes less than coherent in the latter stages of the novel. When Ezeulu says he cannot enact a ritual that will enable new yams to be planted because Ulu has not sanctioned it, a clan delegation urges him to perform the rites anyway and to lay the blame on them. When he refuses, a new choice is mooted:

> So the news spread that anyone who did not want to wait and see all his harvest ruined could take his offering to the god of the Christians who claimed to have power of protection from the anger of Ulu.

The contest is styled as a battle of singularities, one god versus another. It is an essentially Biblical construct; a binary contest between feast and famine, between protection and threat, between the knight and the dragon—and, implicitly, between good and evil. Traditional theology has been undermined by Christian mythology, and subsumed into a Biblical schemata of loss and salvation. Gone are the ordinances of seasonal and festive celebration; gone the multiplicities of divine representation, of elemental hierarchies, of ancestral phantasm and conference. The shape and detail of traditional beliefs have evaporated. Ulu, disconnected from his deific order, must battle for authority in the pavilion of his foe. Of course Ulu will lose. He may offer only the mysterious piety of suffering; Christianity, as it is unfolded and displayed in *Arrow of God*, offers the clear piety of economics, a simple exchange of spiritual faith for material prosperity.

Joseph Swann speculates that the demise of Ulu may have been self-willed, "not for any reason of cultural dissatisfaction, but as a simple historical necessity, to safeguard the bare existence of the clan." But what is existence without faith? In the clan's ancient frame of things it should be as nothing. The fact that it is now feasible attests to a shift in the devotional perspective of the clan members. Knowingly or otherwise, they are trapped into a revisionist interpretation—in effect, a Christianization—of their traditional beliefs. Where once they might have accepted the ruling of the divinity, and starved in the certainty of a mysterious but painful purpose, now an alien creed offers an alluring alternative.

Things Fall Apart reveals a time when this was not so, and goes on to present the temporal nexus point between the ways of the old religion and the ways of a new world order. On the face of it, the new order seems more logical and democratic, and, to contemporary sensibilities, humane. The clanspeople meet and discuss their tactics; the imperatives of action are no longer handed down to them by unseen deities who communicate imperiously through their human emissaries. It is, of course, a superficial freedom. In truth, they now act under a new and equally powerful imperative, a colonial imperative. This new relationship, however, is not founded on mystical ordination or divine machination. It is a relationship of pragmatism and commodity.

That point is made abundantly clear in the abduction of the six clanspeople by the District Commissioner's officers. This may be compared with the abduction of Okonkwo's child, Ezinma, by Agbala's priestess Chielo. After a bizarre odyssey, the child is returned unharmed, and without explanation. The six men, on the other hand, are ransomed. Either the clan pays up the requisite cowrie fine or the six will be hanged. Just as no one questions the motives of Chielo, so no one questions the motives of the District Commissioner. But the reasons for the silences are quite different. Chielo is not challenged because the ways of the gods are beyond mortal comprehension; the District Commissioner is not challenged because, by contrast, his position is abundantly comprehensible. He goes to some lengths to explain the readily discernible economics of commodity transfer: the freedom of six human beings for two hundred bags of cowrie shells. It is a logical, business transaction, and the clan finds it as compelling as it did obedience to the Oracle of the Hills and the Caves.

There is no talk of gods or goddesses or holy wars. The clan's financial penance is part of the new order that has enveloped their traditional life. An egwugwu has been unmasked; their six leaders have been captured through false promises of parley; an extortionate ransom demand has been made—yet the response of the clan is pragmatic. The men of the clan meet at the marketplace and agree to raise the fine without delay. The matter is settled on a commodity basis. Faith in oracular arbitration has been replaced by faith in a new kind of fiscal logic. This eclipse is signed by the fact that the night preceding their decision is a night of the full moon. Normally a time of sacred and secretive communal ritual, it is on this occasion presented as a time of desolation and emptiness.

The economics of religious school education provide momenta no less forceful than the exchange of prisoners for money. This is how the novel describes the impact of Mr. Brown, a missionary educator, on the life and times of the village:

> Mr Brown's school produced quick results. A few months in it were enough to make one a court messenger or even a court clerk. Those who stayed longer became teachers; and from Umuofia labourers went forth into the Lord's vineyard. New churches were established in the surrounding villages and a few schools with them. From the very beginning religion and education went hand in hand.

Mr. Brown's school offers advantages to its enrolment and to the work of the missionary himself. For the local participants it promises advancement within the prevailing socio-economic system; for Mr. Brown it accords the opportunity to convert to Christianity those who have entrusted their education to his care. But the benefits come at a price. The need for court messengers or court clerks, or indeed for people who can read or write, is one generated by the demands of a colonial hegemony, not by the requirements of clan administration. The knowledge and understanding that Mr. Brown's school seeks to promulgate is openly abrasive to the organization and culture of the clan.

Eustace Palmer argues that "[a]s long as a reasonable person like Mr Brown is in charge of the mission station, co-existence is possible between the new religion and traditional society." In fact, the interrelation between the two can never be characterized in terms of co-existence, because the economics of Mr. Brown's religion demand ideological substitution, not concurrence or hybridization. In *Things Fall Apart*, Christianity, like colonialism in general, is depicted as offering a clear rationale of "exchange" for Umuofia. In return for adherence to Christian doctrine, the church offers explicit routes for individual economic advancement.

As the meaning and decisiveness of that interaction dawns on the clan it corrupts the ancient way of things. What use is there in praying to Agbala for the white people to go away when the new order presents so persuasively the dimensions of its power that only co-operation and attempted advancement within its structure seems practicable? Achebe's irony, of course, is that the Umuofi come to believe in the supremacy of the missionary colonizers as devoutly as they once had in their own theater of gods. But these are devotions engendered by quite different experiences: the former, through the compulsion of physical aggression and economic inducement; the latter, through the magnificence and munificence of faith. In the end, the metamorphosis of piety is not a change from belief in one religious system to belief in another religious system but rather a switch from faith in a world where life is given, to commitment to one where security and achievement are measured and earned very differently.

Authors write novels for a multiplicity of reasons, not all of them obvious or cogent. It is possible, as Theo D'haen has suggested, that some postcolonial literatures seek to "take revenge upon the mother country, among other things by means of their shared post-colonial literatures." But *Things Fall Apart* is not about revenge—though Achebe misses few opportunities to satirize the colonial presence. The Nigerian poet Tanure Ojaide offers another possibility:

> Literature might be devoted to leisure in other cultures, but for us Africans who are experiencing the second half of the twentieth century, literature must serve a purpose: to expose, embarrass, and fight corruption and authoritarianism. . . . It is understandable why the African artist is utilitarian. We do not have the luxury of some Western writers, who are apolitical and can afford to write art for art's sake and be confessional (a euphemism for self-therapy).

While no one may accuse Achebe of complacency, Ojaide's premise of utilitarianism is more difficult to decipher in *Things Fall Apart.* The problem is that once things have irrevocably fallen apart, once a unique and intricate construct of a matured civilization has been irreversibly dismantled, then rehearsing the indiscretions of the past can easily be regarded as motiveless reminiscence. Yet, there is clearly a purpose to *Things Fall Apart* and it may be discernible as much in the need for personal therapy as in the quest for historical truth. Achebe perceives a gap between how things were and how things are. The intercessionary phase has been typically fashioned as the sublimation of one culture by another. This is a neat enough postcolonial aphorism but without the detail and minutiae of human circumstance, its veracity can remain only intuitive.

Things Fall Apart, and *Arrow of God* after it, provide the detail, the historical glimpses, of a traditional and colonial past. These are not concurrent glimpses, and not even consecutive. But, in a sense, their temporal dislocations are all the more informative. In particular, the shifting time frame of Umuofia in *Things Fall Apart* delineates not only how things fell apart but theorizes on why they fell apart. It bestows no ebullient credit; it lays no absolute onus of blame. As Aijaz Ahmad has written, history cannot decisively resolve theoretical debate because "[t]he difficulty with theoretical debate . . . is that it can neither ignore the facts nor be simply settled by them; thought . . . tends always to exceed the facts." Obscurities of absolution and blame are of themselves the ironically definitive truths of history. The decline of Umuofia was a decline effected by a concatenation of unfortunate and calamitous and mysterious circumstances. It cannot be argued that the learning of this past is overtly utilitarian for what has been lost will not exist again and therefore cannot be lost again. What can be said is that the novel reconstructs the detail of grand and momentous events, rejecting nineteenth-century ahistorical polarities of Africa and Occident, and asserting a process of metamorphosing piety against a backdrop of seemingly irresistible social and economic imperatives.

JOSEPH McLAREN

Missionaries and Converts: Religion and Colonial Intrusion in Things Fall Apart

Chinua Achebe's treatment of missionaries and the "coming of the white man" can be viewed as a historical critique of colonialism as well as an analysis of the way European Christianity affected traditional Igbo religious and political systems. Though considered a work of fiction, *Things Fall Apart* is also a literary ethnography of Igbo culture and a semihistorical novel implicitly addressing late-nineteenth- and early-twentieth-century developments in Igboland. Achebe's intentions, to counter the record as told through European perspectives and to offer a view of Igbo culture from the inside, can be paralleled to other texts concerned with the Igbo, such as histories and ethnographic studies. As a work supposedly of "fiction," Achebe's novel offers an alternative way of presenting political and anthropological analysis. Similar to the anthropologists, Achebe presents missionaries as "agents of cultural change for whom religion is the ultimate justifying goal."

If it is true that "African writers' response to colonialism began with a guarded, if tacit, affirmation of the assumptions made for it," in certain respects, *Things Fall Apart* is an attempt to revise those assumptions, especially regarding notions of primitivism and religious simplicity. Achebe's depiction of missionaries is consistent with what has become an ongoing theme, to challenge Eurocentric depictions of Africans, as in Achebe's signifying on Conrad's *Heart of Darkness* found in his "An Image of Africa: Racism

From *The Literary Griot* 10, no.2 (Fall 1998). © 1997 *The Literary Griot*.

in Conrad's *Heart of Darkness*" (1977). Achebe describes Conrad's work as presenting "Africa as setting and backdrop which eliminates the African as human factor. Africa as a metaphysical battlefield devoid of all recognizable humanity, into which the wandering European enters at his peril." In the presentation of such issues in Conrad's work, "Africa becomes the spiritual wilderness through which the European hero has to pass on his way to redemption." In *Things Fall Apart*, the British missionaries seek to "redeem" the Igbo; in so doing, they affect the political and social structures.

Things Fall Apart provides characterizations of white missionaries and Igbo converts. In the presentation of British characters Brown, Smith, and the unnamed District Commissioner, the novel contributes to an element of post-Independence African fiction, the presentation of European characters from the perspective of the African writer. If African writers such as Achebe were reacting in part to the one dimensional, limited presentations of Africans found, for example, in the novels of Joseph Conrad and Joyce Cary, do African writers demonstrate a more complex rendering of Europeans as missionaries or agents of the colonial system? In Achebe's depiction of Igbo converts, especially Nwoye, Kiaga, and the *osu*, he interrogates the conversion process involving susceptibility and religious transmission.

The very notion of missionary excursions into Africa can be traced to the sixteenth-century pronouncement of Erasmus, who observed that "There are surely in these vast tracts barbarous and simple tribes who could easily be attracted to Christ if we sent men among them to sow the seed." It might be argued that successful missionary activities were directly related to the strategies of conversion. Also, the acceptance of multiple spiritual elements, a possible argument for the more democratic nature of traditional African religion in contrast to doctrinaire Christianity, may have contributed to accepting Christianity, though it was part of the larger project of colonial intrusion, which affected the social fabric: "Thus ideologically, and to a certain extent in practice, a potentially violent intrusion was made into the social and political world of the Nigerian peoples with the advent of Christian missionaries."

The historical record points to the combination of military excursions and the "halcyon days of Christian missions" in Southern Nigeria and invasions into Eastern Nigeria "from all directions." Both the Roman Catholic Mission of the Holy Ghost Fathers and the Church Missionary Society (CMS) of the Anglican Church were among the missionary groups interested in Igboland. The early missionary developments occurred in consort with the 1841 Niger Expedition.

Things Fall Apart exemplifies the way African fiction can offer literary interpretations of religion and colonialism, showing their complex relationship. Achebe's presentation of Christianity reveals a certain ambivalence regarding its acceptance by Nwoye and the many *osu* outcasts. The characterization of Nwoye shows psychological and cultural arguments for the susceptibility to conversion and suggests reforming certain traditional practices presented in the novel, especially the killing of twins.

Achebe uses Okonkwo as an indirect measure of the entrance of colonialism into Igboland, an area known for the rapid spread of missionary activities in the first decades of the twentieth century. It is through the remarks of Obierika, who visits Okonkwo in exile, that the emerging intrusion is brought forth. The combining of the twofold entry, colonial administration and missionary churches, becomes part of the social history passed on by word of mouth. The aftereffects of resistance in Abame, the hanging of those involved in the destruction of the mission, are, for Okonkwo, the signs of the fissures in the Igbo social structure.

The successful Christianizing of Igboland may have been due in part to the social organization of the Igbo, who tolerated missions:

> Above all, in a community like the Ibo's, where village rivalled village, many village authorities themselves took the initiative in inviting Christian teachers into their villages and towns.

This historical comment is reflected in Achebe's portrayal of numerous villages of Umuofia and the various missionary activities in Abame, Mbanta and Umuofia.

In addition to Abame, the other two Igbo sites of conversion, Mbanta and Umuofia, represent similar patterns of the dual system of entry. In the nineteenth century, conversion and the establishment of churches were the prelude to colonial administration's taking hold:

> For the history of Nigeria, however, it was in this earlier period that the work of the missionaries has its greatest significance. After 1891 their expansion was largely incidental to the establishment of colonial administration. Before 1891 they had a greater measure of initiative and their work had its own decisive influence.

The time frame of *Things Fall Apart* is roughly these transitional years of the late-nineteenth and early-twentieth centuries. Achebe creates an Igboland that witnesses the first phase of missionary activities.

Underlying the gains of missionary endeavors is the susceptibility to or rationale of conversion. The novel in some respects offers reasons to support conversion. These reasons are presented through characters such as Nwoye, who voices his main attraction for Christianity. The early mission sites signified by the developments in Mbanta are the result of exchange and negotiation in which the leaders of Mbanta, those holding titles, priests, priestesses and chiefs, ultimately concede to the missionaries' request for land. It is significant that this initial group of six missionaries, of whom only one is white, is at the onset a mere curiosity, laughable in linguistic terms suggested in the portrayal of translation.

The satirical treatment of these first missionaries in Mbanta is accompanied by details of the linguistic exchange, the use of the Igbo interpreter, whose Igbo dialect is described as "harsh to the ears of Mbanta." The humor is achieved in referring to the Igbo translator's pronouncing of the Igbo word "myself" as "my buttocks." Furthermore, one of the African missionaries does not speak Igbo, a fact that contributes to the implication that the missionary efforts have incorporated other ethnic groups outside of Igboland. As in Achebe's *Arrow of God*, "the Christians present themselves as an alternative cultural system."

The missionary's message is a direct assault on the Igbo religious system. The argument presented is that of a universal brotherhood across race and ethnicity, suggested in the phrase "all sons of God." The Igbo deities are considered "false gods, gods of wood and stone." The novel implies that this early message is merely perceived as a curious and alien event, though there is the connection between the introduction of Christianity and the offering of "Western technology," symbolized by the "iron horse," the bicycle: "I shall bring many iron horses when we have settled down among them," says the white missionary.

The split among the onlookers is represented in the response to the denigration of the Igbo deities, Ani (the earth goddess, Ala), Amadiora (the spirit of thunder), Idemili, and the suggestion of monotheism. These assertions are considered those of a madman, especially to Okonkwo, who interrogates the missionaries concerning the logic of the Trinity. The seeming contradiction of the assertion of monotheism and the concept of the "son" of God is challenged by Okonkwo, who, using the logic of human relations, wonders about the wife of the monotheistic God. Originally interested in repelling the missionaries, "chasing" or "whipping them," Okonkwo's physical aggression is supplanted by his verbal rebuke and satirical mockery, leading to his own conclusion that the British missionary is insane.

The attraction of certain Igbo is attributed to song, that is, the curiosity of hearing in song the Christian message, which is presented as having the "power of plucking at silent and dusty chords in the heart of an Igbo man." The mission in Mbanta and its Christian preachings are perceived as offering answers to problematic cultural decisions, such as the Oracle's ruling that Ikemefuna must be killed, which for Nwoye is connected to the hymn that portrays "brothers who sat in darkness and in fear." Nwoye does not accept the justice of Ikemefuna's death; Nwoye's movement toward Christianity is described as his having been "captivated" not by the theories of Christianity such as the Trinity, but by what the narrator terms the "poetry of the new religion." Rather than the theoretical discourse, the emotive element perceived in the hymn is presented as the causative factor. The killing of twins is also portrayed as part of the "vague and persistent question that haunted [Nwoye's] young soul." The suggestion here is that Nwoye did not have a way of understanding either of those acts, the killing of twins or of Ikemefuna. It is through Nwoye's mother that his conversion is explained to Obierika, but it is the narrator who offers the psychological insights.

When missionaries at Mbanta begin to preach the gospel in the marketplace, they are first concerned with negotiating with the "king of the village," perhaps an indication of other negotiations among ethnic groups where kings were part of the hierarchical structure as in Yorubaland. However in the Igbo political order, distinct clans made their own decisions regarding missionary acceptance, reflecting a decentralized political hierarchy. This decentralization is also indicated by the non-hierarchical order of Igbo deities, as in the gods of nature who "mirror Igbo social structure" in this regard.

The extent to which the decision to offer land in the "Evil Forest" is a key blunder in the negotiations is suggested in the triumph of conversion. The road to conversion is paved with acknowledgments of the resistance to the Igbo spiritual forces and the mythologizing or fetischizing of the white man's spiritual power, as in the reference to the white missionary's eyeglasses as a means to "see and talk to evil spirits," resulting in the conversion of the first three Igbo of Mbanta. Essentially, the struggle surrounding acceptance is waged in the plane of assumed spiritual authority and domination. The perceived "superior" spiritual entity is granted recognition, leading to the seedling church and the presentation of Kiaga.

The twenty-eight day period, or four market weeks, is the trial term, assumed to be the time frame in which the Igbo gods of Mbanta would allow the church to exist in defiance of their own spiritual authority. In this space of time, the gradual assimilation of certain Igbo is symbolized in Nwoye's indoctrination through a kind of indirect and seminal form of colonial or mission school education. Nwoye starts to "know some of the simple stories they told" through the delivery of their message in communal spaces, such as the village playgrounds and the marketplace. These stories represent an alternative oral message overlaying the stories told in a familial setting.

Furthermore, the place of the Mbanta mission, "the little red-earth and thatch building," in the hierarchical structure of the mission church is indicated by the role of Kiaga, whose knowledge of the white man's language and his role as interpreter make him a likely candidate to lead the mission. Kiaga is the agent of Nwoye's conversion. The mission's central seat of authority is, however, Umuofia, where the white missionary has "built his headquarters." The rejection of Igbo deities can be understood within the context of Igbo religion in which humans can "demand from their gods effective service and effective protection," which if not provided could result in "starvation and desertion" of the gods.

Though the Mbanta mission church is perceived through imagery as the "open mouth of the Evil Forest," with fearsome teeth, its triumph at this juncture is based solely on the survival of the missionaries and converts, thus initiating an incremental growth through the attaining of additional converts. For Okonkwo, Nwoye's conversion promotes thoughts of a total betrayal of his male children, resulting in the potentially cataclysmic disjuncture with the ancestors. Okonkwo's vision of a complete rejection of the traditional religion is depicted as a failure to "worship and sacrifice" at the shrine of the ancestors. It is this vision that is perhaps most responsible for Okonkwo's decision to eliminate Christianity by wiping out the missionaries.

In other words, the possibility of coexistence is negated through the threat of near total conversion. In essence, Okonkwo's inability to reason with Nwoye about the elements of Christianity that Nwoye finds appealing—and the subsequent beating of Nwoye—leads to Nwoye's own self-banishing and the beginning of his mission school education in Umuofia, "where the white missionary had set up a school to teach young Christians to read and write." Kiaga perceives this separation as divine will represented in Christ's statement, "Blessed is he who forsakes his father and his mother for my sake." Nwoye redefines his own mission as that of converting his actual mother and father, a literal interpretation of a message that is primarily metaphorical. Though the novel does not necessarily treat the establishment of full-fledged mission schools, it hints at those developments. The establishment of missions eventually leads to the creation of an elite of which Nwoye is a possible projection.

If the "Evil Forest" signifies the center of the clan's location of the unwanted, the damned and the rejected, the site of those spiritual entities considered damaging to the clan, then the survival of the mission under these circumstances represents a spiritual force attractive to those such as Nneka. Her successive birth of twins, who would have been consigned to the "Evil Forest," causes her to view the mission as a refuge. Furthermore, Kiaga's mission preaches a supposedly egalitarian theology—which is enticing to the *osu*. The *osu* are depicted as marginalized outcasts, identifiable by their physical appearance and residence. An *osu*, the narrator tells us,

> was a person dedicated to a god, a thing set apart—a taboo for ever [sic], and his children after him. He could neither marry nor be married by the free-born. He was in fact an outcast, living in a special area of the village, close to the Great Shrine.

The *osu* is defined elsewhere as

> A person dedicated to an arusi [middlemen between Igbo and Chukwu] or a person who has committed a crime and sought sanctuary at an arusi's shrine. Such an individual automatically becomes an outcast barred from communication or relations with any but other osu.

The marginalized *osu* form a portion of the opposing elements of Mbanta, whose actions were both passive and aggressive. At one point, a group of three converts openly defies the traditional gods, and there is the threat of burning these gods; an *osu* allegedly kills the sacred python. This first threat is repelled verbally and physically. The verbal abuse, "Go and burn your mothers' genitals," is similar to the insult battles in the African American form known as "the dozens" or "signifying," where references to the mother form the language of satire and abuse. However, this minimal attack by the converts is easily thwarted physically through beating.

In its appeal to the *osu*, Kiaga's church offers the opportunity for unification of outcasts empowered with a Christian identity considered to have withstood the forces of Igbo religion. Furthermore, Kiaga's defense of the outcasts bolsters the "wavering converts" in a crucial period when the new church could have imploded because of its acceptance of the outcasts. Their new physical identity is observable in the shaving of the hair that marked them as *osu*. It is logical that the violation of the sacred python, addressed ironically as "Our Father," would be carried out by one of the *osu*, allegedly Okoli, though the act is considered as apocryphal.

At this moment in the novel, the decision to ostracize the Christians wins out over the argument of Okonkwo, who argues for physical punishment. The decision not to interfere is explained in terms of Igbo religion and the individual's relation to the gods: "If we put ourselves between the god and his victim we may receive blows intended for the offender." This proverbial statement suggests a strategy of non-interference. Okoli's ultimate death provides a justification for non-interference in proving that "the gods were still able to fight their own battles." The issue here is whether Okonkwo recognizes that in fact the gods do not need the assistance of man in order to control the overzealous elements within the mission.

The hands-off approach in Mbanta indirectly leads to the growth of the mission during a period of eighteen months, after which Mr. Brown, assumed to be the original white missionary, on one of his visits uses the image of the seed, echoing the basic agricultural reality of yam planting, to describe the mission's growth: "I marvel at what the Lord hath wrought," he declares. The novel also presents the spread of Christianity in Umuofia, where the mission has established itself during the first two years of Okonkwo's seven-year exile. The church attracted those who were on the margins of the clan, the *efulefu*, described as "worthless, empty men" who bore no title and had no presence in the communal meetings.

The stalwarts of traditional Igbo religion, such as the priestess Chielo, though unable to exercise physical force to suppress the mission efforts, use language as a way of characterizing the converts, such as "the excrement of the clan." If the metaphor of "falling apart" generally characterizes the dual entry of British hegemony, an additional metaphor is provided by Chielo in which Christianity is perceived as a "mad dog" that will devour the clan. These definitions of converts are relevant to the broad anthropological interpretation of missionary endeavors, in contrast to the colonial bureaucrats and administrators concerned with taxation, profits, cheap labor. The missionary "invariably aimed at overall changes in the beliefs and actions" of the indigenous population, characterized as a "colonization of heart and mind as well as body." Although the presence of the mission is seen as a threat to Umuofia, the assumption, though not stated in the novel, is that the colonial forces would destroy Umuofia if the missionaries were killed, a repetition of the Abame situation.

Mr. Brown and his successor Reverend James Smith are focal points of characterization, implying, respectively, a less invasive and more authoritarian brand of proselytizing. Brown is presented as politically moderate, one who is "very firm in restraining his flock from provoking the wrath of the clan" and who "came to be respected even by the clan." Brown's discussion with Akunna—whose son, similar to Waiyaki in Ngugi's *The River Between* (1965), is sent by his father to learn the "white man's knowledge"—is used to present dialogues of religious debate. Akunna's delineation of Igbo hierarchies stresses the supremacy of Chukwu. Chukwu, the "high god," though "distant and withdrawn, . . . is not completely separated from the affairs of men."

Though Brown prefers to look at Christian hierarchy in non-human terms, "God" as the "head" of the church, Akunna's analogies show the combined elements of missionary efforts and colonial administration. Akunna's allusion to the District Commissioner as an agent of the British nation is a sign of this connection between church and state. The idea of multiple deities and figures is also understandable as "merely manifesting the belief, similar to the Christian theory of the omnipresence of God, that they were present in all aspects of creation through which they could speak to their people."

Though Brown is portrayed as understanding of the Igbo religion, this understanding is a means toward alternate systems of cultural persuasion beyond the gospel, such as the enticement of mission schools and Western medicine. Ironically, the early schools in Umuofia are not considered ladders to elite positions but the locations for "slaves" and "lazy children." Most importantly, Brown suggests that mission education can be a form of resisting the encroaching forces of colonial administration, evident in the Native Court and the gradual entry of strangers, other Africans, from "the distant town of Umuru on the bank of the Great River," perhaps a reference to the Niger Delta as the site of entry by the white man. The mission school will eventually provide the system through which "elites" in the colonial order can be produced, the generation following the court clerks, court messengers and teachers: "From the very beginning religion and education went hand in hand." Brown's mission is interconnected to the emerging colonial administration, resulting in its rapid growth and "social prestige."

Reverend Smith, Brown's successor, is Brown's polar opposite, more concerned with theology than accumulation of converts. His emphasis on "the importance of fewness" and strict adherence to scripture is symbolized by his banning of a woman who, in the narrator's metaphorical terms, was "pouring new wine into old bottles" (not necessarily an Igbo proverb) by allowing the "mutilation" of her dead *ogbanje* child. Smith's zeal is described proverbially, "as a man danced so the drums were beaten for him," implying the matching zeal of converts such as Enoch, whose name shows the transformation to Christian names. (In the Bible Enoch was the eldest son of Cain). Language is also used to characterize Enoch as "the outsider who wept louder than the bereaved," meaning his involvement in Christian proselytizing beyond the intensity of Reverend Smith's activities. Ironically, Enoch is "the son of the snake-priest who was believed to have killed and eaten the sacred python," an echo of Okoli's alleged violation in Mbanta.

The conflict in Umuofia goes beyond the challenges of the outcasts in Mbanta. Enoch's unmasking of an *egwugwu* is seen as the murder of an "ancestral spirit." The retribution, the burning of his compound, is a moment of potential rectification. However, the ultimate destruction of the church, at least in a physical and temporal sense, is a result of the intransigence of Reverend Smith, when Ajofia, the head *egwugwu*, negotiates with Smith, offering an agreement, a compromise and ultimatum: "You can stay with us if you like our ways. You can worship your own god. It is good that a man should worship the gods and the spirits of his fathers."

This religious tolerance of the Igbo has been described elsewhere by Achebe as a sign of the superiority of African religion over Christianity, its acknowledgment of multiple deities (*Writers Talk*), but this tolerance underlies a potential point of fissure. There is a play on language and translation in the interpreter's placating rendering of Smith's firm rebuke: "Tell them to go away from here," interpreted as "The white man says he is happy you have come to him with your grievances," does not pacify the distressed Umuofians.

The arrest of Okonkwo and Ogbuefi Ekwueme shows the other side of the dual system of intrusion, the rapid judicial kangaroo court system. Igbo court messengers are also implicated in the coalescing of colonial authority. The beating of Okonkwo by the court messenger is the climactic moment of the suppression of traditional authority. In the latter chapters of the novel, the colonial system's authority is evident in its power to incarcerate, try, and fine the Igbo. Okonkwo's killing of the court messenger is a last attempt at resistance; though ill-planned and impulsive, it is an act to reclaim agency. The ironic ending of the novel shows that "Achebe's satire grows teeth" in reversing the perspective in the portrayal of the District Commissioner. Achebe uses the language of the British ethnographer to reduce the complex emblem of conversion and colonial ascendency to a paragraph on Okonkwo's demise.

Though portions of the novel could be perceived as merely a view of missionary activity from the position of the Igbo, Achebe achieves a complex characterization of missionaries and converts by demonstrating their variations and interactions. The neglect by anthropological studies in interpreting the colonial administrator and the missionary as an anthropological subject is corrected by Achebe. His rendering of Brown and Smith provides at least a multidimensional understanding of the approaches to conversion. The missionaries are not portrayed as simply a group of intruding white men but as agents of the colonial system, whose personalities and proselytizing strategies are perceived as different by the Igbo themselves, many of whom are also implicated in the missionary endeavor and the colonial administration. Most importantly, *Things Fall Apart* unravels the intricacies of Igbo religion, the complexity of its belief system, debunking the notion of a tabula rasa, addressing the reasons underlying the fractures and discords inherent in nonhierarchical systems. The novel also emphasizes that parallel to missionary intrusion was the larger "mission" of colonization, a political realization evident especially to certain elder factions of the Igbo world.

CLEMENT OKAFOR

Igbo Cosmology and the Parameters of Individual Accomplishment in Things Fall Apart

Since the publication of *Things Fall Apart* in 1958, the novel has developed into a truly remarkable literary phenomenon; it is not only the most widely read book in Africa except for the Bible, but also is now part of the global literary canon. Furthermore, *Things Fall Apart* has sold more than eight million copies and has been translated into fifty-five languages of the world.

As the literary world celebrates the fortieth anniversary of the publication of this classic, it is more important now than ever before that we establish an appropriate epistemological framework that can profitably inform our critical discussions of *Things Fall Apart*.

Since literature is contextual, the interrogation of the setting of a literary opus creates opportunities for a deep and rewarding interpretation of the work under consideration. *Things Fall Apart* is set in Igboland in the second half of the Nineteenth Century, the time when Britain was in the process of colonizing not only Igboland but also the other African territories allotted to her at the Berlin Conference of 1884/85. An exploration of traditional Igbo cosmology is, therefore, a valuable strategy for establishing the desired epistemological framework in which to place our further discourse on the novel.

Throughout this paper, the term "cosmology" is used to convey the sense of a society's perception of the world in which it lives. Such a concept

From *The Literary Griot* 10, no.2 (Fall 1998). © 1998 *The Literary Griot*.

usually explores the complex interlocking relationships between human beings and the pantheon of forces that function within their society's universe.

First, a word about the Igbo. The Igbo inhabit the territory of South-eastern Nigeria, and their homeland is located on both banks of *Orimili* (the great river) the River Niger, from which Nigeria derives her name. According to Basden, "the Ibo nation ranks as one of the largest in the whole of Africa." Igbo people now number about twenty-five million, a population larger than those of Norway, Sweden, and Denmark combined.

Igbo society is historically egalitarian and democratic in the sense that the people have never had rulers with anything approaching autocratic powers. According to Green, the Igbo "have no hierarchy of powers rising from a broad democratic basis through ascending levels to one central peak," rather, "Ibo democracy unlike English, works through a number of juxta-posed groups and a system of balances rather than on a unitary hierarchical principle." This egalitarian principle is expressed in the famous statement: *Igbo enwe eze* (The Igbo do not have kings).

The town, which is the basic unit of Igbo traditional political organization, is made up of various villages that together comprise about twenty to thirty thousand people. Although these towns are "not united by central government authority, nor arranged in any political hierarchy they are none the less interlinked horizontally each with its neighbors by the social bonds of inter-marriage" that is based on the principle of exogamy; thus although the towns are politically independent, they are socially linked by a web of relationships centered around exogamous marriages, which means that everybody has links not only with his own hometown but also, as Green affirms, "with the birthplace of his mother, with that of his wife, and the various places into which his sisters have married," not to mention the towns into which his brothers have married. Every town has a market, which is held every four or eight days and is a socially unifying force; among the Igbo the market is also a place where people socialize.

As Simon Ottenberg has observed in his study, the democratic nature of Igbo society—with its encouragement of healthy individual and group rivalry coupled with the premium it places on individual, personal accomplishment—has enabled its people to adapt rapidly to the modern, western way of life.

Briefly, in Igbo cosmology, there is Chukwu or *ama ama amasi amasi* (the one who can never be fully understood). Below him is a pantheon of deities whose domain may be limited to specific aspects of life on earth. Examples of these are Amadiora, the god of thunder, Ufiojioku, the god of the harvest, and Anyanwu, the sun god. Principal among these deities is Ani, the Earth goddess, who is the arbiter of ethical conduct. The major deities have special shrines and priests dedicated to their worship and it is the duty of human beings to strive at all times to live righteously by conducting their lives in accordance with the ethics of the community and by avoiding societal taboos. If for any reason human beings transgress these rules, they are expected to atone for their offenses by performing prescribed ritual acts of expiation.

When those who live well die, they become ancestors in *ani muo* (land of the dead) provided their living relatives have performed the appropriate funeral rites; it is these rites that initiate the dead into the company of the powerful ancestors. Such ancestors take an active interest in the welfare of the living members of their family, who pour libations to them and make offerings to their memory on certain occasions.

Igbo cosmology admits of the existence of evil spirits, *umunadi*, who are believed to live in the liminal, uninhabited spaces beyond the village settlements and also in the bad bush. It also admits of the existence of *ogbanje*, the spirits of children who reincarnate and are born to die, often in infancy, only to be born again by the same or another unfortunate mother.

Duality or the phenomenology of pairing is another very important aspect of Igbo cosmology. In Igbo thought, nothing can exist by itself, since wherever something exists, something else exists beside it. As the proverb says: *Ife kwulu, ife akwudebe ya* (When one thing stands, something else stands beside it). Thus, there can be no unpaired manifestation of any force or being.

Arising from the duality phenomenon is the Igbo concern for the maintenance of balance in one's life. Because Igbo cosmology envisages the simultaneous functioning of numerous and sometimes antagonistic forces, one is counseled to thread one's way cautiously so as not to offend any of the contending spirits. Extremism of any kind, is thus perceived to be dangerous, as is encapsulated in the following proverb: *ife belu n'oke ka dibia n'agwo* (The healer can cure only something within bounds).

Reincarnation is a cardinal principle in Igbo cosmology. Ancestors who are well cared for by their living offspring may take on new human bodies and be born as loving children to their former sons and daughters. However, reincarnation is not limited to the ancestors. As has been mentioned earlier, the spirits of some children are also believed to reincarnate only to die young.

Central to Igbo cosmology is one's choice of a destiny. This choice is made freely before the moment of incarnation and is witnessed and sealed by one's *chi* or personal guiding spirit. The choice the individual makes usually compensates for the circumstances of his or her previous life. Thus, somebody who is killed by his jealous neighbors on account of his excessive wealth in one life may elect to be poor in his next incarnation. However, once the choice has been made and the child is born, his destiny is guarded throughout his life by his *chi* and cannot be changed. More importantly, once the child is born, he suffers total amnesia with respect to his chosen destiny.

As the child grows, he is socialized into the strong ethos of hard work for which the Igbo people are known, while the egalitarian organization of society encourages him to believe that there is no limit to what he can achieve in life. It is the same ethos of hard work and high self-esteem that Olaudah Equiano refers to in the following description of his Igbo people more than two centuries ago:

> Agriculture is our chief employment; and every one, even the children and women are engaged in it. Thus we are all habituated to labour from our earliest years. Every one contributes something to the common stock; and as we are unacquainted with idleness we have no beggars.

The amnesia at birth ensures that the pre-incarnation choice (as to whether the individual will be a success or a failure) does not deter the person from striving to achieve the best possible life, since only his *chi* knows what destiny he has chosen. Regardless of what one's conscious desires may be, the prior choice made functions as the subconscious drive that predisposes the individual to acting in such a way as to fulfill the individual's destiny. This situation does not make the people fatalistic, however, because in the first place, no one remembers what manner of life he or she has chosen. In the second place, the Igbo also firmly believe that human agency is critical to the actualization of one's destiny and that hard work results in a better life. It is only after a person has been dogged by misfortune, despite his or her best effort, that he begins to suspect that he may not be destined for good things after all. Still, the final judgement is withheld until after the death of the individual. It is only after someone's death that the living can then assess his destiny fully. This practice is encapsulated in the proverb: *Chi ejilu ada akalu ubosi* (One must not condemn the day until it is over).

The foregoing is a brief overview of the Igbo cosmology that was in place at the onset of British colonization of Igboland, the historical setting of *Things Fall Apart*. It remains for us to show how this paradigm is reflected in the novel itself.

Things Fall Apart is like an expansive epic narrative that uses its larger form to frame numerous smaller thematic strands. The main story of the novel is that of Okonkwo, the protagonist, who is introduced in the first word of the first paragraph of the text. At that point, Okonkwo is already famous on account of his personal accomplishments, especially for his earlier spectacular wrestling victory that is likened to that of the legendary founder of his hometown, who is reputed to have wrestled a spirit of the wilderness for seven days and seven nights. Okonkwo's victory over Amalinze, the Cat, who has held the wrestling championship title for seven years, shows his affinity to his town's founding father. Thus, even at eighteen he has shown that he is a worthy son of Umuofia and appears to be marked out for great achievements.

Sadly, Okonkwo's psyche is so traumatized by his father's penury and the poverty of his early childhood that his psyche remains mortally wounded throughout his life, although his hard work enables him to improve his material welfare; hence, he does not see the full range of dual possibilities inherent in every situation. Because he loathes his father, he instinctively hates everything that reminds him of Unoka. Because Unoka is weak, Okonkwo strives at all times to exhibit heroic courage, which pushes him to commit excesses like killing Ikemefuna that drive a wedge between him and his son, Nwoye. From the perspective of Igbo cosmology, Okonkwo's inability to recognize the duality and complexity of life situations is a major handicap, since it reveals a fundamental lack of balance in his life.

Okonkwo's problems also emanate from his inability to practice another Igbo ideal, balance in one's assessment of situations, since he usually takes extremist positions in life. For instance, he cannot understand how a strong man like Ogbuefi Ndulue can do nothing without consulting his wife first. Again, to Okonkwo, the new colonial dispensation is an unmitigated evil that should be expunged from his home and he does not realize that many of his people viewed it differently:

> There were many men and women in Umuofia who did not feel as strongly as Okonkwo about the new dispensation. The white man had indeed brought a lunatic religion, but he had also brought a trading store and for the first time palm oil and kernel became things of great price and much money flowed into Umuofia.
>
> And even in the matter of religion there was a growing feeling that there might be something in it after all, something vaguely akin to method in the overwhelming madness.

This difference in perception of the problem explains why Umuofia does not join Okonkwo in a battle to drive out the new colonial administration and the Christian missionaries. So in the end, Okonkwo's tragic demise arises from his lack of full understanding of his people and their culture.

However, *Things Fall Apart* is not only the story of the protagonist, Okonkwo; it is also the story of an African community, Umuofia. Contrary to the Hegelian ethnocentric theory of history, which posits that Africa has neither a history nor a future, the Igbo society that Achebe portrays in this novel is keenly aware of its history and the legendary feats of its founding father. It is a society in which someone at the beginning of his career can go to an elder and obtain without any collateral the resources with which to establish himself in life. Above all, it is a society that judges a man not by the size of his inheritance, but rather by his own personal accomplishments. Moreover, in Umuofia, the African community portrayed in the novel, there is marital amity and social problems are resolved on the basis of the consensus emanating from open public debate in a manner that protects not only the rights of the individuals concerned but also the corporate interests of the community.

What informs Achebe's portrait of Umuofia is not mawkish sentimentality, since he shows that the community has its share of internal contradictions, as is true of all human societies. These internal contradictions in all societies explain why new laws are being made to deal with new contradictions as well as to revisit old ones. What is remarkable in the African society portrayed in the novel is that it has achieved a great degree of stability by maintaining a balance between its centrifugal and centripetal forces. Indeed, what informs the novelist's portrait of the society is his conviction, which he has expressed on several occasions, that the African needs to tell his own side of the colonial story himself:

> At the University I read some appalling novels about Africa (including Joyce Cary's much praised *Mr. Johnson*) and decided that the story we had to tell could not be told for us by anyone else, no matter how gifted or well-intentioned. ("Named for Victoria")

Like the traditional epics that use the major narratives to frame the many minor ones, *Things Fall Apart* frames numerous minor stories within the major narratives about Okonkwo and his community. One of these minor narratives in the novel is the interrogation of the relationships between fathers and their sons. Igbo society is largely patriarchal and patrilineal; hence, families here depend on the male offspring for succession and the perpetuation of their names. This places a burden on the relationships between fathers and their sons, particularly their first sons. In the novel, Unoka is the founder of his lineage, but he is not successful in agriculture, the principal occupation of his people. His forte is music making and the happiest time of the year for him are those two or three moons after the

harvest when the community relaxes from the rigors of farming and entertains itself with music and dance. Regrettably, he is so improvident that he
owes his neighbors a lot of money. However, he has a tremendous sense of
humor and drama, which he exhibits when one of his creditors, Okoye, asks
him to pay him back the money he owes him:

> As soon as Unoka understood what his friend was driving at, he
> burst out laughing. He laughed loud and long and his voice rang
> out clear as the ogene, and tears stood in his eyes. His visitor was
> amazed, and sat speechless. At the end, Unoka was able to give
> an answer between fresh outbursts of mirth.
>
> "Look at that wall," he said pointing at the far wall of his hut,
> which was rubbed with red earth so it shone. "Look at those line
> of chalk;" and Okoye saw groups of short perpendicular lines.
> There were five groups and the smallest group had ten lines.
> Unoka had a sense of the dramatic; and so he allowed a pause, in
> which he took a pinch of snuff and sneezed noisily and then
> continued: "Each group there represents a debt to someone and
> each stroke is one hundred cowries. You see, I owe that man a
> thousand cowries. But he has not come to wake me up in the
> morning for it. I shall pay you, but not today. Our elders say that
> the sun will shine on those who stand before it shines on those
> who kneel under them. I shall pay my big debts first." And he
> took another pinch of snuff, as if that was paying the big debts
> first. Okoye rolled his goatskin and departed.

Furthermore, Unoka is undoubtedly a coward, and his people regard him as
a failure. He is a burden on his son and the other members of his family;
hence, Okonkwo is thoroughly ashamed of him.

Ironically, the dysfunctional relationship Okonkwo has with his father
is duplicated in the one he has with his own son, Nwoye. Being an Igbo man,
Okonkwo must have dreaded (even without admitting it to himself) the
uncanny resemblance between Nwoye's temperament and that of Unoka. He
must have feared that Nwoye may well be a reincarnation of his father. This
may explain why Okonkwo tries to root out in his young son any personality
trait he despised in his father. Hence, he encourages Nwoye to come to his
dwelling place in order to imbibe the martial traditions of his people.
However, the son prefers listening to the folktales, which the father despises
as being fit for the ears of women only.

Because Nwoye has come to look up to Ikemefuna as if he were an
elder brother, he is devastated by the ritual murder of this role model. This

further aggravates the friction between father and son. In addition, there is something in Nwoye, which cannot find fulfillment within the martial ethos of his society. It is indeed this search for something, which his community cannot satisfy, that leads Nwoye into an exploration of the new religion. Unfortunately, Okonkwo's handling of the news that his son has been seen in the company of the missionaries severs the already weak link between the two and emboldens the son to reject his father completely.

Another minor narrative in *Things Fall Apart* is the portrait of the relationships between fathers and their daughters. Igbo society is mainly patrilineal and succession is through the male offspring, who also perpetuates the family name. The society's concern for the survival of the lineage is expressed in such names like Amaechina (may the compound not perish/disappear) or Obiechina (may the household not perish). As is often the case with such patriarchal societies, they treasure their sons more highly than their daughters. Perhaps, because these families expect more from boys than from girls, they exert greater pressure on the boys to succeed than on the girls.

The irony in *Things Fall Apart* is that the boy, Nwoye, runs away from his father, while his sister, Ezinma, dotes on Okonkwo. It is, thus, not surprising that there is a special bond between father and his daughter and that Okonkwo wishes that Ezinma were a boy, as may be seen in the following dialogue between them:

> "You have not eaten for two days," said his daughter Ezinma when she brought the food to him. "So you must finish this." She sat down and stretched her legs in front of her. Okonkwo ate the food absent-mindedly. "She should have been a boy," he thought as he looked at his ten-year old daughter. He passed her a piece of fish.
>
> "Go and bring me some cold water," he said. Ezinma rushed out of the hut, chewing the fish, and soon returned with a bowl of cool water from the earthen pot in her mother's hut.
>
> . . . .
>
> "She should have been a boy," Okonkwo said to himself again.

Indeed, the bond between Okonkwo and Ezinma is so strong that later when they are in exile a mere word from Okonkwo, expressing his desire that she should hold off getting married until their return to Umuofia makes Ezinma dismiss all good suitors from Mbanta, their place of exile. Thus, it is not unlikely that Okonkwo must have been frustrated that everything he has struggled to accomplish in life will be inherited by his sons, who may not be as deserving as this daughter.

The portrait of the relationships between husbands and their wives is yet another significant narrative framed in *Things Fall Apart*. In Umuofia marriage is more than an affair between two individuals; it is a union of two family groups, who have a mutual interest in preserving that liaison. Marriages here are contracted after elaborate negotiations and public ceremonies, as is exemplified in the *uri* ceremony of Akueke, Obierika's daughter. On this occasion, Obierika's family entertains almost the entire village.

Like marriages all over the world, however, some of the marriages contracted in Umuofia later become dysfunctional, despite the best effort of the two families involved. Some are so bad that they are referred to the community elders for arbitration in the public square, as is the case with the dispute between Uzowulu and his wife. However, even Okonkwo, who abuses his wives, has a very endearing relationship with one of them, Ekwefi—his childhood sweetheart. She has been married before to someone else because Okonkwo was then too poor to finance the required ceremonies. That marriage notwithstanding, Ekwefi one day walks out on her husband and into Okonkwo's home. Thereafter, she becomes his wife. Not surprisingly, the special relationship that exists between Okonkwo and Ekwefi is transferred to their daughter, Ezinma.

Even truly romantic love affairs do exist among some married couples in this society, as is exemplified by the marital bliss of Ogbuefi Ndulue and his wife Ozoemena. So strong is their love for one another that the husband never does anything without consulting his wife first. Indeed, so well known is their love for one another that their community has composed a song about them. The husband and wife are so inseparable, even in their old age, that when Ozoemena learns of the death of her husband, she immediately loses all interest in life. She walks to her house, lies down and passes away that very day.

Another minor narrative that is framed in *Things Fall Apart* is the portrait of the relationships between leadership and followership. In the novel, the highest leadership positions are those of the nine *egwugwu*, who represent the nine villages of the town. Symbolizing the ancestors of the community, these elders arbitrate public disputes and their authority is never challenged, as may be seen in the following formulaic dialogue between Evil Forest, their spokesman, and Uzowulu:

> "Uzowulu's body, I salute you," he said. Spirits always address humans as "bodies." Uzowulu bent down and touched the earth with his right hand as a sign of submission.
> "Our father, my hand has touched the ground," he said.
> "Uzowulu's body, do you know me?" asked the spirit.

"How can I know you, father? You are beyond our knowledge."

In such situations, the *egwugwu* first allow the contending parties to present
their cases and thereafter pronounce a verdict that is not only fair to the
parties, but helps to preserve the solidarity of the community.

In *Things Fall Apart*, matters of public concern are generally discussed
at town meetings that are open to every male adult. Although, the views of
titled men carry infinitely more weight at such public gatherings, yet,
everyone who so desires can express his opinion. Eventually a consensus
emerges through a reconciliation of the competing viewpoints; whereupon,
the consensus becomes the view of the entire community and is, thereafter,
expected to be implemented without dissent. This is the case when Ogbuefi
Udo's wife is killed in Mbaino. The consensus is that Umuofia should give
Mbaino an ultimatum to choose either to pay the agreed upon compensation
or to go to war. On another occasion when the peace of the community is
threatened by the excesses of the fanatical Christians, a meeting is called and
there is a consensus as to how the society should respond. Here again, the
community acts as one and speaks with one unmistakable voice. One may
rightly deduce then that this is the ideal Igbo political process. It follows,
therefore, that good leaders among the Igbo must have consensus building
skills. Viewed from this perspective, Okonkwo's leadership skills fail when he
is unable to build a consensus as to how Umuofia should respond the District
Commissioner's imprisonment of the community's elders.

Thus far we have shown that in *Things Fall Apart*, there are many
minor narratives that are framed by two major ones: the first portrays an
individual's single-minded struggle to rise from the humble circumstances of
birth to a position of prominence in his community; the second is the narrative of a community that has evolved a civilization through the years as it
struggles to adapt to colonial conquest and domination. These two narratives, however, merge into one, since that individual eventually becomes one
of the six leaders imprisoned by the District Commissioner.

It now remains for us to show that the universe of *Things Fall Apart* is a
reflection of the Igbo cosmology described above. A close examination of the
cosmos of *Things Fall Apart* shows that the world portrayed in the novel parallels very closely the universe of Igbo cosmology. For example, in both the Igbo
paradigm and *Things Fall Apart*, the town is the unit of political organization.
In *Things Fall Apart*, towns like Umuofia, Mbaino, Mbanta, Abame, etc. are
also units of political organization since the people see themselves as citizens
of these communities. Ordinarily, these autonomous communities live peacefully with one another, except when cordial relations are disturbed by the

hostile actions of a neighboring town, as in the murder of an Umuofia woman by a citizen of Mbaino. Even in this case, the prompt payment of a ransom restores the good relations that had been consolidated over the generations through numerous exogamous inter-town marriages. Furthermore, councils of elders rule these towns, as is the case in the real Igbo society.

In addition, the events in the lives of the characters in the novel resemble those of the people one encounters in the Igbo cosmos. For instance, the Igbo concept of reincarnation is reflected in Ezinma's life, since she is *ogbanje*—one of those children who are born to die in infancy and re-enter their mother's wombs to be born again and again. This explains the intervention of the medicine man who locates Ezinma's *iyi uwa* in his effort to enable her to break the cycle and live.

Furthermore, the marriages in *Things Fall Apart* are negotiated and celebrated in true Igbo manner. Again, the punishment for Okonkwo's involuntary homicide in the novel is a replica of the Igbo response to such a crime. The corpse of someone who takes his or her own life is an abomination and a source of pollution not only to the earth but also to anyone who comes in contact with it. Indeed, the Igbo consider those who take their lives as being so despicable that they are not mourned and, as in Okonkwo's case, only strangers can handle their bodies. Above all, the pervasive role ascribed to Okonkwo's *chi* is a replica of the dominant role that is ascribed to that guardian spirit in Igbo cosmology. These examples demonstrate incontrovertibly that the universe portrayed in *Things Fall Apart* closely reflects the cosmos delineated above.

If, according to the Igbo paradigm, nobody can accomplish anything without the support of his *chi*, to what extent is Okonkwo then responsible for his tragic end? As Achebe himself explains, although no one can achieve anything without the assistance of his *chi*, the Igbo believe that human agency is essential to the realization of one's destiny. Again, in Igbo cosmology, amnesia at birth ensures that each person is unaware of the choice previously made and leads his life in accordance with the Igbo ethos encapsulated in the following proverb: *Onye kwe chi ya ekwe* (When somebody says yes, his *chi* says yes also).

A review of the career of the protagonist shows that he has a very high self-esteem. On account of his individual accomplishments, Okonkwo sees himself as the legendary lizard which jumped down from the high iroko tree and was able to escape from the seven agile men who were waiting to catch it. Indeed, Okonkwo seems to exemplify the Igbo ethos of hard work; by his hard work he has raised himself from the penury of his childhood to the highest leadership position in his society. He has said yes and it seems that his *chi* also supports his efforts, at least initially. Sadly, his traumatic childhood, however, seems to have permanently wounded his psyche and endowed him with a one-dimensional perception of reality that makes him take the personal decisions that precipitate his calamitous end. The Igbo belief that a person cannot achieve anything without the consent of his *chi* must not mislead one to conclude that Okonkwo is merely a pawn in the hands of his guiding spirit. On the contrary, Okonkwo's personality flaws precipitate his catastrophic demise and nullify his individual accomplishments.

By situating *Things Fall Apart* in its cultural milieu, the exposition above has attempted to create for the ever-growing readership of the master-piece an appropriate epistemological framework that should inform future discourse on its merits and meanings.

IMAFEDIA OKHAMAFE

Genealogical Determinism in Achebe's Things Fall Apart

Things indeed fall apart in Umuofia. The center can no longer hold. But things begin to fall apart in this nine-village Umuofia clan long before a European colonialist missionary culture inserts itself there. The tragedy of Umuofia, therefore, lies not so much in white missionary arrival as in Umuofia's hierarchical failure to fruitfully engage certain internal cultural differences that were already simmering in the general economy of Umuofia long before and even after the presence of any formidable Christian difference in Umuofia. The hierarchical failure derives from an *egwugwu* genealogy that forms and informs the general economy of Umuofia. By general economy I mean the arch network of power relations that structures the thinking and life practices and thus the destiny of Umuofia. The greatest inheritor, defender, promoter, and spokesman of this *egwugwu* culture in Umuofia is Okonkwo.

Read from a genealogical perspective, Chinua Achebe's seminal novel *Things Fall Apart* becomes more about the powers and limits of one dominant interpretation and practice of a certain polygynous and misogynic tradition in Umuofia. This *egwugwu* genealogy defines strength only in martial terms or only in terms of the will to physical power. Furthermore, manhood and this strength are synonymous. The clan recognizes this strength through four titles, the fourth and highest one being lord of the clan. Each title marks

From *Genealogy and Literature*, Lee Quimby, editor. © 1995 by the University of Minnesota Press.

the degree of strength and thus of manhood. Okonkwo's monomaniacal task in life becomes making himself, his sons, and Umuofia males into this kind of man. Manliness so defined is Okonkwo's existential litmus test for himself, his family, and his clan. A male without any title is often called an *agbala* (a woman). Where a male stands in the general economy of Umuofia more or less depends on whether the male is a man or a woman. This *egwugwu* genealogy rests on Umuofia's agricultural economy of yams (men's crops) and non-yams (women's crops, such as cassava). Umuofia's dominant tradition makes Umuofia culture into Umuofia nature, a nature that demands and insists on its subjects' following the line of manliness and womanness as strength and weakness. In Umuofia all females are women and all women are weak. No woman can be strong. Only males can be men and only men are strong. A male who fails to be a man is a woman. Umuofia culture calls on its women to be women and on its males to be men. All women are women. All men are males, but not all males are men. Patriarchy, however, requires the partnership or cooperation of both biological males and biological females. Not even nature itself privileges males or females in the reproductive process. Umuofia does not explain why that which is supposedly potentially strong (the male) would need that which is allegedly inherently weak (the female) to produce those who can become strong (males): that which can be strong needs that which cannot be strong to produce those who can be strong. A woman's proper role is to help Umuofia *reproduce* males who will become men and women who will remain women. There is no room in Umuofia for womanly males or unwomanly women. A man's proper task is to help his women reproduce patriarchy (Umuofia style). A man has to fight constantly not to become a woman. But how does this multiplication process (of strength and weakness so defined) produce a creative (healthy) strength that can indefinitely sustain (on its own terms) Umuofia's patriarchal reality and ideal? This question, which roots itself in the beginning of the novel, is what finally does in both Okonkwo and his Umuofia culture. Umuofia falls because it leaves no space for creative utopian speculation or for the imagination of other ways (from within and without) of being in Umuofia culture. Internal disturbers of the *egwugwu* tradition are dismissed as *agbala*, *efulefu* (effeminate men), or *osu* (outcasts) of some sort and are treated accordingly.

Okonkwo's father (Unoka), we are told, was a woman or a weak male because he never earned any title. He was always in debt and was more interested in being a musician than in being a man. Okonkwo inherited no wealth from his father; in fact, his father was buried in a place reserved for shamed males, female males, and other outcasts. Determined to not be like his father, Okonkwo assumed his manly or economic responsibility very early in life. His goal: to be a man, to be one of the greatest men ever in Umuofia, to obtain all four honorifics Umuofia has to offer to men. His greatest fear: to be a woman or to father a male who becomes a woman. For Okonkwo, to be an Umuofia man means to use physical power in defense or promotion of Umuofia manhood. Anything short of this expectation means cowardice, womanliness, betrayal. When Okonkwo can no longer be an Umuofia man, he takes his own life rather than risk the stigma of being a woman. Umuofia's origin stories and all Okonkwo's ends for his Umuofia culture involve the de-womanizing of men or the de-manizing of women. Okonkwo disowns or disregards the legacy of Unoka because his father allegedly lived like a woman; Okonkwo's father's womanness shames Okonkwo, and he therefore wants a new beginning. He decides to resituate his personal genealogy and thus reclaim a line more in tune with his village and clan's ancestry.

Okonkwo begins and maintains his manhood through the agricultural genealogy/hierarchy already in place in his Umuofia general economy. Umuofia's political economy parallels its yam-centered agricultural economy. Okonkwo's "mother and sisters worked hard enough, but they grew women's crops, like coco-yams, beans and cassava. Yam, the king of crops, was a man's crop." If the most valued crop is the yam, if the yam is the king, then the more yams one has the greater one's kingdom and the greater one's manhood and authority. Yam is man and man is king and all other crops (including women) are subjects. Okonkwo starts sowing seeds of his own kingdom with sixteen hundred seed yams, eight hundred of which he borrows from Nwakibie, a manhood veteran with "three huge barns [of yams], nine wives and thirty children," a man already with three clan titles. Unoka is no longer his father. The new seeds come not from Unoka but Nwakibie, his new father. The narrator has pointed out earlier that Okonkwo's "whole life was dominated by fear, the fear of failure and of weak-ness." His fear here is deeper than a fear of evil or a fear of an awesome being (human or superhuman). This fear "was not external but lay deep within himself. It was the fear of himself, lest he should be found to resemble his father. Even as a little boy he had resented his father's failure and weakness, and even now he still remembered how he had suffered when a playmate had told him that his father was *agbala*. That was how Okonkwo first came to know that *agbala* was not only another name for a woman, it could also mean a man who had taken no title. And so Okonkwo was ruled by one passion: to hate everything that his father Unoka had loved." His father Unoka died without any title. Yet Umuofia does not judge a man's worth by his father's worth, and Okonkwo wastes no time in establishing his own worth. At eigh-teen, he was the champion wrestler in all of Umuofia clan and beyond. At a relatively young age he is already a revered veteran of two intertribal wars, a wealthy farmer with many yams, three wives, many children, and two clan titles. He is indeed an example of the Igbo saying of the elders that "if a child washed his hands he could eat with kings" and his elders.

But Okonkwo does not just want to eat with kings—he also wants to be a king. A king tries to ensure that his subjects follow the values that sustain and perpetuate the kingdom. A king has a fatherly role to beget sons who will be the men to carry on the tradition to the succeeding generations. Because "yam stood for manliness," it is appropriate to initiate boys early into "the difficult art of preparing yams." Manhood and yamhood somewhat create each other. Okonkwo tries to initiate into manhood through yam education his son (Nwoye) and Ikemefuna (the Mbaino boy in Okonkwo's temporary care). Umuofia holds Ikemefuna as ransom for an Umuofia woman who was killed by a Mbaino man in Mbaino market. As Okonkwo prepares his seed yams for sowing, he makes Nwoye and Ikemefuna assist him. Education in yam-raising is an essential part of Umuofia education in manhood. Okonkwo wants to start this manly education of his son early because he is determined to "stamp out the disquieting signs of laziness which he thought he already saw" in Nwoye. He adds, "I will not have a son who cannot hold up his head in the gathering of the clan. I would sooner strangle him with my own hands." Okonkwo's memory of his father is not of a man but a woman; hence Okonkwo the father wants to make sure that he does not fail his son as a manly father. Okonkwo disaffiliates from his womanly father and would not only disaffiliate but even kill any womanly son of his own. He somehow does both: he kills his sonlike Ikemefuna and he manhandles and ultimately disowns his son Nwoye, who likewise disowns Okonkwo the father. The manly thing to do to a male who fails to be a man is to eliminate him. A man who cannot kill a womanly son has to do the manly thing by killing himself. Okonkwo will not have a son who is not a man. Similarly, Okonkwo cannot have a womanly Umuofia, an Umuofia of only women. When Umuofia becomes a woman, Okonkwo also becomes a woman. Okonkwo can no longer live when he ceases to be a man. He would rather die than live as a woman, so he commits suicide.

Planting yams and raising men become synonymous as women become only a means for raising or meeting the ends of Umuofia culture: women as a means for bringing great humans (men) into being. We are told that "the women planted [women's crops] maize, melons and beans between the yam mounds. . . . The women weeded the farm three times at definite periods in the life of the yams." The main task of Umuofia culture is the massive reproduction of male seed crops. Women are the caretakers of yams (and, of course, of men). The weak exist to cater to the needs of the strong. The women's crops were planted between the yam mounds to protect and nurture the yams. The female crops care for the male crops to ensure the stability and continuity of the kingdom of yams. Women exist to reproduce and reinforce patriarchy.

Three days before the New Yam Festival, an occasion for thanking Ani (Umuofia's earth goddess) and other ancestral spirits, Okonkwo shows Ekwefi (his second wife) and others what manhood means for women. When Ekwefi cuts off a few banana-tree leaves to wrap some food, Okonkwo assaults her. When Okonkwo decides to go hunting, Ekwefi, who had just been beaten, talks about a hunter who "had not killed a rat with his gun" and murmurs "something about guns that never shot." This unwomanly remark invites another show of manhood. Okonkwo fires at her but misses. When Okonkwo hears a beat of drums that summons his household to the *ilo* (the village playground), fire fills him up and he trembles "with the desire to conquer and subdue. It was like the desire for women." The desire to conquer whom? To subdue whom? *Woman. Women.* Women are the object of manhood. When strength triumphs, man prevails. When weakness results, women prevail. When Okonkwo's favorite daughter Ezinma brings her mother's dish to her father and sits down beside Obiageli (her younger half-sister), Okonkwo speaks manly to Ezinma, "Sit like a woman!" Ezinma then brings her two legs together and stretches them in front of her. When Ezinma unwittingly tries to function as a "male daughter" by asking to carry her father's chair to the playground for the wrestling contest, she experiences his biological determinism as he responds, "No, that is a boy's job."

Okonkwo's manliness reaches a climax in the case of Ikemefuna, the boy who has lived for three years in Okonkwo's household. Ikemefuna grows "rapidly like a yam tendril" and acts "like an elder brother to Nwoye"; he appeared "to have kindled a new fire" in the younger Nwoye. Ikemefuna "made him feel grown-up; and they no longer spent the evenings in mother's hut while she cooked, but now sat with Okonkwo in his *obi*." Nwoye delighted in being asked by his mother or his father's other wives to do "difficult and masculine tasks in the home," but he "would feign annoyance and grumble aloud about women and their troubles." Nwoye's development "inwardly" pleases Okonkwo, who knows "it was due to Ikemefuna. He wanted Nwoye to grow into a tough young man capable of ruling his father's household when he was dead and gone to join the ancestors. He wanted him to be a prosperous man, having enough in his barn to feed the ancestors with regular sacrifices." Okonkwo "was always happy when he heard" his son "grumbling about women. That showed that in time he would be able to control his women-folk."

Ikemefuna and Nwoye are growing up like brothers, growing up like men, and growing up as the sons of the manly Okonkwo. Okonkwo is becoming confident that he is going to leave behind him a new line, a line of men, a non-Unoka line. Nwoye's signs of manliness please Okonkwo. The narrator states, "No matter how prosperous a man was, if he was unable to rule his women and his children (and especially his women) he was not really a man." Such a man, for Okonkwo and his Umuofia, is an *agbala*, a woman, a failed man. In accordance with this view of men and women, Okonkwo "encouraged the boys to sit with him in his *obi*, and he told them stories of the land: masculine stories of violence and bloodshed." At first Nwoye responds ambivalently to his father's manly economy. The narrator further tells us that "Nwoye knew that it was right to be masculine and to be violent, but somehow he still preferred the stories that his mother used to tell," stories about "the tortoise and his wily ways, and of the bird." His mother's stories are "the kind of story that Nwoye loved. But he now knew that they were for foolish women and children and he knew his father wanted him to be a man. And so he feigned that he no longer cared for women's stories. And when he did this he saw that his father was pleased, and no longer rebuked or beat him." As the women cook, "Nwoye and Ikemefuna would listen to Okonkwo's stories about tribal wars, or how . . . he stalked his victim, over-powered him and obtained his first human head."

The murder of Ikemefuna becomes Okonkwo's last chance to exhibit his definition of manhood, but it is not the last challenge to his manliness. Other challenges to his manhood come, but he would no longer be able to respond manly. Killing Ikemefuna ends Okonkwo's manliness and sets the stage for the beginning of his most feared and most despised weakness: being an *agbala*, being a woman. Ogbuefi Ezeudu, a titled old Umuofia man, one of the most learned and respected interpreters of Umuofia culture, tells Okonkwo that in accordance with the bidding of Agbala (the Oracle of the Hills and Cave), "Umuofia has decided to kill" Ikemefuna. He strongly warns Okonkwo not to participate in the killing, because the boy calls him father. A group of machete-carrying Umuofia men takes Ikemefuna away the following day. Okonkwo joins the party. Ikemefuna carries a black pot of wine on his head. As their journey begins, the men joke about the locusts, about Umuofia "women, and about some effeminate men who had refused to come with them." Ikemefuna feels "uneasy at first" but this uneasiness evap-orates as Okonkwo walks behind him: "He could hardly imagine that Okonkwo was not his real father. He had never been fond of his real father, and at the end of three years he had become very distant indeed." As Ikeme-funa silently reflects about what it would be like to rejoin his mother and younger sister after three years of separation, a man clears his throat. When Ikemefuna looks back, the man orders him to proceed and not look back. Okonkwo withdraws to the rear of the party. As the man who clears his throat strikes Ikemefuna with his machete, Okonkwo looks away. The pot falls and Ikemefuna runs toward Okonkwo for help, crying, "My father, they have killed me!" Okonkwo responds by killing him. He kills him because he "was afraid of being thought weak." He is afraid of becoming a woman. A father figure kills a son figure, and Nwoye the son wonders about this kind of father.

This killing of Ikemefuna also marks the beginning of Nwoye's disaffiliation from his father. Nwoye's disavowal of his father stems from his father's warped sense of manhood and precedes the arrival of any foreign cultural difference in Umuofia or its neighboring clans; the white man or European culture or Christianity had nothing to do with this separation of son and father. Nwoye likens his feeling in the aftermath of his father's killing of Ikemefuna to a feeling he had the year before when he witnessed for the first time another kind of murder: Umuofia's disgusting tradition of discarding infant twins in the forest to die. The agonizing cries of these abandoned, innocent twins made him realize that something was rotten in the clan of Umuofia. This disposition readies Nwoye for an alignment with any bearer of cultural difference (whether from within or outside Umuofia) who speaks to the things that trouble him about his clan's *egwugwu*-dominated culture.

Nwoye's fears of his father arise from his father's concerns over his son's proper manhood. As Okonkwo tells his friend Obierika, "I am worried about Nwoye. . . . His two younger brothers are more promising. But . . . my children do not resemble me. . . . If Ezinma had been a boy I would have been happier. She has the right spirit." But right spirit without the natural proper gender is useless to Okonkwo. Okonkwo laments, "I have done my best to make Nwoye grow into a man, but there is too much of his mother in him." Obierika adds, but only to himself, "Too much of his grandfather in him." For Okonkwo, Nwoye's problem is that he has too much of Nwoye's mother (Okonkwo's first or most senior wife) and too much of Unoka (Okonkwo's womanly father) and little or none of Okonkwo himself (the embodiment of man par excellence). Men are made, but they first have to be born as males before they can be men. If all nature does is decide genetic maleness, culture then has to be held responsible for deciding manhood—and not culture in general but feminine culture. This kind of logic enables Okonkwo to refuse any responsibility for how Nwoye turns out; Okonkwo is indicting Nwoye's mother. She is an unwomanly woman. She fails his test of motherhood. One irony here is that Okonkwo says that he has done his best to make a man out of his son, but the power of weakness (woman) is so much that he the strong Okonkwo fails in his duty as a man, as a father, to make his son a man. Another telling point involves Obierika's linkage of Nwoye's effeminacy with the paternal (Okonkwo's father) rather than the maternal (Nwoye's mother).

In his aside Obierika agrees with Okonkwo that Nwoye is womanly but he does not hold women or Nwoye's mother as solely or mainly responsible as Okonkwo does. Obierika speaks out but only to himself, presumably not to incur unnecessarily the wrath of Okonkwo, who is his guest on this occasion. Even though Obierika, accepts, lives, and contributes to the ongoing sexism of Umuofia, he seems to do so less or nonegregiously. His character serves more as a foil to Okonkwo's character. Almost every dialogue Obierika holds with Okonkwo tells us more about Okonkwo.

Okonkwo often grounds his *egwugwu* patriarchy in a specious biological determinism by linking patriarchy to tradition and tradition to nature or nonhuman powers. For example, Okonkwo insists that in killing Ikemefuna he is only fulfilling tradition. When Okonkwo asks Obierika why he did not join him and the other men who killed Ikemefuna, Obierika answers, "Because I did not want to. I had something better to do." Okonkwo says, "You sound as if you question the authority and the decision of the Oracle, who said he should die." Obierika replies, "I do not. Why should I? But the Oracle did not ask me to carry out its decision." This reason appears to fall on its face given that Ogbuefi Ezeudu, a reputable interpreter of Umuofia culture and Okonkwo's mentor, from his own village (Iguedo), had already explicitly warned him not to participate in the killing of Ikemefuna. Ezeudu's voice here does not speak for the patriarchal culture of Umuofia. Okonkwo tends to read almost every sign only in terms of physical strength (men) and physical weakness (women and womanly men). As he tells Obierika, "But someone had to do it. If we were all afraid of blood, it would not be done. And what do you think the Oracle would do then?" Obierika rejects Okonkwo's charge that he is afraid of blood, adding, "If I were you I would have stayed at home. What you have done will not please the Earth. It is the kind of action for which the goddess wipes out whole families." The sign *Agbala* with a capital *A* names the Oracle that supposedly orders the sacrificing of Ikemefuna. Okonkwo is afraid of becoming the sign *agbala* with a lowercase *a*. Okonkwo kills Ikemefuna in the name of his beloved goddess *Agbala* so that he would not become an *agbala* or die with his most hated name *agbala*. Okonkwo does not want to live or die as a woman. Okonkwo would not want the epitaph or epithet *agbala*. He believes that "the Earth cannot punish me for obeying her messenger. A child's fingers are not scalded by a piece of hot yam which its mother puts into its palm." For Obierika, however, "if the Oracle said that my son should be killed I would neither dispute it nor be the one to do it."

Okonkwo never hesitates to disobey a divine messenger when the message would get in the way of his manhood. He disobeys the Earth (goddess) by violating the sacred week; of course, Okonkwo believes, a man can beat his woman anytime, even during the sacred week, in order to maintain his manhood. The call of manhood is a call to arms (power, physical power). Okonkwo's misogynic reading of his culture is captured succinctly by the incident when he wakes at midnight to scratch the spot where a mosquito has bitten him. As another mosquito wails by his ear, he slaps the ear. He wonders why mosquitoes (women) "always go for one's ears." He then recollects the mosquito and ear story his mother had told him as a child. He dismisses the story "as silly as all women's stories." Okonkwo has no ear for hearing women's stories; he has only mouth and arms for women.

At no time does the Umuofia *egwugwu* elite give a serious hearing or consideration to the causes of the *osu* (outcasts), the *efulefu* (womanly males), parents of twins, and so forth, that abound within Umuofia. Consequently, Umuofia lacks experience in dealing with such internal cultural differences fruitfully. This tradition of not transvaluing the *egwugwu* culture and of not listening to Umuofia's minority bearers of anti-*egwugwu* values makes Umuofia unprepared for or vulnerable to any formidable force (domestic or foreign) that may actively or forcefully challenge its hierarchy. On one occasion the issue of interclan cultural differences surfaces. When Machi (Obierika's brother) points out certain cultural differences between Umuofia and some other clans, Okonkwo says, "I have even heard that in some tribes a man's children belong to his wife and her family." Machi doubts, "That cannot be. You might as well say that the woman lies on top of the man when they are making the children." Obierika then links this question of cultural difference to "the story of white men who, they say, are white like this piece of chalk. And those white men, they say, have no toes." Machi says that one white man (Amadi) passes through the neighborhood frequently. Amadi is a leper, and the euphemism for leprosy is "the white skin." This kind of offhanded discussion of cultural difference suggests the unreadiness of Umuofia leadership to engage with any cultural difference (from within or outside) that insists on inserting and asserting itself on the body politics of Umuofia. Umuofia patriarchal culture never critically considers cultural differences within Umuofia, between Umuofia and other neighboring clans, between Umuofia's Igbo tribe and other tribes, and between African tribes and non-African tribes. Therein arguably lies the heart of Umuofia's tragedy. How can a culture know how to respond most creatively to an opposing cultural difference if the culture is unwilling to consider the rationality and nonrationality of the difference, be it domestic or foreign? I say nonrationality because irrationality is a rationality that another rationality is unable or unwilling to admit into its center. How can one scatter the center of what one offhandedly dismisses as irrational? If rationality is a relationality and if one's culture is unwilling to at least theoretically resituate its own center in order to work out how best to relate to the new or incoming cultural difference, such cultural unwillingness sooner or later congeals into a detrimental inability. What started as a cultural unwillingness begins to look like a natural inability of one culture to withstand a seemingly superior foreign culture. Such is the story of Okonkwo and his Umuofia. The story of the *egwugwu* domination of Umuofia culture is the story of its preeminent son and father: Okonkwo.

The leading most visible inheritor and reinforcer of this dominant androcentric tradition is Umuofia's present *egwugwu*. This body of nine supreme judges and interpreters constitutes the most secret and mystified cult in Umuofia. The *egwugwu* (all male) are nine masked spirits of the ancestors that together represent each of the nine villages of the Umuofia clan. The masking helps to mystify its nature and origins and give it some divine aura. To demystify the *egwugwu*, one first has to unmask the *egwugwu*, which would reveal them as mere mortals rather than spirits with some divine connection; hence it is an egregious offense to unmask an *egwugwu*. Okonkwo is an *egwugwu* representing his Iguedo village: "The nine villages of Umuofia had grown out of the nine sons of the first father of the clan." The *egwugwu* leader (Evil Forest) represents Umueru village; Umueru means the children of Eru, the oldest of the patriarch's nine sons. The *egwugwu* are the fathers, forefathers, ancestors of Umuofia.

The *uri* (dowry-payment ceremony) of Ibe and Akueke (Obierika's daughter) points to the *egwugwu* (men) as the genealogical foundation of Okonkwo's Umuofia and to women as the purveyors of these foundations. In toasting his in-laws, Obierika's oldest brother says, "We are giving you our daughter today. She will be a good wife to you. She will bear you nine sons like the mother of our town." Again women are the instruments for reproducing and perpetuating patriarchy. The oldest man among Ibe's camp looks in Okonkwo's direction and responds: "Prosperous men and great warriors. Your daughter will bear us sons like you." Some of the elders are praised as great farmers, some as clan orators. The young men celebrate Okonkwo as "the greatest wrestler and warrior alive." Men's cultural function of productivity is continually stressed, but for women only their biological function of reproductivity is emphasized again and again.

Umuofia is repeatedly called the land of the brave. When the titled Ogbuefi Ezeudu dies, he is eulogized as a man who met the clan's highest values: he lived as a wealthy, fearless warrior, and he died old. During his funeral, Okonkwo's gun accidentally explodes and kills Ezeudu's sixteen-year-old son. Killing a clansman is a female or male crime against the earth goddess, punishable by exile from one's clan. In Okonkwo's case, he commits a female *ochu* (manslaughter), which carries a seven-year exile. Obierika and others destroy his compound as demanded by Umuofia custom. Okonkwo and his family immediately go into exile in his motherland (Mbanta, just beyond Mbaino territory). Obierika wonders why a man should suffer so much for an offense he commits inadvertently. He arrives at no answer, but he remembers his wife's twins whom he himself threw away and also wonders what crime those abandoned twins committed. This reservation about the fate of twins in Umuofia echoes Okonkwo's son's earlier concern. Nature is evoked, however. Mother earth, we are told, regards twins as "an offense on the land [that] must be destroyed."

With the death of Ezeudu begins the death of Okonkwo as a man, at least Okonkwo's kind of man. Even Okonkwo acknowledges the manliness (greatness) of Ezeudu. But the days and nights of the Ezeudus are over. An Ezeudu son, one of the young Umuofians expected to carry on the tradition of this patriarch, dies with his father through the hands of Okonkwo. Is this apparently accidental death some possibly unconscious desire on the part of Okonkwo to exhibit his manhood? Whatever the case, this triple death (of Ezeudu, Ezeudu's son, and in a sense Okonkwo) hammers a nail in Umuofia's coffin of business as usual. Umuofia's center (of manliness) has been wittingly struck by itself, and things can no longer be the same.

Okonkwo and family now live in exile in Mbanta, Okonkwo's mother's home. The father (Umuofia) has expelled his leading son (Okonkwo) to Mbanta (motherland). In other words, Okonkwo is to live with "women," his dreaded subject(s). Thirty years before, Uchendu (Okonkwo's maternal uncle) went to Umuofia to return the corpse of his younger sister (Okonkwo's mother) to Mbanta for burial. The help given to Okonkwo by his maternal relatives facilitates his transition into resettling in Mbanta. He wants to reroot his *egwugwu* genealogy while he is there, even though he is no longer an *egwugwu*. He builds one *obi* for himself and three huts for his three wives. He installs "the symbols of his departed fathers. Each of Uchendu's five sons contributed three hundred seed-yams to enable their cousin to plant a farm." Okonkwo's life ambition to be a lord of Umuofia clan and thus stand at the top of manhood appears derailed; in Mbanta Okonkwo is a fish on dry land. The beginning of his exile in Mbanta is also the beginning of his effeminization. He tries to transform his family line in order to realign his manliness—which, he realizes, is now in crisis. Uchendu, concerned about his nephew's melancholy, delivers to Okonkwo his first lesson on the meaning of motherhood. He asks Okonkwo why Nneka ("mother is supreme") is one of the most common proper names for Mbanta females even though "a man is the head of the family and his wives do his bidding," even though a "child belongs to its father and his family and not to its mother and her family," and even though "a man belongs to his fatherland and not to his motherland." Okonkwo admits that he does not know why. But here the why is irrelevant and unimportant to Okonkwo because he does not even accept the proposition in either theory or practice. The statement flies in the face of Okonkwo's Umuofia conventional wisdom. Uchendu follows up with another question: "Why is it that when a woman dies she is taken home to be buried with her husband's kinsmen? Why is that? Your mother was brought home to me and buried with my people. Why was that?" Uchendu's declaration of motherhood as supreme is at best nominal or merely linguistic; such verbal reality does not correlate with nonverbal reality in Mbanta or Umuofia. Furthermore, when Okonkwo's mother died, she was not buried with the kinsmen of her husband (Unoka, who is from Umuofia rather than Mbanta, where Okonkwo's maternal grandfather comes from). Unoka was presumably not manly enough to deserve such funereal honor. Uchendu spells out the logic behind the name Nneka when he says that "a child belongs to its father. But when a father beats his child, it seeks sympathy in its mother's hut. A man belongs to his fatherland when things are good and life is sweet. But when there is sorrow and bitterness he finds refuge in his motherland." When a man is in good times he stays and enjoys them with his father(land), but when he falls into bad times he seeks comfort with his mother(land). In times of man's tragedy, tradition demands that mothers console the man. Fathers should not be bothered with such sorrows, which naturally belong to a mother's province.

Beliefs about women in Uchendu's Mbanta do not differ fundamentally from those of Umuofia. For both clans, mother(hood), not woman(hood), is supreme. To say that woman is supreme would of course be another reprehensible or unacceptable equivalent of the presently dominant reality: man(hood) is supreme. If motherhood is supreme, it is supreme only in a benign form. What is fatherhood in relation to this motherhood that is supreme? What is the relationship between fatherhood and manhood? Is fatherhood subordinate to motherhood if motherhood is indeed superior to fatherhood? Such questions point to one direction: in both Umuofia and Mbanta, woman's only basic function remains the same: to reproduce and cater to patriarchy. But Uchendu (unlike Okonkwo) at least tends to recognize (although in an apparently hyperbolic and perhaps patronizing way) the significance of motherhood. Uchendu's etymological explanation does not and perhaps cannot account for the gap between this linguistic adornment of womanhood and the non-*egwugwu* status of this same womanhood. At best the account is seductively condescending. Would a woman who is respected only nominally as a mother be loyal to that same culture that also undermines her motherhood or maternity?

The first Mbanta woman to convert to the white man's faith was Nneka, the pregnant wife of the prosperous farmer Amadi. Nneka experiences motherhood as nadirhood, not supremeness. Nneka the woman, rather than Nneka of language and fable, "had had four previous pregnancies and childbirths. But each time she had borne twins, and they had been immediately thrown away. Her husband and his family were already becoming highly critical of such a woman and were not unduly perturbed when they found she had fled to join the Christians. It was a good riddance." When things are reproductively "bad," blame only the woman. Uchendu's logic works here. If Mbanta culture cannot fruitfully integrate the difference (the coming of twins) occasioned by nature from within the culture, then the ability of Mbanta to withstand an external and more potent cultural difference for which Mbanta is less prepared becomes highly questionable. Similarly, Nwoye's unaddressed questions (Ikemefuna, the twins, and the meaning of manhood) in Umuofia and later in Mbanta contribute heavily to his susceptibility in Mbanta to any new logic (from within or without) that responds creatively to such questions. In Nwoye's case the white Christian missionaries responded satisfactorily to his own difference and issues. For him, the "poetry of the new religion" appears to "answer a vague and persistent question that haunted" his "young soul: the question of the twins crying in the bush and the question of Ikemefuna who was killed." Nneka and Nwoye are soul brother and sister waiting to embrace any force that responds healthily to their agonies and fundamental concerns.

I analyze the power relations in Mbanta and Umuofia before and after the arrival of British Christians and officials against this background of certain Okonkwonian meanings of man and woman. Obierika's first visit to his friend Okonkwo in exile turns out to forebode ironically the end of Okonkwo's life. During this visit to Mbanta, Obierika tells Okonkwo that Abame clan no longer exists because the white man (who "was quite different") has erased it. He tells how the first Abame people "who saw him ran away" and how the white man "stood beckoning to them" and how eventually "the fearless ones went near and even touched him. The elders consulted their Oracle and it told them that the strange man would break their clan and spread destruction among others. And so they killed the white man." Much later "three white men led by a band of ordinary men like us came" to Abame, surrounded the market, and killed everybody "except the old and the sick who were at home and a handful of men and women whose *chi* were wide awake." Okonkwo remarks that Abame people "had been warned that danger was ahead. They should have armed themselves with their guns and machetes even when they went to market." When Okonkwo says he doesn't know how to thank Obierika for continuing to help him take care of his economic interests in Umuofia (tending his yams, and so on), Obierika replies, "Kill one of your sons for me." When Okonkwo responds that "that will not be enough," Obierika tells him, "Then kill yourself." Amid smiles, Okonkwo says, "Forgive me. I shall not talk about thanking you any more." Okonkwo is on a mission to kill any male who becomes a man or who stands in his way to the pinnacle of manhood. He has already killed Ikemefuna. He has already killed Ezeudu's son. He has already virtually killed his own son (Nwoye). When Okonkwo is unable to kill the foreign challenger of his manhood and the manhood of his Umuofia, he kills himself. The white Christian presence brings him face to face with the concrete reality of his worst fear (the fear of becoming an *agbala*, a woman, of becoming his son Nwoye, whom he has already written off as a woman). His logic demands nothing short of suicide as he eventually confronts a cultural difference that tragically confounds and paralyzes him. He kills himself. Okonkwo would rather die than live as a woman, a womanly male. He unwittingly asks his friend Obierika to forgive him in advance for killing himself.

Obierika's first visit announced the womanization of Abame by British white difference. His next crucial visit to Okonkwo announces the spread of this effeminization to Okonkwo's own fatherland (the land of brave men, the land where men are men and women are women). Most significantly for Obierika, this new presence directly implicates the son of Umuofia's symbol of indomitable strength (manhood): Okonkwo. Okonkwo was already aware of Nwoye's membership in the new white missionary church, but he was still unaware (until Obierika's visit) of the British presence in Umuofia, of Umuofia's response to the presence, and of his own son's complicity with whites in the affair. Nwoye's effeminization begins in Mbanta (the motherland). When Okonkwo first learns of Nwoye's involvement with Mbanta Christians, he responds to the situation as a *man*. He grabs Nwoye and asks, "Where have you been?" As Nwoye tries to escape his father's grip, Okonkwo demands, "Answer me before I kill you." He beats him until Uchendu orders him to "Leave the boy at once!" and then asks, "Are you mad?" Nwoye walks away from Mbanta, never to return. Through the help of the local (Mbanta) Christian head and interpreter (Mr. Kiaga), Nwoye leaves motherland for fatherland. Nwoye changes his name to Isaac. Kiaga compliments Nwoye for disowning his father in order to follow the Christian church: "Blessed is he who forsakes his father and his mother for my sake. Those that hear my words are my father and my mother." But according to Okonkwo, "To abandon the gods of one's father and go about with a lot of effeminate men clucking like old hens was the very depth of abomination. Suppose when he died all his male children decided to follow Nwoye's steps and abandon their ancestors?" Okonkwo's initial impulse was to invade "the church and wipe out the entire vile and miscreant gang" with his machete, but he concludes later that "Nwoye was not worth fighting for." He believes that what has happened in Mbanta cannot happen in Umuofia. Okonkwo wonders how he, a flaming fire, could "have begotten a son like Nwoye, degenerate and effeminate. . . . Perhaps he was not his son. No! he could not be. His wife had played him false. . . . But Nwoye resembled his grandfather, Unoka, who was Okonkwo's father. He pushed the thought out of his mind." Soon another explanation comes to Okonkwo: "Living fire begets cold, impotent ash."

Mbanta clan continues to worry about the new faith, while also continuing to dismiss it as "a gang of *efulefu*" who decide to live in the Evil Forest. The Evil Forest appropriately fits the church, for it is traditionally the home of society's undesirable elements. In violation of Mbanta traditional laws, the church rescues abandoned twins. Mbanta villagers, however, do not think that "the earth goddess would . . . visit the sins of the missionaries on the innocent villagers." Stories continue to spread that the white man has come not only with "a religion but also with a government." It is also said that one man who killed a missionary was hanged, but many did not believe or take these stories seriously. The church has welcomed not only twins but also *osu*. This admission of outcasts into the growing Mbanta church (a move spearheaded by Mr. Kiaga) caused much controversy, because many of the other converts vigorously opposed it, at least initially. The first two outcasts converted became "the strongest adherents of the new faith" and "nearly all the *osu* in Mbanta followed their example." One *osu* "in his zeal brought the church into serious conflict with the clan a year later by killing the sacred python." Okonkwo, who now plays a role in Mbanta affairs, has only one response: a manly act. He says that "until the abominable gang was chased out of the village with whips there would be no peace." Other Mbanta see the situation differently from Okonkwo, and their position of ostracizing the Christians by excluding them from the life and privileges of the clan eventually prevails. Okonkwo dismisses opponents of war as cowards and adds, "If a man comes into my hut and defecates on the floor, what do I do? Do I shut my eyes? No! I take a stick and break his head. That is what a man does."

Okonkwo regards Mbanta as "a womanly clan" and thinks that "such a thing could never happen in his fatherland, Umuofia." Obierika's news about the white presence in Umuofia and Nwoye's active cooperation with these white enemies thus demoralize him. Yet he still believes that he can make a difference when he returns to Umuofia, which is presently ruled mostly by women or womanly males. Okonkwo never learns a different sense of womanhood or manhood while in Mbanta. Uchendu's Mbanta has nothing to offer Okonkwo in terms of different conceptions of manhood or woman-hood. The only superficial lesson Okonkwo learns from his days and nights in Mbanta is shown in his giving the name Nneka to the daughter he begets in exile, "out of politeness to his mother's kinsmen." But he names the male child he begets in Mbanta Nwofia ("begotten in the wilderness"). These two names Nneka and Nwofia entrench Okonkwo's definitions of what it means to be a woman or a man in culture. The wilderness evokes manhood and wildness and strength. Nneka suggests motherhood and empty linguistic maternal honorifics. This kind of naming is fully in line with Okonkwo's way of looking at his world, the Umuofia world. He still grieves over the tragedy of the loss of his first son to Christianity, but he takes comfort in the fact that he had "five other sons and he would bring them up in the way of the clan." Shortly before he leaves Mbanta, he assembles these five sons and announces to them his renunciation of Nwoye:

> You have all seen the great abomination of your brother. Now he
> is no longer my son or your brother. I will only have a son who
> is a man, who will hold his head up among my people. If any one
> of you prefers to be a woman, let him follow Nwoye now while I
> am alive so that I can curse him. If you turn against me when I
> am dead I will visit you and break your neck.

Okonkwo constantly wishes Ezinma were a boy and never stops "regretting that Ezinma was a girl." Because the Nwoye line has turned into a woman line, Okonkwo has to eliminate it from his genealogy and start working with the other sons on a new line, a men's line, a line that will continue the *egwugwu* tradition in Umuofia. Mbanta is hopeless for Okonkwo because he is unable to prevail there. Furthermore, Mbanta is not his fatherland, but only a place of sojourn while he is down as a man.

Umuofia responds to Christian invasion in the same way as Mbanta. The missionary development in Umuofia saddens the leaders of Umuofia, "but many of them believed that the strange faith and the white man's god would not last. None of his converts was a man whose word was heeded in the assembly of the people. None of them was a man of title. They were mostly the kind of people that were called *efulefu*, worthless, empty men. . . . Chielo, the priestess of Agbala, called the converts the excrement of the clan, and the new faith was a mad dog that had come to eat it up." Just as in Mbanta, outcasts are among the very first to accept and be agents of this new Christian religion in Umuofia. Obierika recalls to Okonkwo that when he asked Nwoye what he was doing with the white missionaries, he said, "I am one of them." When he asked Nwoye about his father (Okonkwo), Nwoye sadly replied, "I don't know. He is not my father." But Okonkwo refuses to talk with Obierika about Nwoye.

Obierika then briefs him more on the state of the Christian church in Umuofia. Obierika says that Christianity has attracted not just "the low-born and the outcast" but worthy titled men such as Ogbuefi Ugonna. Okonkwo wonders why Umuofians lost the will to fight the Christian missionaries with their guns and machetes. Obierika reminds Okonkwo of the Abame case and lets him know that Umuofians firepower is no match for that of the Christians. Okonkwo insists that Umuofians "would be cowards to compare ourselves with the men of Abame. Their fathers had never dared to stand before our ancestors. We must fight these men and drive them from the land." Obierika tells him that his warrior message comes "too late." Okonkwo's only way of dealing with any difference that threatens the *egwugwu* way of being is to eliminate it by force of arms; he knows no nonmartial approach. Obierika tells him that the white man "has won our brothers, and our clan can no longer act like one. He has put a knife on the things that held us together and we have fallen apart." By paying attention only to the things that supposedly held them together and totally ignoring the other things that divided them, the *egwugwu* hierarchy was ill-equipped to handle the long-brewing internal differences that coalesced into the greatest weapon in the hands of the incoming British Christians.

Many Umuofia men and women do not dislike the new order as strongly as Okonkwo does. For them, the "white men had indeed brought a lunatic religion," but also commerce in palm oil and kernel that now makes much money flow in Umuofia. Even in the matter of religion a growing feeling among some Umuofians admits that there might be a method in the madness. Furthermore, Mr. Brown (the white missionary representative most responsible for this growing reception) warns his followers against excess. His pragmatic principle of "everything was possible, but everything was not expedient" prevails. After debating with Akunna (a theologian of Umuofia religion), he rules out any "frontal attack" on Umuofia religion. Right from the beginning he links his Christian religion with education and commerce and the colonial government and warns Umuofian leadership to take advantage of these seeming opportunities or risk being ruled by strangers from outside Umuofia. He builds churches and schools and hospitals and courthouses. His strategy works, and he takes pride in noting that "the Seed . . . first sown among you" has begun to bear fruit in less than two years. Brown is grounding a new genealogy—also patriarchal and insidious, but differently so. The new church threatens to put an end to Okonkwo's kind of seeds. The days and nights of yams are over. A new crop is in the ground, and a new king is in the making.

Fundamentally unchanged Okonkwo returns to this changed Umuofia. Brown visits him and hopes that Okonkwo would be happy to learn that the Christian church has sent Nwoye (now called Isaac) to Umuru to attend a teacher-training college. Nwoye is to begin a new genealogy. Again, Okonkwo acts as a *man*. He drives Brown away and threatens to kill him should he ever return to his compound. Okonkwo "mourned for the clan, which he saw breaking up and falling apart, and he mourned for the warlike men of Umuofia, who had so unaccountably become soft like women."

Ironically, Rev. James Smith, who succeeds Brown after his return to England, is very different from Brown and very much more like Okonkwo in his view of the world as a war ground. He rejects Brown's compromise and accommodation policy. He sees the world in black and white and associates evil with darkness. For him the world is a battleground between the children of light and the children of darkness, thus resembling Okonkwo, who sees the world only in terms of sheer physical strength (men) versus weakness (women).

Enoch, a fanatical Umuofian follower of Smith, thrives under such regime. He allegedly slays and eats the sacred python. This action sets the stage for the battle that finally does Okonkwo in. Enoch, a Christian, takes on the bastion of Umuofia authority and not only flauntingly commits the unheard of sacrilege of killing and eating an ancestral spirit (the python), but also tauntingly and publicly unmasks the *egwugwu*. In Umuofia the *egwugwu* as the source and dispenser of justice is supreme. This unmasking of an *egwugwu* widens the tension between the Christian church and Umuofia clan. To "unmask an *egwugwu* in public, or to say or do anything which might reduce its immortal prestige in the eyes of the uninitiated," is regarded as one of the most serious human crimes. This double sacrilege prompts the *egwugwu* to incinerate Enoch's compound and move to the church to get him. Ajofia, the leading *egwugwu* and spokesman of the nine ancestors of justice in Umuofia, orders Smith, who is outside the church, to leave so that they can capture Enoch. Smith stood his ground, but to no avail. The *egwugwu* burn down the church that Brown built. This manly measure momentarily pacifies the spirit of Umuofia.

This manly destruction of the Christian church renews Okonkwo's faith in the manliness of Umuofia. Although his fellow clansmen did not agree to kill Smith or expel his Christians, "they had agreed to do something substantial," and they did it. But shortly after this leveling of the church into ashes, the district commissioner summons six Umuofia leaders (including Okonkwo) to his headquarters. Okonkwo warns his fellow leaders: "An Umuofia man does not refuse a call. He may refuse to do what he is asked; he does not refuse to be asked. But the times have changed, and we must be fully prepared." The times have indeed changed, but Okonkwo has not. Okonkwo and the other leaders are handcuffed and imprisoned until they can pay the imposed fine. While they are in jail the prison officials taunt them and shave their heads. Okonkwo chokes with hate and humiliation. Umuofia men pay the fine, and the leaders are released.

The six prisoners return home in silence. With scars of prison torture, Okonkwo swears vengeance. For him, "If Umuofia decided on war, all would be well. But if they chose to be cowards he would go out and avenge himself." Umuofia men meet at the marketplace to decide what to do in light of these recent developments. Okika, an orator and one of the six prisoners, calls for war and laments that some of "our brothers have deserted us and joined a stranger to soil their fatherland."

The sudden appearance of five court messengers interrupts Okika's speech. As soon as Okonkwo recognizes the head messenger, he hatefully and wordlessly confronts him. The head messenger stands his ground and the other four messengers stand behind him. The head court messenger commands Okonkwo, "Let me pass!" Okonkwo has already put himself in a situation where, by his own logic, he has no choice but to let the new order's representative pass. With relish the messenger tells Okonkwo: "The white man whose power you know too well has ordered this meeting to stop." Okonkwo quickly draws his machete and kills the head messenger. Okonkwo now knows that "Umuofia would not go to war" because "they had let the other messengers escape. They had broken into tumult instead of action. He discerned fright in that tumult. He heard voices asking: 'Why did he do it?'" Okonkwo wipes his weapon and goes away. His ailing father's words to him at the beginning of his career as a man eventually come to haunt him. Said his father, "It is more difficult and more bitter when a man fails alone."

Obierika leads the colonial and new leader of Umuofia to the corpse of the dead Umuofia leader. Obierika requests a favor of the new leader: "Perhaps your men can help us bring him down and bury him. We have sent for strangers from another village to do it for us, but they may be a long time coming." One of Obierika's men explains to the commissioner that suicide violates Umuofia tradition, for it offends the Earth, and a man who commits suicide "will not be buried by his kinsmen." Only strangers can touch or bury such a body, which is now regarded as evil. Gazing painfully at his friend's dangling body, Obierika says to the commissioner, "That man was one of the greatest men in Umuofia. You drove him to kill himself; and now he will be buried like a dog."

Okonkwo, the yam of Umuofia earth. Okonkwo, the king of Umuofia men. Okonkwo, the man who lived to be like a god, dies like a dog. His outcast body emblematizes the internal crisis in the *egwugwu* genealogy, an economy of power relations that can no longer maintain their own hierarchy or combat the hierarchy of Christian colonialism. Okonkwo would rather die than be a woman. He does not know how to live except as a man. For Okonkwo, there is no nonmartial way of engaging such enemy force as the Christian missionary. The only alternative to war is capitulation.

Steve Biko has aptly noted that the greatest weapon in the hands of the oppressor is the mind of the oppressed. Chinua Achebe's fiction (including his other four novels) powerfully demonstrates the need for a culture to utilize utopian speculative analytical power if it is to develop fruitfully. Umuofia's tragedy lies not in its fall per se. Things (especially the *egwugwu* tradition) needed to fall apart there. The tragedy of Umuofia lies in the fact that when the center eventually falls apart, it falls to another improperly constituted cultural structure or genealogy. Worse still, it falls without the *egwugwu* leaders ever realizing or recognizing that the *egwugwu* economy has very much to do with the fall and inauguration of a colonial regime in Umuofia.

EUSTACE PALMER

Character and Society in Achebe's Things Fall Apart

The recent publication of a collection of essays on Chinua Achebe edited by Bernth Lindfors and Catherine Innes and entitled *Critical Perspectives on Achebe* clearly demonstrates two main points: the accomplished artistry of the author who now justifiably occupies a central position in African letters and the dominance of his first novel *Things Fall Apart* in the Achebe canon. The essays on *Things Fall Apart* in that volume are not only much better in quality than those on its nearest rival *Arrow of God*, but the authors also go to great lengths to demonstrate its complex artistry. If, however, there is now general agreement about the quality of that novel, opinion is much more divided about the status of its hero Okonkwo and about attitudes (including the author's) towards him. On the one hand are those critics like Killam and the present writer who regard Okonkwo as essentially the embodiment of the major values and norms of his society, essentially a product of his society in fact, while on the other hand there are those like Iyasere, Innes and Carroll who see Okonkwo as deviating from those norms and being essentially out of step with his society.

Solomon Iyasere is most typical of this latter view. In his essay he suggests that the present writer in presenting Okonkwo as the embodiment of his society transforms him from champion to victim, and he goes on to suggest further that far from being an embodiment of the values of his

From *Literary Half-Yearly* 22, no.1 (1981). © 1981 by the University of Mysore.

145

society Okonkwo has only a very limited understanding of those values. Where his society is surprisingly flexible Okonkwo is utterly inflexible; where his society is able to accommodate the lazy and unsuccessful Okonkwo has no patience with them; where his society respects age Okonkwo shows scant regard for age; where his society is noted for its discreet blending of the masculine and feminine principles Okonkwo is openly contemptuous of all things feminine. Iyasere unwittingly transforms Okonkwo into a villain with few redeeming features, instead of the truly tragic hero with a blend of attractive and unattractive qualities that most readers know. The essence of great tragedy, surely, is that the hero possesses certain excellent qualities which arouse the reader's admiration, but he simultaneously possesses certain weaknesses which render him incapable of dealing successfully with the forces and circumstances he is confronted with. It is these which lead to his downfall, but the reader's sympathy is never totally alienated from him because he continues to be aware of those excellent qualities. The tragic hero is never completely villain nor completely victim and his tragedy is always brought about by a combination of his own personal inadequacies and external circumstances. Okonkwo is precisely such a tragic hero.

Like the good critic he is Iyasere senses that that the reader's sympathy is never totally alienated from Okonkwo but the position he has adopted at the start of his essay prevents him from pursuing this hunch to its logical conclusion and realising, firstly that Okonkwo has many more admirable qualities than merely not being at heart a violent man (which is the reason he gives for the retention of the reader's sympathy), and secondly that the very predisposition to violence which he so copiously demonstrates has been conditioned in Okonkwo partly by the need to conform to his society's norms. In his attempt to demonstrate the extent to which Okonkwo deviates from his society Iyasere over-idealises Umuofia society and blinds himself to its harshness. He also has a very narrow interpretation of the term "embodiment." Surely, when one says that Okonkwo is the embodiment of his society's values one does not mean that every single aspect of Okonkwo's character has been conditioned by his society; one means that his public attitudes and ideas like attitudes towards women, customs, children or wealth would have been largely determined by his society's norms, but at the same time he would himself possess certain personal idiosyncracies like impulsiveness, ill-temper or nervousness which might themselves contribute towards his downfall, but which still do not mean that he is not the embodiment of his society's values. When talking about the interrelationship between character and society one must be careful to make the distinction between public attitudes, ideas and beliefs which have been adopted in conformity with the society's norms, and more personal qualities.

It is possible to be the embodiment of one's society and yet possess certain personal individual human qualities. This is the case with Okonkwo. It is the purpose of this paper to demonstrate that Okonkwo's virtues are largely the virtues of his society, just as his weaknesses are largely the weaknesses of his society. In this sense, his tragedy is similar to that of his society, for these weaknesses largely contribute to his downfall, just as they surely lead to the capitulation of his society to an alien force. But of course Okonkwo's own personal qualities, such as his impulsiveness, also play a contributory role, but they do not necessarily suggest that he is a deviant from his society.

It is clear that Okonkwo's admirable qualities, such as courage, fearlessness, determination, industry, energy, perseverance, resilience and tribal pride are either qualities he shares with his society or have been produced in him by the need to respond to the demands of that society. Okonkwo accepts most of his society's major attitudes such as its concern for rank and prestige, its reverence for courage, bravery and success in war or wrestling, and its premium on material and social prosperity. In discussion with Obierika about the law which forbids men of title to climb palm trees Okonkwo can say quite categorically that "the law of the land must be obeyed" and all his actions are determined by this conviction. Even when he breaks the week of peace and unwittingly infringes the law, he accepts that he is wrong and that the law is right, and he submits to his punishment. Okonkwo does not deviate from his society's norms and it is inaccurate to say that he has only a limited understanding of them; rather it is the intelligent Obierika who constantly questions his society's values; it is he who suggests that the law forbidding men of title to climb palm trees is a bad law; it is he who questions the throwing of twins into the evil forest and the banishing of a man for seven years from his fatherland for accidentally killing a kinsman. Okonkwo never does; and yet no one has accused Obierika of deviating from his society's norms.

Very early in the novel there is an episode demonstrating that even in his youth Okonkwo is determined to be the personification of those values that his society holds sacred. He goes to Nwakibie to ask for seed yams and says: "I know what it is to ask a man to trust another with his yams, especially these days when young men are afraid of hard work. I am not afraid of work." Critics like Innes and Iyasere might see this as the most towering conceit on Okonkwo's part, but in reality it shows his confidence in himself and his determination to be different from other young men and conform to his society's aspirations. And Nwakibie who is very much in line with his society's norms and is a pillar of that society, agrees with Okonkwo and confirms the truth of what he has just said: "It pleases me to see a young man like you these days when our youth have gone soft. Many young men have come to me to ask for yams but I have refused because I knew they would just

dump them in the earth and leave them to be choked by weeds." To Nwakibie, Okonkwo stands for everything that he is looking for in a deserving
young man.   Later in Mbanta we see an elder identifying Okonkwo with
the traditional ways of doing things while castigating the younger generation for deviating from the tribe's paths: "It is good in these days when the
younger generation consider themselves wiser than their sires to see a man
doing things in the grand old way." The society's recognition that Okonkwo
is an embodiment of their values is illustrated in their choice of him as the
emissary to Mbaino and the guardian of Ikemefuna. He is also the representative of his village among the nine masked egwugwu of Umuofia. If
anything Okonkwo's tragedy is caused not by his deviation from the norms
of his society, but because he tries to adhere to those norms too completely.

No other issue illustrates Okonkwo's oneness with his society than his
regard for the concept of manliness. Iyasere and Innes would have us believe
that Umuofia society, while adhering to the concept of manliness, holds the
female principle in very high regard, and its world view is based on a subtle
blend of the masculine and feminine principles, a subtlety which Okonkwo
is incapable of understanding. Iyasere cites the aged Uchendu's words of
caution to the exiled Okonkwo when the former tries to explain the meaning
of the adage "mother is supreme", illustrating that the mother, and therefore
the female principle, stands for sympathy and compassion. Furthermore the
importance of the female principle in Umuofia society is illustrated by the
fact that the powerful earth deity Ani is feminine, and the no less powerful
Oracle Agbala is represented as female, as is her mouthpiece—the Priestess
of Agbala. It is true that Umuofia society gives some regard to the female
principle, but there is little doubt that in the novel itself much greater importance is attached to the masculine principle and the concept of manliness.
Okonkwo's regard for manliness is no more and no less than his society's
regard for it. This is particularly demonstrated in the symbolic importance
of the yam. We are told quite early in the novel: "His mother and his sisters
worked hard enough, but they grew women's crops, like coco-yams, beans
and cassava. Yam, the king of crops, was a man's crop." And Achebe's rhetorical guidance suggests that this is the view, not just of Okonkwo, but of his
entire society. This is even more obvious in "Yam stood for manliness, and
he who could feed his family on yams from one harvest to another was a very
great man indeed." The almost proverbial ring in "he who could feed his
family" suggests that this is the point of view of the entire society; it is part
of the tribal wisdom. The New Yam Festival is linked with manly men: "The
New Yam Festival was thus an occasion for joy throughout Umuofia. And
every man whose arm was strong, as the Ibo people say, was expected to
invite large numbers of guests from far and wide." If Okonkwo exalts the

concept of manliness into a kind of shibboleth, it is precisely because his society reveres men whose arms were strong and who in moments of crisis did not behave like shivering old women. On their way to kill the ill-fated Ikemefuna the men of Umuofia pour ridicule on those "effeminate" men who had refused to come with them. It would probably have been more human for Okonkwo to have stayed away as the aged Ezeudu advised him to do, and as Obierika himself did; but there is little doubt that the majority of masculine opinion in Umuofia would have considered him a coward. When at the betrothal of Obierika's daughter's the suitor's family's pots of wine begin to number more than thirty "the hosts nodded in approval and seemed to say 'now they are behaving like men.'" The concept of manliness is paramount. If Okonkwo rules his family with a heavy hand, it is because basically his society believes that women and children must be kept in check: "No matter how prosperous a man was, if he was unable to rule his women and his children (and especially his women) he was not really a man. He was like the man in the song who had ten and one wives and not enough soup for his foofoo." Once more Achebe's rhetorical guidance suggests that this is the point of view, not just of Okonkwo, but of his entire society. The proverbial saying in the song from the oral tradition gives it the weight of tribal wisdom. When Okonkwo encourages his boys to sit with him in his Obi and listen to stories of war and bloodshed it is because his society reveres masculine prowess in war and he feels the boys have reached the stage when they should hear such stories. And the young and rather feminine Nwoye knows what his society believes; he knows it is right to be masculine, even though deep down he prefers his mother's stories. Conclusive proof that this is a male oriented society whose views are very much like Okonkwo's is provided by the discussion during the betrothal proceedings:

> "The world is large", said Okonkwo. "I have even heard that in some tribes a man's children belong to his wife and her family."
> "That cannot be", said Machi. "You might as well say that the woman lies on top of the man when they are making the children."

As in most things he does, Okonkwo probably carries this regard for manliness too far, but it is basically a central tenet of his society's beliefs and in adhering to it one cannot say that he deviates from his society's norms, the subtle discriminations of which he is incapable of understanding. Moreover, the female principle which is supposed to be subtly blended with the masculine and to represent compassion and sympathy, does not, in practice, suggest anything of the kind, does not make for flexibility. The Earth Goddess Ani is a harsh unrelenting deity who is dreaded by the people. It is in obedience to her dictates that twins, suicides and those who die of the swelling sickness are cast off into the evil forest and a man is exiled for seven years for the accidental slaying of a kinsman. Some of the most repulsive and most cruel practices of this society are caused by its adherence to the will of the Earth Goddess, and her will is totally inflexible. The Oracle of Agbala is not much better. If it directs that a young child must be carried away from its mother into the depths of the forest in the dead of night, or that a young and innocent hostage must be killed, then its will must be unquestioningly obeyed. And the Oracle has no more compassion for the lazy Unoka than his male-oriented society. If anything the female principle induces terror. We must never forget that the most active ingredient in Umuofia's war medicine which is the terror of its neighbours is an old woman hopping on one leg. It is inaccurate to suggest that the female principle, representing compassion and sympathy, modifies the masculine and that the two are subtly blended and that Okonkwo is blind to this subtle blending. If anything the female principle merely reinforces the male with its harshness.

One of the mainsprings of Okonkwo's actions is his rather negative revulsion against everything his father had stood for. Humiliated by his father's shameful life and even more shameful death Okonkwo is determined to be everything his father was not. He must be brave and materially successful, he must take the highest titles, he must provide for and rule his womenfolk and children and he must never be thought weak or a coward. In the process he becomes dehumanised, but Okonkwo's determination is conditioned by his society's attitudes and beliefs. If he reacts violently against everything his father stood for, it is because his society despised his father. It is surely inaccurate to suggest, as Iyasere does, that Umuofia society adapts its code to accommodate less successful men. It does not banish them, of course, since they are still members of the clan, but all the evidence suggests that it regards them with the greatest contempt. For instance, all the men are amused by Obiaka's retort when informed that his dead lazy father wants him to sacrifice a goat to him. "Ask my father if he ever had a fowl when he was alive." When Okonkwo hints that his son Nwoye has too much of his mother in him Obierika says inwardly that the young man has too much of his grandfather in him. The priestess of Agbala lashes out at Unoka in the harshest terms when the latter goes to consult the Oracle on the question of his failure. Iyasere suggests that Okonkwo should have given his father the respect due to age in conformity with the norms of his society for "while achievement was revered, age was respected." But Iyasere unwittingly turns the text on its head for the text actually reads: "Age was respected among his people, but achievement was revered. As the elders said, if a child washed his hands he could eat with kings." The drift of the entire passage is the premium that these people place on achievement, rather than on age per se; "among these people a man was judged according to his worth and not according to the worth of his father." There is nothing to suggest that in secretly despising his father and repudiating all he stood for Okonkwo was violating a necessary aspect of the society's code of values. On the contrary, Okonkwo's attitude is completely shared by his society. Of course one would agree with Iyasere that in suppressing his fears and those attributes he considers a sign of weakness Okonkwo denies human responses of love and understanding; and, responding to Achebe's rhetorical guidance, we do realise that Unoka has very human qualities which Okonkwo would have been the better for possessing and that in repudiating him the latter was also repudiating positive qualities of love, compassion and sensitivity. But it is the reader who thinks so, not Okonkwo's society. Many of Okonkwo's weaknesses are also the weaknesses of his society.

There is very little sign of the tolerance and flexibility that critics like Innes and Iyasere see in Umuofia society. Okonkwo's own inflexibility, intolerance and conservatism are merely reflections of his society's. On essential questions of religion, justice and class Umuofia shows no flexibility. The penalties imposed by the gods and by custom must be adhered to. If a cow strays accidentally into somebody's field its owner must pay the full penalty even though no damage has been done and the real culprits are some negligent children who were put in charge of the cow. The question of the osus vividly illustrates the clan's intolerance on essential matters. Even the Christian converts, many of whom are themselves among the underprivileged in their society, refuse to have contact with the osus.

On one matter and one matter alone the clan seems to demonstrate some tolerance, and this is in its attitude towards the new religion. Initially they allow the new converts and their missionaries to practise their religion unmolested, but this is in line with the clan's general courtesy to strangers, and in any case the new converts are still regarded as members of the clan and cannot therefore be ostracised without infringing the clan's own rules. In fact, the clan harbours the most sovereign contempt towards the new converts who in their view are the *efulefu* or worthless excrement of the clan and therefore not worth bothering about. Initially Okonkwo's attitude towards the missionaries is exactly the same as the clan's; it is one of amused tolerance, for he, like the clan, thinks that the missionaries are mad. In reality the tolerance is only apparent, for at Mbanta the clan secretly hopes to bring about the death of the new missionaries. When the latter ask them for land to build their church, they offer them the evil forest in the hope that they will all die there. The clan will not modify its own beliefs and it will allow the new converts to practise their religion only for as long as its own position and religion are not threatened. When some over-zealous converts boast openly that they are prepared to defy the gods by burning all their shrines they are seized and beaten until they stream with blood. When another convert kills the sacred python Okonkwo suggests that the abominable gang should be chased out of the village with whips, but although many do not agree with him, he is certainly not isolated in his view for we are told that many of the elders spoke at great length and in fury. In the end those who suggest gentler measures prevail. And when Okonkwo expresses the view that such a thing would never happen in his own fatherland Umuofia, we must realise that he speaks with the authority of one who knows how his clan would have behaved on such an occasion. Mbanta is by all accounts a gentler clan than Umuofia; but even so the women who are sent for red earth to decorate the church are severely whipped and when they go to the stream for water they find themselves debarred, an unheard of thing. To suggest that the clan is flexible and that Okonkwo's inflexibility is due to a lack of understanding of the subtle variations within the code, is to misread the novel.

The killing of Ikemefuna illustrates the essential inflexibility and brutality not just of Okonkwo, but of the entire clan. It is difficult, in fact, to accept the charge of brutality that critics like Iyasere would bring against Okonkwo in the killing of Ikemefuna. It is the society which is brutal for it is this society which has asked the men to perform a brutal task. On a personal level, perhaps it would have been more human for Okonkwo to have heeded Ezeudu's advice not to have a hand in Ikemefuna's death since the boy regarded him as his father. It is a point we hold against Okonkwo, but we hold it against his society as well, for if Okonkwo decides to accompany the men it is because he knows that if he does not do so he would be considered weak and womanish, and the comments of the men as they take Ikemefuna to his death reinforce this. Some critics feel that in disregarding the aged Ezeudu's advice Okonkwo shows scant regard for age which his society reveres and is therefore going against the norms of that society. But Ezeudu's advice is a personal one which does not necessarily have the backing of his society, for otherwise he would not have felt compelled to offer it. All the evidence suggests on the contrary, that the majority of masculine opinion in Umuofia expects Okonkwo to be a part of the delegation.

In reality, Okonkwo never intended to bear a hand in Ikemefuna's death. He had become extremely fond of the child whom he had come to regard as his own son. Indeed, the relationship with Ikemefuna brings out in Okonkwo those human qualities which we have hitherto missed. When it is announced that the boy must be killed Okonkwo is thrown into the depths of despair and although he accompanies the men on their mission of death he keeps to the rear thus demonstrating that he has no intention of lifting his hand against the boy. He fully intends, in his own way, to heed Ezeudu's advice. When he hears the murderous blow he turns his head; he cannot bear to see a boy whom he regards as his son struck down before his eyes. If that first blow had done its work Okonkwo would never have borne a hand in the killing of Ikemefuna; if Ikemefuna in his terror had not run towards Okonkwo with his anguished cry "they have killed me father" the former would never have cut him down. By making that cry Ikemefuna was invoking the help of Okonkwo as a father and defender against those murderous men and all eyes must have been on Okonkwo to see whether he would yield to what they must consider sentimental ties rather than demonstrate loyalty to his clan and obedience to the dictates of his gods; and for Okonkwo outward displays of sentimentality are out of the question because he does not want his clan to consider him weak; and loyalty to the clan and the dictates of the gods are of over-riding importance. So he cuts Ikemefuna down.

Even so Okonkwo is aware that he has done something which goes against his best instincts and he is racked by internal torment for days afterwards. We see human dimensions here in Okonkwo that we have never suspected before. In his despair he even longs for companionship and sends for the now hostile Nwoye to sit with him in his obi. A number of critics would have us believe that Nwoye's attitude towards his father hardens because he sees the latter as having killed Ikemefuna. This is an oversimplification of the actual position. We are told that the moment Okonkwo walked into the obi Nwoye knew that Ikemefuna had been killed and something seemed to give way inside him like a tightened bow. Nwoye does not, and cannot, accuse his father of having cut down Ikemefuna since he was not present at the killing and could not possibly know that Okonkwo had dealt the final blow. What he blames his father for is taking part in the general clan brutality. That this is so is demonstrated by the anecdote of the twins in the bush which was the first occasion when Nwoye had had the feeling of something giving way inside him. That anecdote also relates to the general brutality of this society and it is this which now impresses itself once more on Nwoye's mind when he has that same feeling. In deciding, in consequence, to join the Christians who are more compassionate and humane, Nwoye rejects not just his father, but his entire society.

The Ikemefuna episode copiously demonstrates that Okonkwo is not really an inhuman person. He does have warm, human feelings, even of compassion and love. If he appears dehumanised and inflexible it is because in order to please his society, conform to its norms and measure up to its demands on him, he is forced to smother his best instincts. This is one of the reasons why we continue to sympathise with him. Okonkwo might bully his boys in order to get them to be manly in line with his society's demands, but he knows inwardly that the boys are still too young to understand fully the difficult art of preparing yams. He might be pleased inwardly at his son's development but he knows he must keep his feelings tightly under control. Okonkwo is what his society has made him, and there is very little support in the text for the view that he is what he is because of a radical misunderstanding of the subtle shades of his society's codes.

Okonkwo, of course, possesses certain harsh personal qualities which are not the result of conditioning by his society. The most conspicuous of these is his uncontrollable temper which is related to his impulsiveness. It almost seems as though there is some irrational ungovernable force within Okonkwo propelling him to insane outbursts of anger and wildly impulsive actions which have increasingly disastrous consequences. In this sense he is rather like Hardy's Michael Henchard. Thus he terrorises the young Ikemefuna when the latter refuses to eat, viciously beats one wife thus breaking the week of peace and murders another with his gun for making disparaging references to his ability as a hunter. We are meant to see the slaying of Ezeudu's son, though an accidental occurrence, as the culmination of a number of increasingly serious and senseless acts partly motivated by his impulsiveness and irrational temper. We are also informed of his brusqueness and impatience with less successful men; he knew how to kill a man's spirit. There is also a basic restlessness in Okonkwo; he always seems to be charged with an overabundance of nervous energy and is always yearning for action. These are qualities, of course, which are related to his impulsiveness and they contribute to his disastrous actions. But Okonkwo is always full of regret for these acts when he comes to himself. His impulsiveness may lead him to forget the week of peace and break the law, but he regrets immediately, accepts that he has been at fault and accepts his punishment. When ever he transgresses against his society's laws, he does so unwittingly or accidentally, never deliberately, and he is quite willing to take full responsibility later. When he insults a clansman by calling him a woman, the people take sides with the man against Okonkwo, and he decently apologises. Okonkwo's harsher personal qualities, therefore, might contribute to his eventual downfall, but they do not suggest that he is a deviant from his society's norms.

A number of people in the novel make disparaging comments about Okonkwo, but we must not necessarily assume that Achebe endorses these; we must follow his rhetorical guidance in order to ascertain his point of view. When Okonkwo insults the man at the meeting for instance, the oldest man present says sternly that "those whose palm-kernels were cracked for them by a benevolent spirit should not forget to be humble." But Achebe's rhetorical guidance suggests that the man's judgement is quite wrong, motivated in all probability by envy at Okonkwo's achievements and sudden rise to prominence though still a young man:

> But it was really not true that Okonkwo's palm-kernels had been cracked for him by a benevolent spirit. He had cracked them himself . . . If ever a man deserved his success, that man was Okonkwo . . . At the most one could say that his *chi* or personal god was good. But the Ibo people have a proverb that when a man says yes his *chi* says yes also. Okonkwo said yes very strongly; so his *chi* agreed. And not only his *chi* but his clan too, because it judged a man by the work of his hands.

The old man fails to give due weight to Okonkwo's personal determination and industry. Similarly when Okonkwo breaks the week of peace his enemies go around saying that he has no respect for the gods of the clan and that his good fortune has gone to his head. But Achebe guides us by openly terming these people 'enemies' and he informs us in any case, that inwardly Okonkwo was repentant. It is simply not true that he has no respect for the gods or that success has gone to his head. Generally Achebe remains most sympathetic towards Okonkwo, while recognising his faults, and he succeeds in generating this sympathy in the reader as well.

Many critics have not been alive to the full significance of Okonkwo's absence for seven years from his fatherland at a time when the new religion is consolidating itself and making inroads into traditional society. That accidental slaying of Ezeudu's son was a shrewd masterstroke of the author's with an important bearing on the plot and on the development of the themes and Okonkwo's character. For during that absence the clan changes profoundly while Okonkwo does not; and it is only now that a gap appears between Okonkwo and his society. But it is not so much Okonkwo who deviates, as his society which is forced to shift from the old paths. Nor is the shift in the society's position due to its flexibility, to a willingness to welcome change. It simply recognises the presence of a militarily superior force, and it is cowed in spite of itself into submission. Furthermore it has been racked by internal disunity enhanced by its own rigidity and lack of compassion. The osus, the mothers of twins and all those who are outcasts from this society or who have something to dread from its harsh unrelenting laws flock to the new religion. There are those, of course, who welcome the new regime, because it has brought trade and prosperity, and we know that Umuofia society has always been materialistic. The downfall of the society is already in progress when Okonkwo returns, and it is brought about, in part, by those very qualities which will also contribute to Okonkwo's own disaster.

So far is Okonkwo from deviating from his society's norms that on his return he is one of the very few who still hold on to the old values—the belief in courage, tribal independence, and pride in the tribe's traditions. That these values have not entirely been lost sight of, that the tribe does not willingly submit to change and to the white man's rule and that Okonkwo's attitude is not such an aberration as commonly supposed, is authenticated by the discussion at the great meeting called to discuss the white man's humiliation of the clan's elders. Sensing the resurgence of the tribal spirit Okonkwo takes heart and gets down his war gear. At the meeting itself Okika the great orator speaks out powerfully for war, thus suggesting that Okonkwo is not entirely isolated in his championing of the old values.

The killing of the messenger is one of Okonkwo's impulsive and foolish acts which have disastrous consequences. This is why certain voices ask why he did it. He attempts to force his society's hand by an act which would almost certainly result in war, whereas his clan would have wanted to take the decision in a more rational way. But there is little doubt that the old Umuofia would have backed Okonkwo, for this would not have been a war of blame since the court messengers were not really messengers but haughty aggressors attempting to stop the meeting by force. But the present, much changed Umuofia would never go to war, as Okonkwo correctly realises; it is cowed by this manifestation of the white man's power into final submission. This is the real death knell of traditional Umuofia society. It is his realisation of this which leads to Obierika's impassioned outburst against the uncomprehending District Commissioner: "That man was one of the greatest men in Umuofia. You drove him to kill himself; and now he will be buried like a dog . . ." Iyasere is surely wrong in suggesting that Obierika at this point loses all sense of objectivity. Obierika has been the sanest and the most sensible man throughout the novel and we can be sure that at this stage he carries Achebe's endorsement. Okonkwo has been one of the greatest men in Umuofia, endorsing all of his society's norms to the very last, even when others are cowed into submission. He is neither victim, nor villain, but a truly tragic hero, a man with admirable qualities reflecting those of his society, and weaknesses also reflecting those of his society; but in spite of these he never loses the author's or the reader's sympathy. His tragedy resides partly in the fact that the society which he has championed for so long is forced to change, while he finds that he cannot.

RICHARD K. PRIEBE

The Proverb, Realism and Achebe:
A Study of Ethical Consciousness

Mⁱore people have read Chinua Achebe than any other African writer. This is no less true outside the continent than it is within it. And this is constantly reflected in the fact that more critical attention is paid to his novels than to the work of any other writer. Find someone who has read but one African literary work, and the odds are that the work will be Achebe's *Things Fall Apart*. The reasons for this are not hard to surmise. Achebe writes in a style that is at once accessible to the individual who knows nothing of Africa and intensely compelling to even the most knowledgeable Africanist. He was one of the first writers to effectively dramatize the most important historical, political and cultural issues facing Africa, and he has remained among the best. Moreover, he is a consumate artist; he always tells a good story.

One result of his accessibility and popularity is that Achebe has become something of a standard against which other African writers are measured. Often when writers like Soyinka and Armah are attacked for their obscurity, or their use of scatological imagery, there is the implicit, if not explicit comparison with the "model" writer, Achebe. In saying this I wish to take nothing away from Achebe's well-deserved reputation. In fact, the act of pre-judging what a writer should do has led to problems in interpreting Achebe as well as Soyinka and Armah. Approaching the mythic consciousness is

From *Myth, Realism and the West African Writer*. © 1998 by Richard K. Priebe.

indeed much more difficult than approaching the ethical consciousness, and thus most of my attention in this book is focused on the former. Still, I would maintain that if we can approach the ethical in a clearer manner, we will have far less trouble in approaching the mythic.

By turns Achebe has been both praised and condemned for his didacticism. Regardless of how it is judged, perhaps the least controversial statement anyone could make in the field of African literature is that Chinua Achebe is a didactic writer. By his own statements and through his work, Achebe clearly shows his belief in the role of the artist as teacher. The pejoration of the word "didactic" in Western criticism, however, makes this statement rather misleading for many readers. Achebe's artistic concerns are with presenting a holistic view of the ethos of his people in an entirely vital, dynamic mode that is expressive of his culture in terms of form no less than content. His works progress in a linear manner and are set in an historical framework that reveals the persistence of cultural continuity despite internal and external threats to the society. Yet, as Soyinka noted, there is never a mere photographic rendering of the world he gives us. We confront an ethical consciousness, an authorial presence that leads us into the societal structures of Ibo life and proceeds in a realistic, linear and historical manner, while revealing the depth and breadth of strategies open to the individual and society for coping with reality. Achebe's works are didactic, but not in the manner of a facile, two-dimensional realism where all ethical choices are clear cut.

Kenneth Burke has suggested that complex literary works can be considered "proverbs writ large." On more than one level Achebe is clearly engaged in writing proverbs. As Burke has explained, the proverb is a very primary unit through which we can see art as equipment for living. Proverbs name and encompass ranges of strategies or attitudes for handling recurrent situations. A strategy, if it is worth anything, must be functional and realistic—in other words, it must size things up rather accurately. Above all, the proverb must have vitality: "The point of issue is not to find categories that 'place' the proverbs once and for all. What I want is categories that suggest their active nature. Here is no 'realism for its own sake.' Here is realism for promise, admonition, solace, foretelling, instruction, charting, all for the direct bearing that such acts have upon matters of welfare."

Few who have seriously looked at Achebe's work would argue with the aptness of Burke's comment on the proverb as a description of the activity Achebe has been engaged in. That Achebe artistically employs proverbs in his writing is not even the central question; it merely underscores my point about the complexity of the ethical consciousness reflected in his work. Proverbs are reflective of the values of a society, and the proverbs that

Achebe employs are important elements in the whole system of values that *Things Fall Apart* reflects, elements as it were of a very large proverb. So careful is Achebe in putting the elements together, that we have an empirically valid statement about Ibo society at a given period of time, the 1890s. In other words, we have a work that is not only a distinctive piece of literature, it is also an important piece of meta-history, meta-ethnography, and meta-theology. I will look at the way Achebe reveals the human tragedy of an individual, Okonkwo, who cannot come to terms with the values of his society, that is to say, the strategies for surviving in that society. It is possible to understand the more encompassing tragedy, that of the group, in terms of the historical circumstances of European colonialism, but colonialism can only be seen as a catalyst for what happens to Okonkwo. To try to explain his tragedy outside of the meta-ethnographic and meta-theological framework Achebe provides, is not simply to misread the work, but to rob Okonkwo of his tragic dignity and explain what happened to him in terms of historical determinism.

For the non-African reader the subtleties and complexities of Achebe may indeed be rather difficult to perceive at first. The clues are there, however, and careful reading can lead to an understanding of a great deal that is distinctly African, though comprehensible within Western terms.

In a monograph entitled *Oedipus and Job in West African Religion*, Meyer Fortes explores the way fate and divine justice operate in West African religion. The title sounds arrogantly ethnocentric, but Fortes is careful to avoid any superficially descriptive comparisons of the kind Sir James Frazer made. Instead, he considers the stories of Oedipus and Job from an analytical perspective and shows how they together form a useful paradigm for understanding the paradoxically contradictory and complementary concepts of prenatal fate or destiny, and supernatural justice in West Africa. I will show that this paradigm is one we can also extract from Achebe's *Things Fall Apart*. The point is not to reduce an aspect of Achebe's work to a Eurocentric archetype, for we are actually pulling two rather disparate ideas together to create a metaphor that will facilitate an understanding of a religious strategy artistically rendered by an African writer. A tighter argument might be made by taking an emic approach and first going into Ibo religious thought, but the justification for my etic approach lies in what such exegesis will reveal about the accessible pattern in this novel.

A common observation by Western critics has been that *Things Fall Apart* is very much like a Greek tragedy. Okonkwo, like his Greek counterpart, appears to be brought down by a fatal flaw that is beyond his control. Without any doubt Oedipus is the victim of Destiny; personal responsibility or guilt has nothing to do with what happens to him. We also find that Okonkwo's *chi*, his personal god, has quite a lot to do with his destiny, but we are stopped at the very beginning of the novel from pursuing a descriptive comparison for we are told that a man can, in part, shape his own destiny: "If ever a man deserved his success, that man was Okonkwo. At an early age he had achieved fame as the greatest wrestler in all the land. That was not luck. At the most one could say that his *chi* or personal god was good. But the Ibo people have a proverb that when a man says yes his *chi* says yes also. Okonkwo said yes very strongly; so his *chi* agreed. And not only his *chi* but his clan too, because it judged a man by the work of his hands."

Having learned that a man can assert control over his *chi*, we learn a few pages later that the *chi* controls the man. Okonkwo is compared to "the little bird *nza* who so far forgot himself after a heavy meal that he challenged his *chi*." As there are limitations on how strong the "yes" can be, we are left with an apparent contradiction that seems to raise questions about the nature of Okonkwo's tragedy. How much can he be held responsible for his end and how much can be attributed to an overpowering Destiny?

In order to answer this question I must make a closer comparison of the structural parallels in the lives of Oedipus and Okonkwo. The summary Meyer Fortes gives of Oedipus's life clearly shows where these parallels lie. Oedipus enters life with an ominous foreboding of an evil Destiny as he is rejected by his parents who physically cast him away. Only for brief moments in his life does he ever escape being an outcast; ultimately his fate overwhelms him.

> His tragedy can be described as that of a man blindly seeking to achieve his legitimate place in society, first as son, then as husband, father and citizen against the unconscious opposition of an inborn urge to avenge himself by repudiating his parents, his spouse, and his children. When in the end, he succeeds to this fate he shows his revulsion against himself by mutilating his own eyes and so blotting out his relationship with his kind and his society. He dies in exile, almost like a ghost departing from this world rather than like an ordinary man.

With a few changes of detail, Meyer Fortes could have been talking about Okonkwo. By material standards Okonkwo's father, Unoka, is an outcast in Umuofian society, and by any spiritual measure, he dies one: "He had a bad *chi* . . . and evil fortune followed him to the grave, or rather to his death, for he had no grave." Okonkwo spends his life trying to avoid his father's fate only to succumb to a death that also severs him spiritually from his society. In the course of his life, while attempting to repudiate the "feminine" characteristics of his father, he is respectively alienated from his father, one of his wives, his son (Nwoye), and finally his clan. He treats the memory of his father with contempt; he beats Ojiugo during the Week of Peace; he is horrified by Nwoye's attraction to Christianity; and he is physically exiled when he accidentally kills a young man. His suicide, moreover, is a clear correlative to Oedipus's self-mutilation.

Granted, I am still operating on a rather tenuous descriptive level, but behind both men there is definitely a strong force of Destiny controlling their lives, their parents and their children. With Oedipus this control is complete and with Okonkwo it is partial, though in both cases "it serves to exonerate both society and the sufferer by fixing ultimate responsibility on the ancestors and on a pre-natal, that is pre-social, event." No careful reader of *Things Fall Apart*, any more than a character within Umuofian society, could hold Okonkwo to blame for his fate, despite the fact that a good argument can be made for the idea that there are implicit authorial criticisms of both Okonkwo and his society. Within that society we are shown that a man can have either a good or a bad *chi*—Okonkwo's life is simply controlled by an evil Destiny.

Yet such knowledge about a man's fate can only be known for certain after the fact. Moreover, neither the novel, the society, nor Okonkwo's life is all that simple. As Bernth Lindfors has very cogently shown, a very large proportion of the proverbs used by Achebe in *Things Fall Apart* have to do with achievement. Many of these proverbs confirm the idea that in Ibo society a man is not necessarily foredoomed by an evil *chi*. Providing he acts in the appropriate manner, he can say "yes" to a *chi* that says "no": "the sun will shine on those who stand before it shines on those who kneel under them"; "if a child washed his hands he could eat with kings"; "a man who pays respect to the great paves the way for his own greatness"; "as a man danced so the drums were beaten for him."

These proverbs encompass strategies for individual equity that are antithetical to the closed system of prenatal destiny we find in the story of Oedipus. They are, however, rather incisive leads into another dimension of the religious framework of Okonkwo's society—a dimension that can be understood in terms of the patterns of divine justice we find in Job.

Nothing has been pre-established for the course of Job's life. He is free to choose between good and evil, and whatever consequences result from his choices are the rewards and punishments of an omnipotent God. Though personified, and ultimately just and merciful, this God cannot always be comprehended in terms of what the individual perceives as just. Job never admits, nor does he need to admit, any

guilt in the sense of responsibility for actions that are wicked by
ordinary human standards. What he admits is having placed
himself on a footing of equality with God, judging for himself
what conduct is righteous and what wicked. This wrong relationship was his sin . . . Job's sufferings are like severe measures
of discipline that a father might use to correct a son who, while
exemplary in his conduct, was getting too big for his boots and ,
arrogating to himself a status equal to his father's; and Job's salvation might be compared to the son's realizing and accepting his
filial dependence.

As we are dealing with a paradigmatic and not a simple descriptive
comparison, it might help to momentarily reverse perspectives. Job, in other
words, can be seen as one who wrestled with his *chi*, realized his mistake before
it was too late, and took the necessary steps to rectify his relationship with his
God. Again, the idea here is not in some missionary-like manner to find one-
sided "universal" correspondences, but to show that the Western reader should
be able to get into the aesthetic complexity of Achebe's work. No injustice to
the integrity of the work need be committed by this artificial atomizing so long
as we see the process only as a key to a holistic understanding of a work that in
its totality is very unlike the stories of either Oedipus or Job.

The parallel between Job and Okonkwo that is significant to us is the
idea that the ancestors, just as Job's God, can be angered or pleased in such
a way that they either confirm or override an individual's Destiny, bringing
him disaster or good fortune. In discussing this in relation to the religious
thought of the Tale, Meyer Fortes makes three generalizations about Tale
ancestral belief that we can also draw out of *Things Fall Apart*. These generalizations concern

axiomatic values from which all ideal conduct is deemed to flow.
The first is the rule that kinship is binding in an absolute sense.
From this follows the second rule, that kinship implies amity in
an absolute sense. The third rule is the fundamental one. It
postulates that the essential relationship of parent and child,
expressed in the parent's devoted care and the child's affectionate
dependence, may never be violated and is, in that sense, sacred.
It is indeed the source of the other rules.

Thus, when Okonkwo is exiled from Umuofia he must flee to the village of
his mother. He must accept his relatives there, and they are bound to accept
him in complete friendship. Moreover, they are seen almost literally as living
extensions of his mother.

Beyond any strict legalistic adherence to these values it is imperative that one have a proper attitude towards the moral relationships that follow from them. Like Job, Okonkwo is an upright and honest man, guilty not of any willfully unjust actions, but of an unbending self-righteousness in his relations with his gods, his ancestors and his kin. Moreover, he cannot accept the suffering he is forced to bear. While in exile he is angrily castigated by his kinsman, Uchendu:

> You think you are the greatest sufferer in the world. Do you know that men are sometimes banished for life? Do you know that men sometimes lose all their yams and even their children? I had six wives once. I have none now except that young girl who knows not her right from her left. Do you know how many children I have buried—children I begot in my youth and strength? Twenty-two. I did not hang myself, and I am still alive. If you think you are the greatest sufferer in the world, ask my daughter, Akueni, how many twins she has borne and thrown away. Have you not heard the song they sing when a woman dies?
>
> "For whom is it well, for whom is it well?
> There is no one for whom it is well."

Though Job's relation to his god is unilaterally contractual and Okonkwo's relation is a bilateral one of mutual dependence, the attitudes of both men pose a threat to the religious fabric of their society. God had a bet with Satan that had to be won; Umuofia had its very survival at stake in its confrontation with the white man. This survival of gods, ancestors and kin was more important than the inflexible will of one man: "What the ancestors demand and enforce on pain of death is conformity with the basic moral axiom in fulfilling the requirements of all social relationships; and these are the counterpart, in the domain of kinship, of the obligations posited between persons and their ancestors in the religious domain."

The first thing we learn about Okonkwo is that "his fame rested on solid personal achievements." It is noteworthy that this is followed by our seeing that "he had no patience with his father." Considering the value placed on personal achievement in his society, Okonkwo certainly had no obligation to have patience with his father, who had no rank at all in the society. But there is a more fundamental kinship value that Okonkwo ignores. In a very subtle manner Achebe introduces this tension between individual and communal values and carefully orchestrates its buildup. The proverb that "age was respected . . . achievement . . . revered" lays emphasis on achievement, but indicates a balance between respect and reverence that Okonkwo ignores. His father praises him for his proud heart, but warns him of the difficulty in failing alone, advice that Okonkwo is unable to accept. When a joke is made about a man who refused to sacrifice a goat to his father, Okonkwo is uncomfortable, ironically because it reminds him of his father's poverty and not of his own neglect of his father's memory. An old man commenting on Okonkwo's success quotes the proverb "Looking at a king's mouth . . . one would think he never sucked at his mother's breast." The proverb is not used here in any derogatory manner, but is one more sign to the reader that Okonkwo lives much of his life as if he had no kin.

All this is revealed within the first few chapters. The subsequent action sharpens our insight into the tragic ordering of values that should be complementary, but in Okonkwo become completely oppositional. Communal and individual values must be in carefully ordered balance. In his extremist actions Okonkwo shows "no respect for the gods of the clan." Though he may feel contrite, as he did after beating his wife during the Week of Peace, he never shows it. The group itself must adjust and change when it is threatened by its customs; it expects no less of the individual. This point is indirectly, but firmly underlined by Ezeudu's recounting of the heavy punishments that were once exacted whenever the Week of Peace was broken. After a while the custom had to be altered as it destroyed what it was intended to protect.

Without going very far into a Lévi-Straussian type of structural analysis, it is very obvious that we have here yet another aspect of Okonkwo that can be understood in terms of the Oedipal paradigm, namely the underrating of blood relations. Unlike Oedipus in his incestuous relationship with his mother, Okonkwo never overrates blood relations. Yet comparable to Oedipus's parricide is Okonkwo's rejection of his father and all things feminine. Okonkwo continually acts in a manner that leads to an absolute rejection of his autochthonous origin. In his participation in the killing of Ikemefuna and in his reluctant acceptance of his exile in his mother's land, he shows a willful refusal to submit to the Earth Goddess; in his beating of his wife during the Week of Peace and in his accidental killing of the boy during Ezeudu's funeral, he commits overt offenses against the goddess.

During a feast at the end of Okonkwo's exile, an old kinsman rises to give a speech to thank Okonkwo for the great banquet. Very discreetly, however, he gives a talk on the strength of kinship bonds, which while a general warning to the clan, must also be construed as a specific warning to Okonkwo: "A man who calls his kinsman to a feast does not do so to save them from starving. They all have food in their own homes. When we gather together in the moonlit village ground it is not because of the moon. . . . We come together because it is good for kinsmen to do so." The words, in effect, are beyond Okonkwo's comprehension. When he returns to Umuofia, he is entirely out of step with his clan. A clear, inexorable logic thus leads him to the ultimate offense against the Earth Goddess, his own suicide.

The logic, however, was inexorable only because of Okonkwo's unbending will. Had he submitted to the will of the clan, a will dictated by survival, he too might have avoided a tragic end. Okonkwo's daughter, Ezinma, is born with an evil Destiny. A diviner is consulted and he informs the family that the child is an *ogbanje*, a spirit that continually returns to the mother's womb in a cycle of birth and death. Once the proper ritual measures are taken, the evil *chi* is propitiated and survival from its threat is insured. The implication is clear—Okonkwo never fully propitiates his *chi*.

What Meyer Fortes had noted in a general way we can see very specifically, namely an Oedipal predisposition figuratively transformed into a Jobian fulfillment. Okonkwo is a strong man, but he has limited vision and is caught in the singleminded pursuit of his ambitions and escape from his fears. Only in the end, after he has killed the messenger, does he achieve some tragic recognition: "Okonkwo stood looking at the dead man. He knew that Umuofia would not go to war. He knew because they had let the other messengers escape. . . . He wiped his matchet on the sand and went away." But even then, Okonkwo sees only the futility of his own course of action. Complete understanding would entail the perception that "the system as a whole is impregnable, particularly since the criterion invoked is ritual service, not conduct that can be judged by men themselves. Whatever the ancestors do must therefore be, and is, accepted as just, and men have no choice but to submit."

Two scenes that the Western reader is likely to find annoyingly inexplicable can be easily understood in relation to the function they serve in underscoring the need to submit to ancestral control. No reason is given for the Oracle's decision that Ikemefuna must be sacrificed—nor is any reason given for the Oracle's decision to take Ezinma to Agbala's cave for an evening and then bring her home. A boy appears to be senselessly killed and a young girl taken on a seemingly meaningless journey. The point is, however, that man's understanding cannot encompass the ancestor's justice. When Okonkwo attempts to interfere with the Oracle's decision and prevent her from taking his daughter, the priestess warns: "Beware Okonkwo! . . . Beware of exchanging words with Agbala. Does a man speak when a god speaks? Beware!"

We can see, then, that while prenatal destiny and divine justice appear to be completely oppositional, even antithetical concepts, they are in fact complementary aspects of a logical, well-balanced system in which masculine and feminine values as well as individual and communal values are incorporated without any sense of contradiction. Okonkwo's tragedy is that he fails to recognize this. Like the tortoise in the folktale narrated by Ezinma's mother, Okonkwo tried to have everything his own way. His greed may not be as devious as that of the tortoise, who calls himself "All of you," but in the same fundamental sense of selfish desire he sets himself against the group. Likewise, he rejects everything that is feminine in his own nature and others; the group is left with no recourse but to reject him. On the other hand, the imposition of Christianity and the incursion of the European colonial administration afford a great shock to the system, but they do not shatter it.

To return to Burke's idea of novels as proverbs writ large, we can see that *Things Fall Apart* names a strategy for dealing with change. Divine justice and prenatal destiny, the basic components of this strategy, are also the woof and warp of an extremely flexible social fabric. Okonkwo, in his political conservatism and obsession with status, poses a threat to the fabric. Existing almost entirely on a physical, material plane, and concerned solely with maintaining the status quo, Okonkwo gets into a death lock with his *chi*. The strategy, and mainly the component of prenatal destiny, insures for society that survival is accepted over stasis. It is worth taking note that the last proverb in *Things Fall Apart* is about the bird who is always on the wing: "Men have learnt to shoot without missing their mark and I have learnt to fly without perching on a twig."

JOKO SENGOVA

Native Identity and Alienation in Richard Wright's Native Son *and Chinua Achebe's* Things Fall Apart: *A Cross-Cultural Analysis*

This essay deals with the use of "native" identity and "alienation" as literary themes in Richard Wright's novel *Native Son* and Chinua Achebe's pioneering African novel *Things Fall Apart*. I will attempt to examine how society's denial of native status and identity with full citizenship to Wright's chief protagonist, Bigger Thomas, and to people of his community and background, leads to alienation and certain violent responses to it. In a cross-cultural comparative analysis, I will similarly examine the case of Achebe's hero, Okonkwo. Okonkwo's character heralds and celebrates the theme of ethnic African identity, yet Okonkwo is shown to have inherent weaknesses that make him vulnerable to irrational and tragic behavior. As historical prototypes, Bigger and Okonkwo seem to share a common genesis: their African ancestry. As cross-cultural symbols of contemporary society, what motivates their behavior and personality is inherent in the state of affairs defined by their respective societies.

Conceived and written nearly two decades apart under what are in many ways different social conditions and cultural contexts, *Native Son* and *Things Fall Apart* present an interesting pair of "star" characters in their chief protagonists. Despite their strong portrayals as men with the ability and volition to influence or determine their own destinies, Bigger and Okonkwo are forced in the end to succumb to much greater agencies of power immanent

From *Mississippi Quarterly* 50, no. 2 (Spring 1997). © 1997 by the Mississippi State University Press.

in or incumbent upon their respective societies. In Bigger Thomas's case, this agency is immanent racism as Wright lived, saw, and sensed it himself, with all its accoutrements. In "How 'Bigger' Was Born," his lucid introduction to the novel, Wright wrote of Bigger, highlighting the complexity in social consciousness which informs Bigger's turbulent journey through life:

> Bigger, as I saw and felt him, was a snarl of many realities; he had in him many levels of life. . . .—What made Bigger's conscious- ness most complex was the fact that he was hovering unwanted between two worlds—between powerful America and his own stunted place in life.

Characterizing his own writing as communicating a state of mind reflecting a world of bitter sensations, and one akin to that in which Bigger finds himself, Wright's voice is unmistakable in the following lines from *Black Boy (American Hunger)* when the narrator Richard says, "My writing was my way of seeing, my way of living, my way of feeling; and who could change his sight, his notion of direction, his senses."

Okonkwo's world, on the other hand, at least as he saw it, comprised a single harmonious order and reality: one defined almost exclusively within the cultural boundary and traditional value system of his village, ethnic group, clan, *obi*, family, and extended family ties. Beyond these, nothing else was conceivably rational. This world view is also compatible with many precolonial systems not only in Africa but in other parts of the world that experienced a similar phase of human history. Okonkwo's world did not extend beyond the traditional realm of Igbo villages that constituted the basis of everyday interaction and contact among his people. The incumbent power of colonialism and its attendant Christian evangelism soon descends upon this traditional setting and promulgates its demise.

In a sense, therefore, both Bigger and Okonkwo are "native" sons in their communities who are challenged, albeit in different ways, by powerful forces which help not only to mould their characters but also to determine how they negotiate the circumstances and events of their immediate surroundings, indeed, their very lives. Wright's use of the term "native son" as title of the novel as well as symbolic reference to the chief protagonist, however, carries with it a strongly intended tone of irony and mockery which may not be quite the case with Achebe's novel. Nonetheless, the carefully designed plots and narrative movements in both novels successfully create interesting complexities in the two chief characters as they struggle to authenticate or uphold their nativism (used here in the sense of identity as native), as well as battle against forms of alienation that pose threats to it.

Such are the worrying challenges of our contemporary societies that deserve to be examined closely in literary discourse, whether their subject focus is couched in fiction or non-fiction.

The three main sections of my essay focus on the themes of native identity and alienation. First, I will discuss native identity with relation to my view of the relevant historical and socio-cultural backgrounds that inform the novels' narrative contexts and characterizations of the chief protagonists. I shall attempt to integrate into my discussion the theory of "creolization" and its accompanying "nativization" hypothesis as the terms currently apply in Creole linguistics, to explain the linguistic competencies of the chief protagonists. The subject of "Pidgin" and "Creole" languages has recently generated much interest in African diaspora studies and research. Second, I will base my analysis of the two main characters, Bigger Thomas and Okonkwo, upon the preceding background discussion, as well as upon the comparative perspective of three psychological concepts used as motifs in the structure of the narratives. In *Native Son*, Wright overtly links his narrative strands and advances character development upon these three notions: "Fear; Flight; and Fate." Achebe, similarly, infuses these concepts into his narrative plot, character formation and development, especially in the events that surround the rise and "fall" of his chief protagonist, Okonkwo. Finally, I will examine the role and use of language in creating the powerful plots and strong themes in both novels. This perspective so often overlooked by critics is of special interest to me, because I find a great deal of significance in the varieties of English utilized in both the narrative and the conversational styles of the novels. I will try to show that in addition to several literary tools and techniques available to these authors, there is also a principal concern and preoccupation with delivering the message by means of unique linguistic symbols and strategies representing the indigenous or "native" competencies of the novels' cultural settings, as well as the linguistic background of Bigger and Okonkwo.

Native Identity and the Creole Hypothesis

There is so much fluidity in the use of language today that we are frequently allowed the privilege to develop our own idiosyncrasies of style and lexical choice without necessarily transmitting a poor impression of our communicative ability to our interlocutors in any given speech event or situation. The words we choose as part of larger communicative utterances in speech may sometimes have quite controversial implications. One such word with a variety of manifestations is the word "native," used in reference to indigenous origin, ethnic/cultural identity, political status, linguistic heritage, and so forth. A similar term of controversy utilized specifically, in American English, is the word "nativism," often denoting ethnocentrism or intolerance to more recent immigrant populations. Contemporary American English, for instance, refers to America's indigenous population no longer as Indian/American Indian, but rather as "Native American." On the other hand, African Americans are yet to agree on whether the consensus term for their total or common identity shall be African-American, African American, Afro-American, or some other locution.

Elsewhere, for instance in Africa, where hundreds of languages may be spoken within a small geographic area, it is conventional wisdom and practice to identify first with one's so-called "native" language, before any other in the polyglotta inventory is acknowledged. It is interesting that people in those circumstances hardly ever make reference to themselves as "natives," in the sense Defoe or Conrad, for instance, would use the word in their fiction. Probably there is not a word equivalent to the English word "native" in many of those languages, but, rather, lexical items matching the designation of ethnicity, language, clan/lineage affiliation and so forth. Needless to say, earlier usage of the word at least on the African continent is associated with the precolonial and colonial eras on that continent, periods during which European-African contact was greatest.

As a result of the first of these contacts at a yet undetermined period in history, mixed cultures and languages were evolving alongside the commercial activities involving Europeans and Africans. Linguists speculate that many Atlantic Creole languages emerged as a result of such contact, especially along the West African coast, where trade was at one time heaviest. They speculate that first there was an early "pidginization" phase involving some type of makeshift jargon used purposely to facilitate inter-group communication during trade. This jargon or "pidgin," as it came to be known in Pidgin and Creole linguistics or, recently, by its even more fashionable term "creolistics," later developed into a full-blown "creole" language with a fully developed grammar, lexicon, and phonology of its own. This is even more so they claim if or when it had "birthed" first-generation "native" speakers who spoke it as their first language, identified with its mixed cultural heritage, and claimed it as their own ethnicity.

We find creole populations of this type in coastal Africa, the Caribbean, and the Americas. The Gullahs of the South Carolina-Georgia Low country (sometimes also called Geechee), the Krio of Sierra Leone, and West Indian Creole communities are probably all descendants of this unique cultural linguistic heritage. Scattered communities of Geechees can also be found in parts of Oklahoma and Brackettville, Texas.

How does all this apply to the historical and sociocultural contexts involved in Wright's and Achebe's novels? For one thing, each work is staged at the dawn of some important transformation in human relations both internally and externally. In America, especially in the Jim Crow South, racial segregation was still the order of the day when blacks and whites had no common arena or sphere in which to live their daily normal lives. At the same time, America was at the threshold of another socially disruptive world war. Achebe's novel is informed by the events of two closely related time frames: the advent of colonialism and Christianity on the one hand, and the ushering in of independence on the other. Achebe skillfully weaves these changes together as if they had occurred in a single time frame.

While blacks like the fictional Bigger Thomas struggled to gain recognition as true native sons of the soil in America, African blacks were engaged in a similar struggle for political emancipation and self-determination. In this sense, people of a common history and heritage were bound within the same time frame in a struggle to assert themselves as equal partners of their respective "native" identities. Bigger's identity crisis is precisely of a "New World" type that emerged from the historical blend of multiple cultures and heritages. Okonkwo's is of an "Old World" order, the very genesis of Bigger's world now transformed into new realities. Mocked and battered as if by design, Okonkwo believes he must cover every ground to defend it just as he always stood firm to defend his clan and *obi* against any intrusion from the outside. I shall discuss some cultural-linguistic nuances involved in this type of scenario later in the essay.

Native Sons and Fallen Aliens

It should be interesting not only to trace Fear, Flight and Fate in the life cycles of both Bigger Thomas and Okonkwo but also to show how each persona's role in the narrative is figured around the authorial constructs of native versus alien.

A vivid but striking image of Bigger Thomas to my mind is one of an unsupervised, exuberant, impulsive, "just don't giv' a damn" black kid, whose frighteningly poor socio-economic background and upbringing prepare him for one thing only: loathing intensely the citadel of power, including its putative population, its values, and other symbols that identify it. These, by Bigger's estimation, are the things that have stifled all his attempts to reach out for the "American pie," that same package of boundless opportunities promised to all in limitless abundance, regardless of race, creed, color, ethnicity, and so forth. Measured along these lines, society is to blame entirely on every count for Bigger's psychological disorientation, a condition which drives him nearly insane and leaves open to him the clear option: kill in order to show defiance and disdain for the things that stand and have stood in his way, the insurmountable barriers that force him to think he is merely a "no man," and nothing else.

Bigger's characterization appears to involve two distinct constructs: first, an almost parabolical dossier of multiple personalities identified as universal "Bigger Thomases," transcending geopolitical, racial and ethnic borders around the globe. At this level, Wright, in a prophetic voice, presents us with a troubled sub-population of malcontents, some of whom had already reached their point of explosion at the time he wrote, while others were still to come. About this universal prototype, Wright wrote in "How 'Bigger' Was Born," for example: "Bigger Thomas was not black all the time, he was white, too, and there were literally millions of him everywhere." But in the genesis of the novel's chief protagonist, we also find the bully, the black renegade, the "bad nigger," a mentally ill and defiant Negro, a point of view captured by John Reilly in his "Afterword" to Wright's book.

On a second level of characterization, however, that of the expressive and referential content of Bigger's textual communication, we see Bigger as he presents himself to us verbally in terms of an individual personality identifiable within the specific socio-cultural context of American society. In Book Three of the novel ("Fate"), for example, where according to Reilly, Bigger's chosen attorney, Max, is introduced "to organize Bigger's intuitions into systematic statements," Bigger attempts an explanation of why he felt such resentment against white America, a tune still sounded in the communication of contemporary African-American youth:

> I wanted to be an aviator once. But they wouldn't let me go to school where I was suppose' to learn it. They built a big school and then drew a line around it and said that nobody could go to it but those who lived within the line. They kept all the colored boys out.

This direct communication also echoes an important element in Bigger's first reaction to life beyond the line of segregation at the suburban Chicago home of the wealthy Daltons, where, in a set of twisted events, he murders his first victim, Mary Dalton. This is Book One, the first stage in Bigger's life cycle, which Wright designates as "Fear."

Bigger rejects his society not only at this systemic level but, in nearly the same way, at the individualized "natural supports" level: that of his immediate family, extended kinsfolk, and friends. He feels hopelessly claustrophobic in the filthy and dilapidated one-bedroom apartment he must share with his single-parent mother, his sister, Vera, and brother, Buddy, and often explodes in anger or seeks abode outside in the streets to hang out with his gang, Gus, Jack and G.H. During his incarceration for the murders he committed, Bigger refuses to be counseled by a known family preacher from his neighborhood, and rejects any voluntary friendships offered by whites. We first get a real feeling for Bigger's instinctive fear in his early confrontation with Gus, for failing to show up at the appointed time to rob Blum's store. It is here that Wright first paints the real picture of his terrified hero, twenty years old, and having managed to make it only to the eighth grade in school. As we will see, this assessment of Bigger's fear is similar to that portrayed in Achebe's Okonkwo:

> His confused emotions had made him feel instinctively that it would be better to fight Gus and spoil the plan of the robbery than to confront a white man with a gun. But he kept his knowledge of his fear thrust firmly down in him; his courage to live depended upon how successfully his fear was hidden from his consciousness.

Fear eventually has its last gripping hold on Bigger as he confronts the intoxicated and limp body of Mary Dalton after the spontaneous night out with her and her boyfriend Jan. Bigger's senses tell him that on this side of the fence no matter how favored a Negro boy has been in the benefactor's household, it is unacceptable to touch any belonging of his, especially those things human. Thus faced with the possibility of being discovered alone with Mary in her bedroom by the keen tactile senses of her blind mother, Bigger suffocates the girl as he tries to muffle any sounds she might make responding to her mother's call. "Fear," says the narrative voice, drove this perpetrator to murder and to the subsequent incineration of Mary's body to ward off any suspicions and eventual conviction for the murder. The narrator conveys the "cold facts" of Bigger's fears in a matter-of-fact tone of reporting through this concatenation of declarative clauses: "She was dead; she was white, she was a woman; he had killed her; he was black; he might be caught; if he were they would kill him."

But Bigger seems to overcome this fear once he has committed the first act of murder, even though he realizes that it will be only a matter of time before he is caught. And now he feels no remorse for what he has done. Rather, a new sense of elation, a sort of ascension to a higher consciousness now overtakes him. The narrative voice describes it this way in two separate internal monologues reflecting the double murders of Mary Dalton and Bigger's black girlfriend, Bessie Mears, whose violent killing at the hands of one she trusted is equally shocking to the reader. This is Book Two, the section titled "Flight":

> In all of his life these two murders were the most meaningful
> things that had ever happened to him. . . . and never in all his life,
> with this black skin of his, had the two worlds, thought and
> feeling, will and mind, aspiration and satisfaction been together;
> never had he felt a sense of wholeness.

The final solution to Bigger Thomas's turbulent life is depicted in Book Three, the section titled "Fate," where he confronts justice for his crimes, but more so for the murder of Mary Dalton than the equally grue-some killing of his girlfriend, Bessie Mears. In a series of futile defense hear-ings during Bigger's trial, his attorney, Max from "the Labor Defenders," leads him and the court on a path of self-vindication by blaming the crimes not squarely on the perpetrator but on the wrong-doings of society. But state prosecutor Bentley, who is also running for re-election, is not to be robbed of the opportunity to validate the status quo, the very thing he represents on behalf of the people. Max bases one of his pleas for mercy for his client upon what he calls "the fundamental problem involved, a background of oppres-sion. This boy comes from an oppressed people. Even if he's done wrong, we must take that into consideration."

Of course, mercy is never bestowed and Bigger faces the full penalty of the law for his crimes. Even at this stage in his life, Bigger cuts the figure of a "loner," in spite of the fact that he has a poor, caring mother, a loving sister and brother from whom he is distant throughout. Bigger is raised, or rather grows up in a poor, single-parent, African-American family, an appropriate psychological climate for children's and adolescents' severe emotional chal-lenges and mental illness.

As he goes to his death still fearful of its actual unknown mechanics, Bigger hysterically asks Max what it is like to die. He seeks "knowledge of how to die" as if he would then discover "knowledge of how to live," not real-izing that the complementarity of both lies precisely in a fundamentally meaningful life well-lived alongside those with whom one has co-existed. Max tells him, "Men die alone," just as they are born alone, and this truth will go along with Bigger Thomas all the way to the electric chair.

Achebe's Okonkwo

Chinua Achebe's *Things Fall Apart* is critically acclaimed one of Africa's best pioneering literary works, as well as one of its major critical responses to colonialism and the Christian evangelization of African peoples. The hero of the novel, Okonkwo of Umuofia village, offers the central challenge to the new European politics and religion, since he champions traditional African Igbo customs and values. He lives within his community and runs his family exclusively on those precepts. Anything outside the axioms and accepted ways of his native traditions, especially its oracular precepts, is absolutely unacceptable to him.

Like Wright, Achebe writes a three-part story in his novel, which I think we can compare with Wright's in thematic structure and movement based upon the three concepts: "Fear," "Flight," and "Fate," involving the chief protagonist, Okonkwo. Like Bigger Thomas, Okonkwo commits murders which lead to his eventual downfall. In his case, there are three of them: first the ritualistic killing of the hostage boy, Ikemefuna "—a lad of fifteen—," surrendered to Umuofia by the neighboring village of Mbaino in recompense for the reported murder of "a daughter of Umuofia" by inhabitants of that village; second, the second-degree murder of a clansman, the sixteen-year-old son of Ezeudu, a renowned village warrior; and third, the somewhat lone, vigilante murder of one of the white district commissioner's court messengers in what Okonkwo believed to be a defense of his village of Umuofia. All three murders are thematically charged with motifs parallel with the three concepts: Fear, Flight and Fate.

In Okonkwo, Achebe creates a physically strong male character with a stout heart, one who is unwilling to have or make any excuses for physical weaknesses as he perceives them in his own father, Unoka, and his son, Nwoye. Those are abnormalities that he associates with women. He is at once both the village champion wrestler, winner of many (*ilo*) arena titles, as well as vigorous tiller of the soil who faithfully brings home fruitful harvests to sustain his large family. Seeing and believing in himself as supreme father figure, he is also sole custodian of his family and household or compound, and he administers all therein with a blend of very firm hands and paternal caring and nurturing. Perhaps, of all Achebe's characters in this novel, Okonkwo is the most steadfast and glued to his tradition, especially in following its precepts closely, as if by the book. Together with his quick and irate spirit, these consuming qualities will plummet Okonkwo into one skirmish after another until his final *nadir*.

And underneath all his greatness and power, Okonkwo, like some real life contemporary archetypes, has his weaknesses, the greatest of which is "Fear." Fear of falling prey to the things he views as undesirable in men constantly haunts him. Ironically, in order to avoid such a fall, he conducts himself through a channeled course of self-destruction and tragedy. It is such a pervading consciousness that drives him, for instance, when he pulls his machete and strikes a blow, first killing Ikemefuna and later the court messenger. The same temperament drives him to spousal abuse and the near fatal shooting of his youngest wife. Early in Part One Achebe captures the totality of his hero's drive to the impulsive:

> Perhaps down in his heart Okonkwo was not a cruel man. But his whole life was dominated by fear, the fear of failure and of weakness. It was deeper and more intimate than the fear of evil and capricious gods and of magic, the fear of the forest, and the forces of nature, malevolent, red in tooth and claw. Okonkwo's fear was greater than these. It was not external but lay deep within himself. It was the fear of himself, lest he should be found to resemble his father—a playmate had told him that his father was *agbala*—another name for a woman—also a man who had taken no title. And so Okonkwo was ruled by one passion—to hate everything that his father Unoka had loved. One of those things was gentleness and another was idleness.

In another instance, the narrative voice carves a *machismo* image of Okonkwo, nonetheless flavored with the human quality of love inside him. His relationship with the lad Ikemefuna is a mixture of hidden emotion and caring with an iron will to resist bending the laws of tradition decreed by "The oracle of the Hills and Caves." Thus, even though Okonkwo "inwardly—became very fond of the boy—," the narrator says: "Okonkwo never showed any emotion openly, unless it be the emotion of anger. To show emotion was a sign of weakness, the only thing worth demonstrating was strength."

When it is time for the boy's roadside murder, Okonkwo goes to work easily with the rest of the village team to whom the gruesome task is assigned as a duty. He totally ignores the advice of Ogbuefi Ezeudu, the oldest man in his quarter of the village, not to participate in the act. Ezeudu, whose son will become Okonkwo's second murder victim, puts the warning this way:

> That boy calls you father. Do not bear a hand in his death.—Yes, Umuofia has decided to kill him. The Oracle of the Hills and the Caves has pronounced it. They will take him outside Umuofia as is the custom, and kill him there. But I want you to have nothing to do with it. He calls you father.

Okonkwo's "Flight" comes, in fact, not after the murder of Ikemefuna but after that of Ezeudu's sixteen-year-old son, whom he shoots accidentally at the elder statesman's funerary celebrations. He gets very little admonishment for participating in the killing of the boy Ikemefuna, who had not only lived in his custody but had also cultivated a friendship and sibling relationship with Okonkwo's first son, Nwoye, who was about his own age. Nwoye's growing resentment toward his father for taking part in Ikemefuna's murder becomes instrumental in making him decide to become one of the village's earliest Christian converts. For the accidental slaying of Ezeudu's son, Okonkwo and his entire family are sent into exile for seven years to his maternal village of Mbanta. The narrator tells it this way in the closing chapter of Part One:

> The only course open to Okonkwo was to flee from the clan. It was a crime against the earth goddess [Ani] to kill a clansman, a man who committed it must flee from the land. The crime was of two kinds, male and female. Okonkwo had committed the female, because it had been inadvertent. He could return to the clan after seven years.

Unlike Bigger's hounded flight from justice, however, Okonkwo's flight is supernaturally ordained by the putative spirituality of the earth goddess, Ani. It is a flight designed by traditional religious order to achieve positive outcomes, namely, Okonkwo's spiritual and social rehabilitation to resume his place in society after seven years has elapsed. Bigger, on the other hand, stood no chance of rehabilitation. He would only pay dearly for his crimes according to the penal code of American justice. Whether there is any parity in the gravity of murders committed by both men is again an issue of sociocultural relativity, yet universal human standards of morality often reject the taking away of human life, no matter where or what the circumstances are.

Once Okonkwo is pronounced an exile, his own "Fate" is sealed in the hands of the very traditions he fosters. I think the beginning of Okonkwo's end is signaled by the symbolic cleansing of the land "which Okonkwo had polluted with the blood of a clansman." It is men from the quarter of the murder victim's father who carry out the ritual of appeasement of the earth goddess, Ani, the ritual itself resembling an act of war, albeit aimed at rehabilitating the murderer:

> They set fire to his houses, demolished his red walls, killed his animals and destroyed his barn. It was the justice of the earth goddess, and they were merely her messengers. They had no hatred in their hearts against Okonkwo. His greatest friend, Obierika, was among them. They were merely cleansing the land which Okonkwo had polluted with the blood of a clansman.

Henceforth, Okonkwo will be facing a new force, an "alien" adversary posing a totally new challenge to the old order. In the eyes of this new order and those among people who embrace or welcome its new religion and form of government, the old ways now seem repressive and backward. As Christianity firmly gains ground, its most enthusiastic followers become the outcast *osu*, men ostracized and alienated from mainstream society by traditional law and religion. The *osu* are important in the total transformation of this African society because it is one of them who initiates the violation of one of the clan's most sacred laws: "killing the sacred [royal] python, the emanation of the god of water." This incident causes a direct confrontation between the forces of African tradition headed by Okonkwo himself, and those of early colonialism and Christianity. What complicates events for men of the old order is that the Christians have a formidable political collaborator in the new colonial administration which backs the expansion and evangelism of Christianity all the way.

Okonkwo's final tragedy is staged in Book Three, when, amidst a number of calculated losses in his socio-political status among the clans, he begins a steady fall toward self-destruction. These losses are calculated in the narrative in terms of three domains: loss in spiritual and political power; loss in military prowess and leadership, the very weapon needed to fight against "the new religion"; and a loss in terms of setbacks in gaining "the highest titles in the clan." On the other hand, some of these losses translate as gains for others in the clan who would have been no match for Okonkwo if not for his years in exile. Thus, Okonkwo's ordained flight took a heavier toll from him than his society's rehabilitative agenda and its intended outcomes. The narrative voice measures Okonkwo's exile from his clan parabolically, in terms of quite realistic losses in traditional power and stature:

> Seven years was a long time to be away from one's clan. A man's place was not always waiting for him. As soon as he left, someone else rose and filled it. The clan was like a lizard; if it lost its tail it soon grew another.—Okonkwo knew these things. He knew that he had lost his place among the nine masked spirits who administered justice in the clan. He had lost the chance to lead his warlike clan against the new religion, which, he was told, had gained ground. He had lost the years in which he might have taken the highest titles in the clan.

Okonkwo finally meets with death at his own hands after hacking to death a uniformed messenger sent to break up a meeting he and others are having about opposing the new order and expelling its perpetrators from the community. Okonkwo hangs himself from a tree behind his compound rather than be subjected to the white man's own form of justice: hanging by his own rather than the hangman's rope. In committing suicide, however, Okonkwo commits another sin against the earth goddess. By his manner of death, he had desecrated the land, sanctuary for earth goddess Ani. For this, he will also have to pay another severe penalty according to custom. One of the men on the search party looking for the obvious murder suspect in the killing of the court messenger explains it this way to the District Commissioner: "It is against our custom. It is an abomination for a man to take his own life. It is an offense against the Earth, and a man who commits it will not be buried by his clansmen. His body is evil, and only strangers may touch it."

But Okonkwo seems to maintain his former stature in life even in death. In the final eulogy in his honor, his dear friend of many years, Obierika (technically with Achebe's authorial permission), blames European encroachment, symbolized by the District Commissioner's presence, for his friend's tragic end: "That man was one of the greatest men in Umuofia. You drove him to kill himself; and now he will be buried like a dog. . . ."

Thus, whereas Bigger Thomas contemplates suicide briefly and then dismisses it after he realizes the futility of Max's defense strategies, Okonkwo uses it as last resort to convey a strong message about his strength and character. Yet, in a sense, each man accepts his fate and comes to meet its consequences without a grudge against himself or others.

The Language of Native Identity and Alienation

Two varieties of English exist in the textual context of Wright's novel: first, there is what one might call "standard" English, the type of English approximating the speech of the educated as well as the majority of mainstream Americans; and second, levels of stereotypical "Black Vernacular English."

In *Native Son*, the dichotomy in communicative behavior is as obvious as daylight. Everyone in the novel speaks in the standard vogue, including the narrative voice in its multiple manifestations, except for Bigger and other blacks. But it is the variety of Black English which Bigger speaks that catches the reader's attention as well as its uniqueness as part of an autonomous linguistic system, a creole language. I am not sure, for example, how much Wright himself knew about the creole features of tense and aspect which recur in Bigger's syntax, especially among interlocutors of his race. This variety of Black English may be compared to what linguists refer to as "decreolized Gullah," the remnant of a once viable means of communication among black slave populations of predominant Southern provenance. The following are examples of some creole features found in the speech of Bigger and his "native" speech community. Sentences under [a] are from the novel; those under [b] are Sierra Leone Krio equivalents showing similarities in structure between the two. The creole features are also shown in italics and labeled with linguistic descriptors:

1. [a].   You done said that ten times
   [b].   Yu don se dat ten tem (Perfect aspect)
          "You have said that ten times."
2. [a].   *You get the job?*
   [b].   Yu get di job? (Question without inversion)
          "Did you get the job?"
3. [a].   *You in it* as deep as me
   [b].   Yu de insai de dip wan lek mi (Zero Copula marking in [a])
          "You are (neck-deep) in this as well as I am."
4. [a].   —We thank thee for *the food you done placed* before us—
   [b].   Wi tel yu tenki fo di it we yu don put bifo wi (Zero Relative marker Plus perfect marker in [a]).
          "We thank you for the food you have provided us."

In the following passage however (from Book Three "Fate"), Bigger's reflective statement to his attorney, Max, about himself and his crimes, has a more popular syntactic flavor to it. It is typically contracted or reduced speech splattered with the free use of double negation and unmatched agreement rules, often frowned upon as unsophisticated, and not easily associated with race, but, rather, with socio-economic status. The fact that Bigger can switch from a style typical of utterances in 1 through 4 to this style and register is indicative of the linguistic ability of members of pluralistic speech communities to "code-switch" from one medium of speech to another, be it language internal or external:

> 5.—Really I never wanted to hurt nobody. That's the truth, Mr. Max. I hurt folks' cause I felt I had to; that's all. They was crowding me too close; they wouldn't give me no room. Lots of times, I tried to forget 'em, but I couldn't. They wouldn't let me—

Nonetheless, these varieties present an interesting case of language continuity reflected in the examples shown above. That continuity appears to favor the argument that African-American speech patterns contain certain residual features of some African languages, retained in various forms through a cultural linguistic process such as creolization.

What remains problematic about such speech varieties no matter their socio-cultural context is their non-acceptability as means of communication by the mainstream societies in which they are found. Several examples abound from speech communities all over the world but the specific case of Bigger Thomas is sufficient to elucidate our American situation. Three oddities based upon a speaker's variety of English are often perceived in American communication: non-standard usage (sometimes synonymous with "sub-standard"), racial/ethnic/linguistic origin, and socio-economic status. Any variety of English that exhibits features of phonology, syntax, and idiomatic usage that are unacceptable to speakers of mainstream American English is often classified as one or (in some instances) all of the above oddities. Thus bilingual citizens/residents, the less educated, as well as many recent immigrants from non-English-speaking countries may fall easily into this or that category. Bigger seems to fit in all three categories, because he is black, semi-literate/educated, and woefully low in socio-economic standing. At once, his social status is determined by these factors. He does not have the necessary linguistic tools of socio-political or cultural empowerment such as Okonkwo has to negotiate his social status. His communicative repertoire reflects, as Wright himself puts it, "his own stunted place in life," from which there is no viable platform to negotiate his social destiny. After all, all he speaks is "Black Vernacular English," a code totally incomprehensible and unacceptable in arenas such as aviation, where Bigger once aspired to be. Okonkwo's empowerment, on the other hand, emanates largely from his cultural linguistic skills among those with whom he has to negotiate his social destiny.

Language in *Things Fall Apart*

Language takes on a totally different meaning in Achebe's novel. It is the very life-line and spine of the narrative, and weaves carefully its character portrayal, thematic movement and plot from a dual perspective: African and European. Achebe's language, therefore, attempts to capture everything from the visible ecology and climate of the environment to cultural titles, names and axioms. Though written in fine narrative English, the novel never ceases to be African in its cultural semantic form and content. Critics often ask why Achebe did not simply write the novel in Igbo since it abounds with codes and images that are predominantly African and not English. Of these codes and images, it is Achebe's and the Igbo people's penchant for using proverbs and parables which, even when translated into English, never quite lose their African flavor and cultural nuances. I find these most captivating to read in this novel.

A proverb is a didactic maxim or saying based upon principles and ideals held by a community or group such as an ethnic group and is intended to influence behavior. Among many African societies, these proverbs are considered vital in communication, especially in their conciseness, and are often complementary with riddles and parables. Here are some examples of proverbs that point specifically to the three themes (fear, flight, and fate) in the novel:

6. —A toad does not run in the daytime for nothing—
7. —an old woman is always uneasy when dry bones are mentioned in a proverb.
8. —A chick that will grow into a cock can be spotted the very day it hatches.

In these proverbs, and many others in the novel, the referential agency is animate. In 6 and 8, they are animals, whereas in 7, it is human, "an old woman," a repository of reverence and links with the spirit world. But no matter the overtly named agency, proverbs are aimed at society. Okonkwo's inner fears over certain weaknesses he associates with his deceased father, Unoka, as well as his son Nwoye, seem to be highlighted in all these proverbs. Although in its literal sense the toad refers to "the palm-wine tapper, Obiako, who suddenly gave up his trade," for fear of falling off a pine tree and killing himself, its indirect referent is Okonkwo. Abandoning his trade meant a sort of "flight" as a result of a rumored warning said to have been ordained by the oracle concerning Obiako's life. So the agency of opaque reference in the proverb is Okonkwo himself. It is he who should beware of some unnamed danger lurking somewhere in the alley.

Similarly, reference in the same context to Obiako's father, who had the same frailties as Unoka, makes Okonkwo uneasy in the second proverb. The chick in 8 is symbolic of the "fate" of Nwoye as his father sees it—or, perhaps, of his destiny, marked early in life, as a weakling who would desert his father's manly ways and join the Christian missionaries in spreading their faith among his people. There are dozens of such proverbs, riddles, parables and text stories that depict Igbo culture. Their style of written English is literal, yet so fluid that they are easily comprehensible to a non-"native" Igbo reader. For instance, responding to his friend Obierika's criticism of him for participating in the ritual murder of the boy, Ikemefuna, Okonkwo says the following proverb to defend his act as well as justify it as one ordained by supernatural power:

9. The earth cannot punish me for obeying her messenger—A child's fingers are not scalded by a piece of hot yam which its mother puts into its palm.

The reader, who knows by now that *Ani* is earth goddess in this Igbo culture, understands without difficulty the meaning of the first line of this proverb. Similarly, yam-like palm oil is recognizable as the Igbo staple vegetable from several references to food culture in the novel. Beyond its literal meaning, therefore, the proverb itself tells of a parent-child bonding at a higher level in this culture: one between deity and human being. Just as a mother is nurturer and protector of her child, so is Mother Earth (*Ani* in the Igbo context) and all her children, the Igbo people. Certainly, this relationship finds parallels in many of the world's religions and cultures.

Perhaps an even more universal sociological reality is portrayed in the next proverb, spoken by Obierika when he leads a group of supporters on a friendly visit to their great ally Okonkwo, during his second year in exile. The proverb, both literally and figuratively, addresses the issue of "timeliness" or time-appropriate behavior in most human interactions, probably at all levels. It warns its intended audience in proverbial yet context-sensitive language: do not intrude in a newly wed couple's honeymoon agenda, while in its deeper sense, it offers a caveat about how we should arrange our affairs and follow protocol in social interaction with the dignity of all parties concerned strictly kept in mind:

10. Never make an early morning appointment with a man who has just married a new wife.

There are other African cultural markers in the novel such as time indicators: "the two or three moons after the harvest," indicating a time lapse in the agricultural cycle; "three of four markets," indicative of a cycle of commercial events resembling "flea markets" in America, and so forth. All kinds of traditional artifacts and symbols are given their Igbo names to signify their cultural meanings appropriately, and the author provides a useful glossary of key Igbo words and phrases that are significant for the reader's understanding of themes. Above all, it is the significance among the Igbo of the art of engaging in discourse and communication similarly common to numerous African cultures that Achebe also wishes to highlight in his own work, in addition to practicing his career at the time as a journalist and broadcaster. One proverb which states this unequivocally in the novel is found in its opening pages:

11. Having spoken plainly so far, Okoye said the next half a

dozen sentences in proverbs. Among the Ibo the art of conversation is regarded very highly, and proverbs are the palm-oil with
which words are eaten—

As complex as it may read, this proverb marks in a literal sense a significant
aspect of West African food culture, the main ingredient of sauce dishes
that accompany the staple. Not only is palm oil eaten on a daily basis, but
it also has religious significance in mediating with spirits and supernatural
forces through food offerings. In its figurative use here, it is a complementary vehicular ingredient to words in the mediation of social intercourse
through discourse. Thus, the parity of this equation of proverbs and palm
oil conveys to the reader important elements of Igbo culture the understanding of which is equally important in appreciating Achebe's overall
message: that this is a world of dualities, where things must stand together
for or against one another.

To what extent is such semiotic system of putative Igbo culture
reflected in Okonkwo's own style of communication in the novel? First, as a
firmly established member and sort of celebrity in his culture, Okonkwo is
part and parcel of this traditional system and equally well versed in its art of
verbal communication and discourse. This culturally oratorical ability is
displayed equally in communications with his clan and village leaders, his
spiritual peers and superiors, his three wives and eleven children, outsiders,
and so forth. Such communication is often designed and delivered appropriately, in the form and content that suits its purpose as well as context. Thus,
as empowered as he is, Okonkwo must carefully manipulate his communicative style and vocabulary to suit gods and goddesses, the old and the young
(strictly based on gender), and so forth.

Below, examples 12 through 15 attempt to capture this hierarchy of
communication. In 12, Okonkwo is engaged in a greeting formula that
includes the ceremonial breaking and sharing of kola nut with wealthy village
leader Nwakibie, with whom he must first establish some sort of "phatic
communion" before embarking on the real purpose of his visit, to ask for a
loan of yam seeds to cultivate his farm.

Then in 13, as he prepares to leave his maternal village of Mbanta after
seven years in exile, Okonkwo expresses extensive gratitude to all for their
great hospitality toward his family and himself. In 14, Okonkwo tries to stir
adults of his rank in Mbanta to support and engage in a rebellion against
what he sees as a disruptive band of Christians tearing his people and their
lives apart. Finally, in 15, Okonkwo speaks to his other sons, expressing
disappointment over his oldest son Nwoye's desertion of his family and
village to become a member and follower of the new Christian religion (he
had also taken a new baptismal name, Isaac):

12. He presented a kola nut and an alligator pepper—He broke it saying:—'We shall all live. We pray for life, children, a good harvest and happiness. You will have what is good for you and I will have what is good for me. Let the kite perch and let the eagle perch too. If one says no to the other, let his wing break—I have come to you for help—I have cleared a farm but have no yams to sow. I know what it is to ask a man to trust another with his yams, especially these days when young men are afraid of hard work. I am not afraid of work. The lizard that jumped from the high iroko tree to the ground said he would praise himself if no one else did. I began to fend for myself at an age when most people still suck at their mother's breasts. If you give me some yam seeds I shall not fail you.'

13. 'My mother's [i.e., "you"] people have been good to me and I must show my Gratitude—I beg you to accept this little kola— It is not to pay you back for all you did for me in these seven years. A child cannot pay for its mother's milk. I have only called you together because it is good for kinsmen to meet.'

14. 'Let us not reason like cowards—If a man comes into my hut and defecates on the floor, what do I do? Do I shut my eyes? No! I take a stick and break his head. That is what a man does. These people are daily pouring filth over us, and Okeke says we should pretend not to see.'

15. He sent for the five sons and they came and sat in his *obi*. The youngest of them was four years old.—'You have all seen the great abomination of your brother. Now he is no longer my son or your brother. I will only have a son who is a man, who will hold his head up among my people. If any one of you prefers to be a woman, let him follow Nwoye now while I am alive so that I can curse him. If you turn against me when I am dead I will visit you and break your neck.'

In all these quotations, Achebe shows how firmly entrenched in his culture and language system Okonkwo is. From this position of empowerment, he is literally equipped to handle anyone, insider or outsider, and does not have to change or adapt to a new system of communication to survive. If anything, it is the stranger, in this sense the "white man," who must adopt new strategies of communication in order to achieve his political and religious goals. Thus, as the new missionaries and administrators arrive in the villages, they must bring along with them able interpreters to facilitate communication with the "natives," many of whom, though "natives" themselves, may not be as competent in the Igbo dialect of Okonkwo's people. This is clearly the case in the story about the missionaries' arrival in Umuofia, as Okonkwo hears it from the lips of his friend Obierika in Mbanta during the second year of his exile:

> 16. When they all had gathered, the white man began to speak to them. He spoke through an interpreter who was an Ibo man, though his dialect was different and harsh to the ears of Mbanta. Many people laughed at his dialect and the way he used words strangely. Instead of saying "myself" he always said "my buttocks."

Then with added mockery to this missed communication, the people of Umuofia begin to make jokes built around the buttocks phenomenon, first about the white man's inability to speak Igbo, and second, the interpreter's own poor rendition of the "God-Jesus Christ" distinction often made in Christianity:

> 17. 'Your buttocks understand our language,' said someone light-heartedly and the crowd laughed.
> 18. 'Your buttocks said he had a son,' said the joker. 'So he must have a wife and all of them must have buttocks.'

As a native African, I can myself relate to this linguistic situation of missed communicative events where one's ability to understand the nuances of another language can easily lead to incorrect expressions, which can sometimes be amusing or offensive. I am reminded of one particular example in Mende language greeting, which when uttered with the wrong sounds can easily result in offensive language. Compare the two Mende sentences below: 19 is acceptable but not 20. A simple difference in the initial consonants in the last word in each sentence makes the crucial difference in meaning.

> 19. Gboo bi gaahu?—'How are you/how do you feel?' (Literally what is in your bones?)
> *20. Gboobi gbaahu?—'What is between your legs?'

Thus equipped with such advantages of language competence, Okonkwo's cultural situation is less burdensome than Bigger's, both in establishing the legitimacy of his native identity and in meeting any challenges that pose formidable threats to it.

Conclusion

The inherent thrust of this essay has been on the significance of the antithetical concepts of "native" identity and "alienation" embedded in the structure of *Native Son* and *Things Fall Apart*. Given the systemic issues of racism, colonialism, Christianity, and traditional African cultures, these antithetical concepts are indeed a reality. They constitute major dichotomous entities of what Achebe himself calls "a world of dualities," no matter what we think of them. For Achebe then, these were realities which the colonizer failed to perceive during his planned agenda of colonization and evangelism, just as he did with slavery. Ironically, even Bigger and Okonkwo failed to recognize such a duality in the patterning of life. Like the white man, they too failed to see a world beyond theirs, and, together, they each must pay dearly for their calculated visions and realities. Perhaps the concept of duality envisioned by Achebe is vividly portrayed in the words of Okonkwo's uncle, Uchendu, during their reflective conversation with Obierika and others visiting Mbanta:

21. 'There is no story that is not true,' said Uchendu. 'The world has no end, and what is good among one people is an abomination with others—.'

On the other hand, Wright's point of view seems to visualize a world in which the Bigger Thomases and their folks are entrapped, with very little hope of escape. Indeed, one of Bigger's greatest setbacks is an atrophied communication system, a less sophisticated and acceptable sub-code of the oppressor's language system over which he can show no mastery. So, as for a caged prey, the only option is to hit hard (in violent terms) against this enemy when the opportunity arises. Unlike Achebe, however, Wright's firsthand experiences with racism could make him see all of its sociopolitical dimensions, especially as a carefully programmed systemic offensive against his people. For Achebe, everywhere such an offensive rears its head, "something else will stand against it." Thus, alongside Christianity and the new politics must stand the old ways of African culture and tradition. These two men, however, share something in common: their celebrated roles as story-tellers of things witnessed, not romanticized from their individual fantasies. For it is stories of those things which survive for future generations and reveal the way things were that they are both so willing to tell.

Chronology

1930   Born November 16 in the village of Ogidi in eastern Nigeria to Janet Hoegbunam Achebe and Isaiah Okafor Achebe, a catechist for the Church Missionary Society. The name Chinua is an abbreviation for Chinualumogu ("may God fight on my behalf"), in effect a prayer and a philosophical statement reflecting a belief in and desire for stability in life.

1935   The Achebe family returns to Ogidi. The storytelling tradition now exists side by side with book reading sessions in Society's school. Later on, when looking back at his early days, Chinua remembers living in two worlds at once – the Christian world of hymns in church and the poetry of the litany, and the traditional religion of the Igbo culture, where masquerades and festival foods play an important role.

1936   Achebe begins school at St. Philip's Central School, Akpakaogwe Ogidi. The school itself was constructed of mud blocks in the shape of a T and surrounded by mango trees which provided snacks for the children. After a week in religious class, the Rev. Nelson Ezekwesili sends him to a higher infant school because of his intelligence.

1938   Achebe learns English. He is in Standard Two when World War II begins.

1939–43   Chinua is taught by the inspirational S. N. C. Okonkwo from Standard Two upwards. He excels in reading English and, among other things, earns Okonkwo's respect for his knowledge of the Igbo version of the Bible. Among the books Chinua reads during his primary school days are *A Midsummer Night's Dream* and *Pilgrim's Progress*.

1944   Chinua enters Government College, Umuahia, one of the best schools in West Africa. The new principal, named Hicks, said to be a kind and gentle soul, carried on the tradition of Robert Fisher, emphasizing a careful selection of qualified boys for admission and academic excellence. The boys are expected to lead a very organized life, at times at the pace of a military school.

In late 1944, William Simpson replaces Hicks as principal. Simpson, a Cambridge graduate who has spent about twenty-six years in the colonial service in Nigeria, was dedicated to improving the already high academic standards at Umuahia. During his tenure, Simpson introduces the "Text-book Act" which states certain times during which text-book reading is not permissible, leaving sports, physical exercise or time to become acquainted with the extensive college library, as the only alternative. Chinua benefits from the Simpson "method," reading such books as *Up from Slavery, Gulliver's Travels, The Prisoner of Zenda, Oliver Twist, Tom Brown's Schooldays* and *Treasure Island*.

Among Chinua's professors are Adrian P. L. Slater, who teaches logic by emphasizing scientific methods of observation and experimentation, and inculcates the habits of writing correct English, and Charles Low, an Australian educated at Melbourne and Oxford universities, both a poet and playwright, and who has practically memorized *Paradise Lost*.

1948–53   In 1948, Achebe enrolls at University College, Ibadan, as a member of the first class to attend this new school. Although his original intention is to study medicine, Achebe soon switches to English literary studies with a syllabus that is almost identical to the honors degree program at the University of London. Towards the end of his career at Ibadan, Chinua is greatly influenced by the lectures of Alex Rodgers on Thomas Hardy's *Far from the Madding Crowd*.

1950   As a student in the Faculty of Arts, Chinua begins to express himself as a writer. He contributes stories, essays and sketches to the *University Herald*. These stories are later published in 1972 in *Girls at War and Other Stories*.

1953   Achebe graduates from the University College, Ibadan. The degree examinations reflect the strict and rigid desire of the university to maintain the highest standards. By the time he graduates, his intellectual horizon and social understanding have been enhanced through his interaction with a variety of Nigerians and foreigners.

1954   Begins teaching English at the Merchants of Light School at Oba under the supervision of A. E. D. Mgbemena. As the school was in its infancy, the quarters for staff and students were inadequate. The dormitories were made of mud and coated with cement and there was at that time neither electricity nor piped water—the students had to fetch the water from either a neighboring village or a stream. His tenure at the Merchants of Light Secondary School is brief. About four months after his arrival, he receives a letter from the Nigerian Broadcasting Service inviting him for an interview which is quickly followed by an offer of employment as senior broadcasting officer from the around the middle of 1954.

1955   In the January issue of *Radio Times*, Chinua and Angela Beattie receive acknowledgment for their role in educating their listeners.

1956   Early in the year, Chinua Achebe and Bisi Onabanjo, editor of the *Radio Times*, are nominated by the NBS, Lagos to attend the BBC Staff School in London organized for participants from Africa, Australia, New Zealand, Canada and Asia. The training was intended to emphasize "hands-on" experience within the UK Broadcasting system.

1957   Goes to London to embark on a twelve-year career as producer for the British Broadcasting Corporation Staff School where he meets the British novelist and literary critic Gilbert Phelps.

1958   *Things Fall Apart* published in London: Heinemann; and in New York: McDowell, Obolensky (1959). The novel is published two years before Nigerian independence is gained in 1960.

1960   Writes two short stories, one entitled "Chike's School Days" which appears in the *Rotarian*, and "Akueke," which is published in the anthology *Reflections*, edited by Frances Ademola, who was working at the NBS in Lagos as head of Talks. Also publishes *No Longer at Ease* in London: Heinemann and in New York: McDowell, Obolensky (1961).

1961   Achebe appointed director of the Voice of Nigeria (external broadcasting) by the Nigerian Broadcasting Corporation. On December 10, he marries Christie Chinwe Okoli at Ibadan.

1962   Birth of his first child, a daughter named Chinelo, on July 11. *The Sacrificial Egg, and Other Short Stories* published in Onitsha, Nigeria: Etudo (1962).

1964   Birth of his second child, a boy named Ikechukwu. His name means "through the might of God."

    Arrow of God published in London: Heinemann; in New York: Day, 1967; revised, London: Heinemann (1974).

    Publishes "The Role of the Writer in the New Nation," *Nigeria Magazine*, June 1964.

    In September, Chinua participates in the first Commonwealth Literature Conference to be held at the University of Leeds where he presents a paper on "The Novelist as Teacher."

1966   *A Man of the People* published in January in London: Heinemann and New York: Day. Date of publication closely coincides with the first military coup d'état in Nigeria. Achebe resigns from his job with the Nigerian Broadcasting Corporation due to the increasing persecution of Nigerians and returns to his homeland.

    Chike and the River published in Cambridge: Cambridge University Press (1966).

1967   On May 24, his third child, a son named Chidi, is born. His name means "There is a God." The Eastern Region of Nigeria declares itself an independent state called Biafra following a thirty-month civil war. Achebe gives unwavering support for the young nation, so much so that he declines an offer by Northwestern University to teach in the Gwendolen M. Carter Program of African Studies.

1968   Achebe declines a second offer, made by letter dated January 9, from Gwendolen Carter. On August 25, delivers paper on "The African Writer and the Biafran Cause" to a political science seminar at Makere University College, Kampala.

1969   Serves as Chairman of National Guidance Committee at Umuahia. In January, writes a poem entitled "Air Raid," a requiem on a devastating air strike at Umuahia.

1970   On March 7, his fourth child, Nwando, is born. Her name, which means "a child under which the parents would shelter," signifies their anticipation of a time after the war.

1971   *Beware, Soul Brother, and Other Poems* published in Enugu, Nigeria: Nwankwo-Ifejika; revised and enlarged edition, London: Heinemann, 1972; and Enugu, Nigeria: Nwamufe, 1972; republished as *Christmas in Biafra and Other Poems*. Garden City, N.Y.: Anchor/Doubleday (1973).

Publishes *The Insider: Stories of War and Peace from Nigeria*, edited by Achebe and others. Enugu, Nigeria: Nwankwo-Ifejika.

1972   Publishes *Girls at War and Other Stories* in London: Heinemann (1972) and Garden City, N.Y.: Doubleday (1973).

Achebe receives D.Litt. degree from Dartmouth College.

1973   Achebe's impact in France is apparent with the publication of *Chinua Achebe et la tragédie de l'historie*, a critical study of his work by Thomas Melone.

1974   Achebe lecturing at the University of Massachusetts, Amherst.

1975   Achebe publishes a volume of fifteen essays, *Morning Yet on Creation Day*, written between 1962 and 1973, on various literary and political subjects. Achebe decides to accept an appointment at the University of Connecticut in Storrs.

1976   Achebe leaves University of Connecticut to return to Nigeria. Among many responsibilities, he teaches a course in modern African fiction at the University of Nigeria, Nsukka.

1977   Publishes two children's books, *The Flute* and *The Drum*, based on Igboland folktales.

1978   Publishes a poem, "The American Youngster in Rags," in *Okike* and writes essay, "The Truth of Fiction," presented at the University of Ife.

1979   Delivers his essay, "Impediments to Dialogue Between North and South," at Berlin International Literature Festival held June 21 to July 15.

1980   In April, attends conference of the African Literature Association in Gainesville, Florida. Meets James Baldwin for the first time.

1982   Attends meetings and engages in discussions regarding general elections to be held in 1983. Joins People's Redemption Party (PRP) in late 1982.

1983   *The Trouble with Nigeria* published in Enugu, Nigeria: Fourth Dimension; and London and Exeter, N.H.: Heinemann.

1984   Achebe gives lecture at University of Port Harcourt, "Reflections on Nigeria's Political Culture."

1985   Heinemann publishes *Short Stories* edited by Achebe and Lyn Innes.

1986   *The World of the Ogbanje* published in Enugu, Nigeria: Fourth Dimension.

            Achebe awarded the Nigerian National Merit Award for the second time. In his acceptance speech, Achebe notes the essential role played by literature in the comprehensive goal of a developing nation like Nigeria.

1987   *Anthills of the Savannah* published in London: Heinemann; and New York: Anchor/Doubleday (1988).

1988   *The University and the Leadership Factor in Nigerian Politics* published in Enugu, Nigeria: Abic (1988).

            Hopes and Impediments: Selected Essays, 1965–1987 published in London: Heinemann; in New York: Doubleday (1989).

1989   *A Tribute to James Baldwin* published in Amherst: University of Massachusetts Press (1989). Appointed a Distinguished Professor of English at City College of the City University of New York. Receives Callaloo Award for his contributions to World Literature. Publishes first issue of *African Commentary: A Journal for People of African Descent*, in America.

1990   Achebe birthday symposium held at the University of Nigeria, Nsukka, under the direction of Edith Ihekweazu. Achebe also accepts invitation to become Charles P. Stevenson Professor of Literature at Bard College. Many new critical works on Achebe are published.

1993   Achebe travels to University of Cambridge in January to deliver the annual Asby Lecture at Clare Hall on "The Education of a 'British Protected Child,'" which was subsequently published in the *Cambridge Review*. Towards the end of the year, the political situation in Nigeria has degenerated with the military government canceling a scheduled election. In November, Achebe is awarded the Langston Hughes Medallion at a celebration sponsored by the City University of New York.

2000   Publishes *Home and Exile*, a collection of essays presented as the McMillian-Steward Lectures at Harvard University in 1998.

Contributors

HAROLD BLOOM is Sterling Professor of the Humanities at Yale University and Henry W. and Albert A. Berg Professor of English at the New York University Graduate School. He is the author of over 20 books, including *Shelley's Mythmaking* (1959), *The Visionary Company* (1961), *Blake's Apocalypse* (1963), *Yeats* (1970), *A Map of Misreading* (1975), *Kabbalah and Criticism* (1975), *Agon: Toward a Theory of Revisionism* (1982), *The American Religion* (1992), *The Western Canon* (1994), and *Omens of Millennium: The Gnosis of Angels, Dreams, and Resurrection* (1996). *The Anxiety of Influence* (1973) sets forth Professor Bloom's provocative theory of the literary relationships between the great writers and their predecessors. His most recent books include *Shakespeare: The Invention of the Human*, a 1998 National Book Award finalist, and *How to Read and Why*, which was published in 2000. In 1999, Professor Bloom received the prestigious American Academy of Arts and Letters Gold Medal for Criticism.

RICHARD BEGAM teaches in the English Department at the University of Wisconsin in Madison. He is the author of *Samuel Beckett and the End of Modernity* (1996) and "Toward a Posthistorical Novel" (1997).

RHONDA COBHAM has held a teaching position at Bayreuth University, West Germany. She is the author of "Revisioning Our Kumblas: Transforming Feminist and Nationalist Agendas in Three Caribbean Women's Texts" (2000) and "Jekyll and Claude: The Erotics of Patronage in Claude McKay's *Banana Bottom*" (2000).

EMMANUEL EDAME EGAR is Assistant Professor of English at Paul Quinn College in Dallas, Texas. He is the author of *The Rhetorical Implications of Chinua Achebe's "Things Fall Apart."*

ABDUL JANMOHAMED is the author of *Manichean Aesthetics: The Politics of Literature in Colonial Africa* (1983) and *The Nature and Context of Minority Discourse* (1990).

ANTHONIA C. KALU is Professor of Black Studies at the University of Northern Colorado in Greely, Colorado.

NEIL TEN KORTENAAR teaches in the English Department at Scarborough College, Scarborough Ontario. He is the author of "Foreign Possessions: Erna Brodber's 'Myal,' the Medium, and Her Message" (1999) and "Doubles and Others in Two Zimbabwean Novels" (1997).

CLAYTON G. MacKENZIE is the author of "Thomas Carlyle's 'The Negro Question': Black Ireland and the Rhetoric of Famine" (1997) and "Girding the Gods: Mythologies of Mars in *Coriolanus*" (1994).

JOSEPH McCLAREN is Associate Professor of English at Hofstra University. He is the author of "*Cotton Comes to Harlem:* The Novel, the Film and the Critics" (1994) and *Langston Hughes: Folk Dramatist in the Protest Tradition, 1921–1943* (1998).

CLEMENT OKAFOR teaches English at the University of Maryland, Eastern Shore. He is the author of *The Banished Child: A Study in Tonga Oral Literature* (1983) and "Chinua Achebe: His Novels and the Environment" (1989).

IMAFEDIA OKHAMAFE holds a double Ph.D. from Purdue University and teaches philosophy and English at the University of Nebraska at Omaha. His work has appeared in such publications as *Research in African Literatures* and *Soundings: An Interdisciplinary Journal.*

EUSTACE PALMER teaches in the Department of English, Speech and Journalism at Georgia College & State University in Milledgeville and is an associate editor of *Critical Theory and African Literature Today: A Review* (1994).

RICHARD K. PRIEBE teaches in the English Department at Virginia Commonwealth University in Richmond. He is the author of "The Canonization of Texts: The Childhood and Allegories of Salvage and Change" (1990) and editor of *Ghanaian Literatures* (1988).

JOKO SENGOVA is affiliated with the University of South Florida and is a research associate at the Florida Mental Health Institute in Tampa.

Bibliography

Agetua, John, ed. *Critics on Chinua Achebe, 1970–76*. Benin City, Nigeria: Agetua, 1977.

Carroll, David. *Chinua Achebe*. New York: St. Martin's Press, 1980.

Egudu, Romanus N. "Achebe and the Igbo Narrative Tradition." *Research in African Literatures* 12 (1981): 43–54.

Emenyonu, Ernest. *The Rise of the Igbo Novel*. Ibadan: Oxford University Press, 1978.

Ezenwa-Ohaeto. *Chinua Achebe: A Biography*. Oxford: James Currey; Bloomington: Indiana University Press, 1997.

Gagiano, Annie H. *Achebe, Head, Marechera: On Power and Change in Africa*. Boulder: Lynne Rienner Publishers, 2000.

Gates, Henry Louis, Jr., ed. *Black Literature and Literary Theory*. New York: Methuen, 1984.

Gikandi, Simon. *Reading Chinua Achebe: Language and Ideology in Fiction*. London; Portsmouth, New Hampshire; Nairobi: J. Currey; Heinemann; Heinemann Kenya, 1991.

Githae-Mugo, Micere. *Visions of Africa: The Fiction of Chinua Achebe, Margaret Laurence, Elspeth Huxley, and Ngugi wa Thiong'o*. Nairobi: Kenya Literature Bureau, 1978.

Gunner, Elizabeth. *A Handbook for Teaching African Literature*. London: Heinemann Educational, 1984.

Herdeck, Donald E. *African Authors: A Companion to Black African Writing. Vol 1: 1300–1973*. Washington: Black Orpheus, 1973.

Heywood, Christopher. *Chinua Achebe's* Things Fall Apart: *A Critical View*. London: Collins, 1985.

Innes, Catherine Lynette and Bernth Lindfors, eds. *Critical Perspectives on Chinua Achebe*. Washington, D.C.: Three Continents Press, 1978.

Innes, Catherine Lynette. *Chinua Achebe*. New York: Cambridge University Press, 1990.

Irele, Abiola. *The African Experience in Literature and Ideology*. London: Heinemann, 1979.

Iyasere, Solomon O., ed. *Understanding* Things Fall Apart: *Selected Essays and Criticism*. Troy, New York: Whitston Publishing Company, 1998.

————. "Narrative Techniques in *Things Fall Apart*." *Obsidian* 1.3 (1975): 73–93.

Jabbi, Bu-Buakei. "Fire and Transition in *Things Fall Apart*." *Obsidian* 1.3 (1975): 22–36.

JanMohamed, Abdul R. "Sophisticated Primitivism: The Syncretism of Oral and Literate Modes in Achebe's *Things Fall Apart*." *Ariel* 15.4 (1984): 19–39.

Jeyifo, Biodun. Contemporary *Nigerian Literature: A Retrospective and Prospective Exploration*. Lagos: Nigeria Magazine, 1985.

Jones, Eldred. "Language and Theme in *Things Fall Apart*." *Review of English Literature* 5.4 (1964): 39–43.

Kemoli, Arthur and Leteipa Ole Sunkuli. *Notes on Chinua Achebe's* Things Fall Apart. Nairobi: Heinemann Kenya, 1989.

Kronenfeld, J. Z. "The 'Communalistic' African and the 'Individualistic' Westerner: Some Comments on Misleading Generalizations in Western Criticism of Soyinka and Achebe." *Research in African Literatures* 6 (1975): 199–225.

Lindsfors, Bernth. *Conversations with Chinua Achebe*. Jackson: University Press of Mississippi, 1997.

————. "The Palm-Oil with Which Achebe's Words Are Eaten." *African Literature Today* 1 (1968): 3–18.

Mbiti, John. *Introduction to African Religion*. London: Heinemann, 1975.

Morrell, Karen L., ed. *In Person: Achebe, Awoonor, and Soyinka at the University of Washington*. Seattle: African Studies Program, Institute for Comparative and Foreign Area Studies, University of Washington, 1975.

Moses, Michael Valdez. *The Novel and the Globalization of Culture*. New York: Oxford University Press, 1995.

Mudimbe, V. Y. *The Invention of Africa: Gnosis, Philosophy, and the Order of Knowledge*. Bloomington: Indiana University Press, 1988.

Njoku, Benedict Chiaka. *The Four Novels of Chinua Achebe: A Critical Study*. New York: P. Lang, 1984.

Nnolim, Charles. "Achebe's *Things Fall Apart:* An Igbo National Epic." *Modern Black Literature*. New York: Black Academy, 1971: 55–60.

Obiechina, Emmanuel. "Structure and Significance in Achebe's *Things Fall Apart*." *English in Africa* 2.2 (1975): 39–44.

Ogbaa, Kalu. *Understanding* Things Fall Apart: *A Student Casebook to Issues, Sources and Historical Documents*. Westport, Conn.: Greenwood Press, 1999.

————. *Gods, Oracles and Divination: Folkways in Chinua Achebe's Novels*. Trenton, New Jersey: Africa World Press, 1992.

————. "A Cultural Note on Okonkwo's Suicide." *Kunapipi* 3.2 (1981): 126–34.

Ojinmah, Umelo. *Chinua Achebe: New Perspectives*. Ibadan: Spectrum Books Limited, 1991.

Okoye, Emmanuel Meziemadu. *The Traditional Religion and Its Encounter with Christianity in Achebe's Novels*. Bern: New York: Lang, 1987.

Omotso, Kole. *Achebe or Soyinka?: A Study in Contrasts*. London; Northvale, New Jersey: Hans Zell Publishers, 1996.

Ottenberg, Simon. "The Present State of Igbo Studies." *Journal of the Historical Society of Nigeria* 2.2 (1961): 211–30.

Owomoyela, Oyekan. "Chinua Achebe on the Individual in Society." *Journal of African Studies* 12 (1985): 53–65.

Parker, Michael and Roger Starkey. *Postcolonial Literatures: Achebe, Ngugi, Desai, Walcott*. New York: St. Martin's Press, 1995.

Peters, Jonathan. *A Dance of Masks: Senghor, Achebe, Soyinka*. Washington, D.C.: Three Continents Press, 1978.

Petersen, Kirsten Holst and Anna Rutherford, eds. *Chinua Achebe: A Celebration*. Oxford, England; Portsmouth, New Hampshire; Syndey, Australia; Heinemann: Dangeroo Press, 1990.

Podis, Leonard A. and Yakubu Saaka, eds. *Challenging Hierarchies: Issues and Themes in Colonial and Postcolonial African Literature*. New York: P. Lang, 1998.

Robertson, P. J. M. "*Things Fall Apart* and *Heart of Darkness:* A Creative Dialogue." *International Fiction Review* 7 (1980): 106–11.

Shelton, Austin J. "'The Palm-Oil' of Language: Proverbs in Chinua Achebe's Novels." *Modern Language Quarterly* 30 (1969): 86–111.

Simola, Raisa. *World Views in Chinua Achebe's Works*. Frankfurt am Main; New York: P. Lang, 1995.

Stock, A. G. "Yeats and Achebe." *Journal of Commonwealth Literature* 5 (1968): 105–11.

Turkington, Kate. *Chinua Achebe:* Things Fall Apart. London: Arnold, 1977.

Ugah, Ada. *In the Beginning . . . : Chinua Achebe at Work*. Ibadan: Heinemann Educational, 1990.

Uwechie, Cele, Moses, Ugwoke, et al., eds. *Chinua Achebe: A Bio-Bibliography*. Nsukka: Faculty of Arts, University of Nigeria, 1990.

Weinstock, Donald J. "The Two Swarms of Locusts: Judgment by Indirection in *Things Fall Apart*." *Studies in Black Literature* 2.1 (1972): 14–19.

Winters, Marjorie. "Morning Yet on Judgment Day: The Critics of Chinua Achebe." *Journal of the Literary Society of Nigeria* 1 (1981): 26–39.

Wren, Robert M. *Achebe's World: The Historical and Cultural Context of the Novels of Chinua Achebe*. Washington, D.C.: Three Continents Press, 1980.

Wynter, Sylvia. "History, Ideology and the Reinvention of the Past in Achebe's *Things Fall Apart* and Laye's *The Dark Child*." *Minority Voices* 2.1 (1978): 43–61.

Yankson, Kofi E. *Chinua Achebe's Novels: A Sociolinguistic Perspective*. Uruowulu-Obosi, Nigeria: Pacific, 1990.

Acknowledgments

"Achebe's Sense of an Ending: History and Tragedy in *Things Fall Apart*" by Richard Begam from *Studies in the Novel*, vol. 29, no. 3 (Fall 1997). ©1997 by University of North Texas. Reprinted by permission.

"Problems of Gender and History in the Teaching of *Things Fall Apart*" by Rhonda Cobham from *Canonization and Teaching of African Literatures*, Raoul Granqvist, ed. Amsterdam and Atlanta, Georgia: Rodopi, 1990. © 1990 by Editions Rodopi B.V. Reprinted by permission.

"Rhetorical Implications of the Theme in *Things Fall Apart*" by Emmanual Edame Egar from *The Rhetorical Implications of Chinua Achebe's "Things Fall Apart."* Lanham, Maryland and Oxford: University Press of America, 2000. © 2000 University Press Of America. Reprinted by permission.

"Sophisticated Primitivism: The Syncretism of Oral and Literate Modes in Achebe's *Things Fall Apart*" by Abdul JanMohamed from *Ariel*, vol. 15 no.4 (October 1984) © 1984 by The Board of Governors, University of Calgary. Reprinted by permission.

"Achebe and Duality in Igbo Thought" by Anthonia C. Kalu from The *Literary Griot*, vol. 10, no. 2 (Fall 1998). ©1998 by *The Literary Griot*. Reprinted by permission.

"How the Centre Is Made to Hold in *Things Fall Apart*" by Neil Ten Korte-naar from *English Studies in Canada*, vol. 17, no. 3 (September 1991). © 1991 by Carleton University. Reprinted by permission.

"The Metamorphosis of Piety in Chinua Achebe's *Things Fall Apart*" by Clayton G. MacKenzie from *Research in African Literature*, vol. 27, no. 2 (Summer 1996). © 1996 by Indiana University Press. Reprinted by permission.

"Missionaries and Converts: Religion and Colonial Intrusion in *Things Fall Apart*" by Joseph McLaren from *The Literary Griot*, vol. 10, no.2 (Fall 1998). © 1998 *The Literary Griot*. Reprinted by permission.

"Igbo Cosmology and the Parameters of Individual Accomplishment in *Things Fall Apart*" by Clement Okafor from the *The Literary Griot*, vol. 10, no. 2 (Fall 1998). © 1998 *The Literary Griot*. Reprinted by permission.

"Genealogial Determinism in Achebe's *Things Fall Apart*" by Imafedia Okhamafe from *Genealogy and Literature*, Lee Quimby, editor. Minneapolis and London: University of Minnesota Press, 1995. © 1995 by University of Minnesota Press. Reprinted by permission.

"Character and Society in Achebe's *Things Fall Apart*" by Eustace Palmer from *Literary Half-Yearly*, vol. 22, no. 1 (1981). [Published in Mysore, India by The University of Mysore, POB 407, Mysore 570005, Karnataka.] ©1981 by University of Mysore. Reprinted by permission.

"The Proverb, Realism and Achebe: A Study of Ethical Consciousness" by Richard K. Priebe from *Myth, Realism and the West African Writer*. Trenton, New Jersey: Africa World Press, Inc., 1988. © 1998 by Richard K Priebe. Reprinted by permission.

"Native Identity and Alienation in Richard Wright's *Native Son* and Chinua Achebe's *Things Fall Apart:* A Cross-Cultural Analysis" by Joko Sengova From *Mississippi Quarterly*, vol. 50, no. 2 (Spring 1997). © 1997 by Mississippi State University Press. Reprinted by permission.

Index